PRISONER OF POWER

To 'Nick' – 'Samantha'

Hope you enjoy the book.

Sorry about the watch.

Happy Reading.

Best wishes

[illegible]

With warm good wishes

Rex Gibson

May 25 1997.

Neil Antony Roff

PRISONER OF POWER

The Greg Blank Story

Rex Gibson

ZEBRA

ZEBRA

Published by Zebra Press
a division of Struik Book Distributors (Pty) Ltd
(a member of the Struik Publishing Group (Pty) Ltd)
32 Thora Crescent, Wynberg, Sandton

Reg. No.: 63/06481/07

First published in May 1997

The author and publishers gratefully acknowledge permission to quote articles from the following publications: *Business Day, Finance Week, Financial Mail, Sunday Times, The Star* and *The Sunday Independent.*

Editor Tamsin Shelton
DTP and cover design Neels Bezuidenhout
Cover photograph Libby Edwards
Author photograph Peter Nash

Reproduction by Disc Express cc, Johannesburg
Printed and bound by Creda Press (Pty) Ltd, PO Box 200, Thornton 7485

ISBN 1 86870 048 8

Contents

Foreword

This book was conceived in Krugersdorp prison. I first met Gregory Lex Blank through the good offices of a mutual friend, Peter Reynolds, father of the girl Blank hoped to marry and legal adviser to *The Star*, where I worked for many years. Reynolds thought Blank's story should be told. I agreed.

Blank and I talked for many hours in the visitors' courtyard at the jail over a period of more than a year. He was remarkably frank. So were the numerous friends and associates I interviewed; I could not find any enemies. But this book is, I hope, more than just 'his story'. I have tried to place it in the perspective of the times. I have tried to address the question of whether Blank was a scapegoat, as he believes, or something else – a menace to society, as his judge believed. Society may not have deserved Blank, but did Blank deserve society?

The brilliant young stockbroker touched two worlds. Both were altered radically by the contact. Those words would make a handsome eulogy at the end of a long life. Blank achieved this distinction before his thirty-eighth birthday. He is one of those people born to make a difference, sometimes for the better, sometimes for the worse. The first world he altered was the world of investment and high finance, a shady world indeed. He flew too close to the sun and got burnt. The second world he altered was in reality an underworld – the underworld of a jail.

Put another way, Greg Blank got two chances. The first, the easy one, he blew, and paid the price for it. The second, the hard one, he seized gloriously. His is a story of regret and triumph, weakness and invincibility.

We made just one deal when Blank agreed to co-operate with the writing of this book. He would be completely open, evade nothing, but he would have no say over what I wrote. I, for my part, would not whitewash what he did, but I would try to be fair and put it in context.

He kept scrupulously to his side of the bargain. I hope I have done so too.

Several people helped by casting a critical eye over parts of this book. They deserve anonymity lest they be associated with unwitting errors I might have made. Peter Reynolds – a loyal and brave friend, as this book will show – made it happen; Harvey Tyson went beyond the call of duty and read much of it, contributing even more; Tamsin Shelton read all of it – and sometimes saved me from myself. My thanks to them all.

Rex Gibson
SANDTON, APRIL 1997

PART ONE

1

The Midnight Callers

Gregory Lex Blank's richly-packaged world caved in on him for the first time at 17 minutes to midnight on Sunday, 10 March 1991. That, at any rate, was when the bell at the front gate chimed in his home.

At 11.43 on this particular night, the world was a sleeping place. Nothing – nothing visible, anyway – was happening to disturb the serenity of the residents of Khyber Rock, a small exclusive suburb of the satellite town of Sandton, on the northern fringes of Johannesburg. The air was still and warm, summer not yet gone. Soothing white noise, rather like the sound of a distant sea, filtered from the concrete highway a few kilometres away. Outside Greg Blank's elegant and spacious cluster house – No. 17 in the complex called Khyber Rock Village on Lincoln Street – a single tall palm stood like a giant sentry, warding off harm. Blank was upstairs in the master bedroom that overlooked the near-tropical greenery of an enclosed garden and a small splash pool. Like most of the rooms in the house, his bedroom was dominated by large paintings. Some were originals, some were prints, all were valuable. He liked being surrounded by works of art; they comforted him and reassured him of his worth.

For Blank, it had been a pretty ordinary Sunday – a 60-kilometre cycle ride in the morning, followed by a shower and steambath, then off to his father's home in Lower Houghton, Johannesburg, for the ritual lunch with family and friends, about 20 people in all. It was, as ever, a cheerful and undemanding occasion. In the evening, he had played stud poker with friends. A fun game, not big stakes – R5 to play, limit of three raises on the pot. On a bad night a player could possibly lose R2 000 or so, which was peanuts to Blank. But he was feeling vaguely unwell that evening, and had pulled out of the game at 10.45 p.m. He had driven home, showered, then crept into bed contemplating the unusual pleasure of a relatively early night.

Normally he worked 16 to 18 hours a day, a punishing but stimulating routine that had become almost a drug to him. However, tonight he would take it easy, recharge his batteries. He was not sure why he felt off-colour. Yes, it had been a tense few weeks, all the speculation, the anxiety, the sense of foreboding. It must have preyed on his mind more than he cared to admit. But it seemed to be all over now, he could breathe easy again.

The sound of the front-gate chime was sudden and alien. It jarred in the way that unexpected noises in the night do. Blank couldn't think of anyone who might come calling at this odd hour, but he was not unduly alarmed. He used the intercom that connects from his bedroom to his front garden gate.

'Hullo?'

'Hullo, Greg. It's General Hulme. Remember me?'

Of course he remembered General Nollie Hulme. Former head of the South African Police Fraud Squad and now in charge of the newly-established Office for Serious Economic Offences. He had spoken to him only the week before when they had parted on amiable terms. Now Hulme was saying: 'Frank Kahn just needs you to sign some papers here. It won't take a minute. Please let us in.'

He knew Frank Kahn too. Attorney-general of the Cape. Leader of the investigation team probing alleged irregularities at the Johannesburg Stock Exchange. Only a few days before he had 'helped Kahn out', as he liked to think of it, by explaining a complicated set of JSE deals that some people thought might be fraudulent. Blank thought he must have forgotten to sign some document or other after their meeting. Darn nuisance. Why couldn't the signature wait until tomorrow? He climbed out of bed, put on a dressing gown and walked unsuspectingly downstairs to open the front door.

He did not even begin to guess that he was about to be sandbagged.

When General Nollie Hulme and Major Max Olckers arrived at Blank's home 17 minutes before midnight they were in civilian clothes – neat ties and jackets. They seemed curiously ill-at-ease, almost as if they were uncomfortable about the subterfuge they had decided to resort to. A few papers to sign indeed! Of course there were no documents for signing. The deceit had been deemed necessary to ensure that the two investigators were able to get through the front door and down the two steps into the luxurious lounge before showing their hand.

Blank gave his late-night callers a moderately civil welcome.

'Would you like some tea?'

The general replied: 'No thank you, Greg. We've got a warrant of arrest. You'll have to come with us.'

'What for?' said Blank. 'You've got to be hallucinating.'

But they weren't. The warrant proved that. The policemen said a bail application would not be opposed, but the bail amount would be high, as befitted the gravity of the charges they proposed to bring. Blank would have to find R500 000 before they would let him go. R500 000 – on a Sunday night! Blank felt vulnerable, nervous and unbelieving by turns. This surely couldn't be happening, it had to be a bad joke. Policemen simply didn't come and arrest charming young stockbrokers in the dead of night. Not in the enclave of Khyber Rock anyway. Blank was naked under his dressing gown. He wanted to go to his bedroom to fetch clothing and a cheque book. The policemen took up station behind him as he climbed the stairs.

'Why are you following me?'

'You're under arrest now. We've got to go with you.'

'But why are you arresting me?'

'You had your chance to tell them everything,' said General Hulme.

'What are you talking about? I told them what they wanted to know. I spoke on a tape recorder for hours. Nobody asked me for anything else.'

Blank was genuinely bemused. Of course he knew who 'them' were. 'Them' were the people investigating what might be a large-scale fraud involving equities. The whole of the Johannesburg Stock Exchange was buzzing with information and rumours about the investigation and what it might uncover. The newspapers were writing about it too. He had even submitted himself to questioning on the matter by Attorney-General Kahn and his staff. That's what General Hulme was referring to when he said: 'You had your chance…' Blank ran over in his mind the circumstances leading up to his rather odd meeting with Kahn the previous week.

Some time in January 1991, someone at the JSE with a score to settle had drawn the stock exchange's attention to a number of 'unusual-looking deals' done on behalf of Old Mutual, the insurance and unit trust giant. Old Mutual – formally registered as the South African Mutual Life Assurance Society – was the biggest player on the JSE. Its Investors Fund was the single largest unit trust operation in the country, managing hundreds of billions of rands of public money. On top of that, it operated nine other unit trust funds, not to mention the fortunes administered in life insurance, endowment funds and the like.

Old Mutual had been invited to look more deeply into the matter of the unusual deals. What it uncovered had caused it to suspend two of its top people – 'sweet guy' Marco Celotti, a senior portfolio manager, and 'nice guy' David Schapiro, a dealer in the investment department. That's where the probe had come to a dead end. Old Mutual had known there was something fishy, but as it had no authority to follow the trail any further it had decided to seek government help. It had sent a delegation to Minister of Justice Kobie Coetsee and Minister of Finance Barend du Plessis to urge them to set up a wider-ranging investigation. That's when Attorney-General Kahn had come into the picture. It was also when Sweet Guy Celotti and Nice Guy Schapiro had slipped out of the picture – and the country.

Greg Blank was a logical source from whom to seek information on the deals. As one of the youngest stockbrokers ever to be given a licence and possibly the youngest-ever director of a stockbroking firm, he had won the confidence of Old Mutual to the extent that it became his, and his firm's, biggest client. He alone, by dint of hard work and persistence, had hooked this big fish. Old Mutual trusted him enough to use him fairly regularly for acquiring or selling large parcels of shares. He thought he had done a good job for his most valued client.

He had been almost pleased when the stock exchange urged him to co-operate with the Kahn inquiry. He was sure he could explain away the suspect deals to the entire satisfaction of all concerned. Besides, he rather liked being the centre of attention, the whiz-kid stockbroker with an almost uncanny gift for dealing.

At 2.05 p.m. on Wednesday, 6 March, Blank had been ushered into the first-floor office at the JSE which served as temporary headquarters for the investigating team. There he had found Kahn, a rumpled, chain-smoking figure with his tie loosened and his shirt-tails out. He had the face and style of a hostile bulldog. With him were a couple of advocates and Major Max Olckers. Kahn had produced a document which contained a list of stock exchange deals, left the room, come back with a tape recorder and said: 'Right, please explain these deals to me.' Then, after a few more words, all the investigators had departed, leaving Blank alone.

Blank had been disconcerted by the peremptory style. It wasn't at all what he had expected. But, what the hell, he'd give them the answers they were looking for.

Unsure even whether the tape recorder was working, he had begun to talk to it. It was like talking into a vacuum. After an hour or so, he thought he had done rather well; provided a comprehensive and lucid explanation of each deal. So he had gone looking for the absent interrogators, found Kahn and had told him: 'Look, if you need any more help I'll come back tomorrow.' Kahn had replied, somewhat absent-mindedly: 'Fine.'

Yet when Blank had called the next day to check whether he was needed, he was told that Kahn had gone back to Cape Town. Blank's services were no longer required.

What he did not know – could not know – was that the attorney-general had been stringing him along, playing a cat-and-mouse game with him. Kahn was noted for his short attention span. After listening to the young stockbroker for a few minutes he had pulled General Hulme aside and said: 'Look, we've got all the information we need. I'm not going to listen to this bullshit any more. Let him tell his story to a tape recorder.'

But Blank never doubted that he had satisfied everyone. Even General Hulme, to whom he had spoken a few days before the Kahn interrogation. He remembered that interview very clearly too. Hulme had also been involved in the stock exchange investigation. He too had approached Blank for information. The interview had been friendly and unthreatening, and after their little talk the general had said: 'Okay, you've got nothing to worry about.'

All the more bizarre, then, was the indisputable fact that Hulme and another policeman were now standing in Blank's lounge, waiting to take him away. Why was he under arrest? Northern suburbs high-fliers didn't usually get arrested in midnight raids. He must have satisfied the attorney-general's office, or they would have questioned him again. What had gone wrong?

He didn't know it then, but a former senior Old Mutual dealer called Colin Harper had gone wrong. Harper was a nervous fellow who had recently left the employ of Old Mutual. When he had heard about the abrupt departure of his former underlings, Celotti and Schapiro, he had concluded that Europe in late winter was a very attractive place to go for an extended holiday and a long think about his own future. One day early in March – a week before Blank's arrest – he had come to a conclusion. It was to save his own neck if he could. He had phoned Frank Kahn and said: 'What's it worth if I spill the beans?'

'Show us the beans first,' Kahn had replied.

Harper had responded with a small flurry of unsigned affidavits and statements detailing the information he had to offer. He would sign them, but only if Kahn would strike a deal. Kahn and a select delegation of investigators had flown to London. They saw Harper first, then they saw a man called Peter Rawson. Rawson was a Zimbabwean who had made his home in the United Kingdom. He too had a story to tell and a neck to save. He was ready to talk. So now Kahn had Harper and Rawson and another source in Johannesburg, Chris Logan of the Old Mutual dealing department; he didn't need more snitches.

When he had finally come face to face with Celotti and Schapiro in London, and they had asked him what deal he would offer them, he had told them bluntly: 'I don't need you to deal for anything. Come back and face the music.'

On Saturday, 9 March, Harper had returned to South Africa and been met by the attorney-general. They talked, and Kahn reached for the arrest warrants. There were five names on the warrants: Rawson, who could not be extradited; Schapiro and Celotti, who had fled; and Greg Blank and Kenny Fouche, another stockbroker, who were available.

But none of this, of course, was known to Blank at the time of his arrest, and so he was left to rack his brains for explanations while the policemen waited in his home. Perhaps the arrest was just a device to put him under pressure, see if he would crack. That might explain the late-night raid – a form of psychological warfare. Perhaps they would release him tomorrow. No hard feelings, Greg, just needed to be sure you were innocent. He was confident he could answer any questions. Hadn't he done so with Kahn?

For the rest of that long night, Blank's emotions fought a war with his intellect. He determined not to brood on his plight. He had always prided himself on his ability to divide his mind, store his thoughts into neat compartments. It was a trick he had taught himself as a youngster, a simple trick really. First he would face his problem head-on, construct a worst-case scenario and consider options, which would be carefully dissected. Then they, and the whole problem, would be dispatched to some deep-freeze corner of his mind, to be buried but not forgotten.

Experience had taught him that even large problems sometimes disappeared with time, solving themselves. If that happened, well and good. If it did not, at least he had his contingency plan ready and waiting in his mental deep-freeze. He called the process his 'survival kit'. It was not an evasion of reality, just a device to enable him to turn his mind to other matters, even in a crisis.

Being arrested was a reality. What could he do about it practically? The worst case was that he would be stuck in a cell for a night or so while he raised bail, or the police came to their senses. They would surely come to see that they were over-reacting to what was, in his eyes, at most a small misdemeanour. But, more immediately, he needed to consider how quickly he could raise the money for bail. Quite fast, he reckoned. For once, his inventive mind missed a trick. Even in his darkest fears, he never considered – not for a moment – that when he and the arresting officers took those first steps away from his front door he had begun a long walk to jail.

Survival, at this miserable midnight moment, meant accepting the fact of arrest without becoming demolished by it. But intellectual defences can often yield to emotions, and so it was with Blank from time to time through that endless night and in the months to follow. Thoughts and feelings crept unbidden into his head. Suddenly, unexpectedly, he felt the humiliation, the shame and torment his loved ones would suffer at his arrest. The realisation was sharp, hard to dislodge, but after a while he managed to suppress it.

Blank put on jeans, a jersey and shoes, but he didn't bother with socks. He went downstairs to his younger brother's bedroom and said casually: 'Listen, Vaughan, I've been arrested. Phone Mom and Dad and tell them what's going on.' Vaughan nearly fell out of bed at the announcement.

The little procession – two policemen and their captive – made its way down the path to the awaiting vehicle, a Mercedes-Benz. Blank felt irrationally cheered for a moment. That's nice, he thought, they're taking me away in a nice car, and without handcuffs.

Inside the car was a huddled figure, not quite sober, near to tears and whimpering: 'Oh fuck...oh fuck...' The figure turned out to be Kenny Fouche, a 42-year-old employee of the stockbroking firm of Ed Hern, Rudolph. Fouche, who was married with two children, was known as a quiet man in the office and a jokey fun-lover after hours. The police had picked him up at a braai and he too was under arrest. He had eaten onions and his lamentations were punctuated by burps.

First stop was the Johannesburg Stock Exchange building on Diagonal Street in the central business district. General Hulme wanted to collect some documents from the offices of stockbroker Ed Hern. The building was normally empty at this hour but there was no problem gaining entry. The investigators had their own key and the security guard was accustomed to their erratic hours. They put Blank in their makeshift office and instructed him not to use the phone. The moment they were out of sight, Blank decided to ignore the instruction. Realising at last that he might need a lawyer, he decided it was time to wake his employer, Sidney Frankel, head of the stockbroking firm of Frankel, Max Pollak, Vinderine Inc.

Blank recalls: 'I'd never used a lawyer in my life. I thought I had better phone Sidney. I said: "Sidney, I've just been arrested." I think he knew what was going on because he said: "Oh jeez, what do you mean you've been arrested?" and I said: "You'd better organise me a lawyer." Next minute, the lawyer was there, dressed. It was now like half past twelve. The lawyer phones Sidney himself. Sidney says: "We've got to work out how to dissociate Greg from the business." I shouted out: "How can you dissociate me from the business?" I was getting really cross now. Next thing, Sidney appears, shaven, in a jacket, almost as if he had been waiting, expecting it to happen.'

Blank made three more calls, one to a friend, another to his brother and the third to his father. The call to his father was particularly painful.

'Imagine phoning your father and saying: "Listen, Dad, I've just been arrested. Not for drunk driving or something. For fraud." You feel like you've let everyone down, especially when you've been riding so high. You're not worried so much for yourself as for them. I don't cry easily, but that was the first time that tears came to my eyes.'

Just then General Hulme came back into the office to find Blank putting the phone receiver down. Gone was the amiable front. Now Hulme was aggressive.

'I told you not to use the phone.'

'Sorry, General…'

'You know, you Jews are all the same.'

'What do you mean?'

'You're just out to make more money. Where's your Portuguese passport?'

'I haven't got one.'

'Of course you have. All you people have Portuguese passports.'

'Listen, General, I haven't got one!'

Silence. Blank wondered whether the general believed him. He hoped so.

He turned his attention to the problem of raising bail of R500 000. He knew he had about R1,3 million on call in current bank accounts. Why, only last Friday he had verified that he had about R1 million in his current account at the Stock Exchange branch of First National Bank. What was the name of the woman who had attended to him? Hook? Veronica Hook – that was it.

It was now close to 2 a.m. When the general left the office again, Blank phoned four of the 16 Hooks in the Johannesburg phone directory before finding the right one. He asked Ms Hook if she would verify that his cheque was good for the R500 000 bail money. Ms Hook said she remembered rolling over a balance of about R1 million in his current account for another 30 days the previous Friday. But how, she wanted to know, could she be sure Blank had not withdrawn it on Saturday? 'Don't bother,' said Blank curtly.

Nedbank bank manager Iris Seabrook was more obliging. 'No problem,' she said. 'Sign the cheque and we will guarantee it.'

From the JSE, a somewhat subdued procession made its way to the Johannesburg magistrate's courts to explore the possibility of getting bail. Even at 2.45 a.m. the courthouse was busy, people everywhere, noise and activity. Evidently, justice did not sleep.

Kenny Fouche's lawyer was arguing that his client couldn't afford the R500 000 bail; Sidney Frankel's lawyer, representing Blank, was insisting that Blank would pay twice that much if need be to avoid spending the rest of the night in jail. Blank wondered again whether the whole incident was designed to soften him up, make him crack. A frisson of alarm prickled his spine, but it was gone in a moment. What was the worst that could happen? If, indeed, he had infringed a stock exchange rule or two, well then, he would be rapped over the knuckles and perhaps suspended from the JSE for a few days. It was a storm in a teacup. Besides, he had done nothing that others weren't doing as well.

But, again, a little alarm bell rang. What was happening to him was over the top. He had been hauled from his home at midnight like a common thief. He was captive in an echoing hall of justice. He was about to be charged with what the policemen were telling him was a major crime. How could all this be happening to him? He wavered between disbelief, despair and a half-hope that he was dreaming.

In the chill hours before dawn, Blank and Fouche walked down the gleaming corridors to a bleak court. Magistrate D. 'Langboet' van der Wath was informed that they faced fraud charges involving alleged irregular share transactions affecting both the JSE and Old Mutual. The charges were serious, said the policemen. Magistrate Van der Wath agreed, and set bail at the recommended figure of R500 000 each.

Now it was back to John Vorster Square police station for fingerprinting, and to await confirmation that bail cheques would be honoured. A policeman took pity on Blank. 'I can see you aren't the normal type of criminal. You don't have to wait in a cell.' So Blank stretched out on a charge office bench.

Just being in a police station felt strange to him. There seemed to be millions of people coming and going. Eyes closed, he listened to the voices, the problems. A woman complained that she had not heard from her husband since he went to jail three months ago. Could the police help? The last sound he heard was Kenny Fouche, sleepless on a chair, beating his head against a table and saying: 'Oh shit…oh shit.' Then exhaustion overcame him.

At 5.30 a.m. on Monday, 11 March 1991, Greg Blank awoke from his tortured sleep at John Vorster Square to a gentle, feminine touch. Di Reynolds had answered the call he had made to her from the stock exchange office, as he knew she would.

2

A Legend Is Born

Halfway between sleep and wakefulness, reassured by the touch of a comforting hand, Blank forgot where he was for a moment. The arrival of Di Reynolds gave him a feeling of normality, even of wellbeing. She had responded to his call, what else could be wrong?

Dianne Margaret Reynolds was special to him. He wasn't quite sure why. Their relationship had been strange, turbulent, unsettled. Some things had drawn them together and some things had pulled them apart. They made a handsome couple and Blank's even-tempered attitude was a foil to her more volatile, emotional personality. But the relationship foundered time and again because something was missing. Di was hungry for reassurance and commitment, which Blank seemed unable to give. Naturally affectionate though he was, his emotional responses were somewhat stilted. He seemed scared to open himself up, to make himself vulnerable. Something in his genes or his environment had taught him an iron self-control. Perhaps he had been hurt once too often as a youngster. And yet, in his withdrawn, self-contained way, he loved her. Indeed, Di was the one who taught him how to have fun, how to fall in love.

The couple were introduced at Steffanie's coffee shop in Hyde Park in 1987. He was approaching 30, she was a few years younger. Di had spotted him the previous evening at a night club and wanted to meet him. Blank invited the coffee-table party to his house for tea, and soon he and Di began to date. Says Di: 'There was a spark between us from the beginning. We started dating quite seriously, but I think that Gregory had never dated anyone very seriously before, so for him it was a big thing. All the same, I think work was first and foremost in his life at that point.'

Some time in 1989, a man from Di's past came back into the picture. Di found herself torn between an old flame and a new one. 'It was a very confusing time in my life. I think it was more like an obsession with this other person. It was a bad relationship but I couldn't get out of it. I knew I would never marry him.'

When Blank asked her to marry him that year, she said she couldn't; she was too confused about her association with the other man. One day they confronted the issue of betrayal. For the first time, Blank's mask slipped. She saw tears in his eyes. She had never seen that before.

'He prided himself on never showing his feelings. He would never show if he was upset. He pretended to be a very unemotional kind of person. You never really knew with Gregory where you stood. I actually find that difficult. I need to know where I stand. With Gregory, you don't.'

Blank did precisely what Di feared he would do. He cut her out of his life, not once but several times.

'When someone tells you they're not seeing you any more, that's the only person you want to see,' Di remembers. 'You know what it's like. The breakups were always traumatic for me. Gregory is just an amazing human being. Nobody would put up with what I put him through. I mean, I'm not proud of it but I think I was just a very mixed-up kid.'

Forgiveness never came easily. 'When he cut me out, he cut me out. It was like closing a book. There was nothing I could say or do – that was it! He wasn't interested. We used to go for months on end, and he would refuse to take phone calls from me, or else he would be very stiff and formal. I used to beg and plead for him to take me back, and I'd nearly drive him mad. Eventually he would agree.'

They were midway between friendship and commitment after another breakup when Di got Blank's phone call on the night of the arrest.

'We weren't together, but we were definitely seeing each other. I remember him coming home from his meeting with Kahn on the Wednesday and telling me he'd seen this guy and given him information. I asked: "What happened?" And he said to me: "No, nothing. He thinks I'm a hell of a nice guy." We had dinner together on the Saturday night but I didn't see him on Sunday because he was playing cards.

'About 2.30 a.m. on Sunday night – I mean early Monday morning – he phoned me and said he'd been arrested and was at an office at the stock exchange. It took me completely by surprise. I said I'd meet him there, but he said: "No, go to John Vorster Square, because that's where they're going to take me." Until that moment I'd had absolutely no idea he might be in trouble. He had never given me an inkling.

'I was completely horrified. I mean, here was this amazing young guy who seemed invincible. Everything he touched turned to gold. He was a lucky person. If he took a raffle, he won. He always won at the races. I actually couldn't believe that something like this could happen to someone so lucky. His arrest came as a total shock.'

There was to be another, near-final, breakup. This time it would not be Di Reynolds's fault. It was occasioned by Blank's arrest and was destined to become the most traumatic by far for both of them.

Some time during their on-off affair, Blank discovered the aphrodisiac effect of wealth and power. Women seemed fascinated by the young whiz kid with the Midas touch. He was good-looking in a lithe, fresh way that was disarming. He moved lightly, with an athlete's gait. Mothers would instinctively think of him as clean-cut and personable. He was that kind of man.

It was his sheer pleasantness that male friends noted. Women saw something else. He breathed power and authority, though he could be naïve and even unsophisticated. He was self-confident without being cocky; tough without being ruthless, generous without being ostentatious. If he had fears and insecurities, he hid them well. But it is also true that some women detected the little boy in him, and it made him seem more desirable still. One such woman was Gail Carruthers, whom he dated during one of the 'off' phases in the relationship with Di.

Gail Carruthers made no secret of it. She adored her new boyfriend. Within a few days of his arrest, Blank would pick up the *Sunday Times*, there to be confronted by a front-page, full-colour picture of Carruthers, a fashion model and former runner-up in the Miss South Africa contest. Carruthers was happy to inform an avid audience of her feelings for the man who had earned overnight notoriety when he was arrested. 'I am mad about Greg,' she said. 'He is the most unbelievable person. I think about him constantly. I phoned him as soon as I heard, but he didn't want to talk. We met at the Sandton Health and Racquet Club and started dating when he and Dianne Reynolds broke up four months ago.'

Carruthers was merely one of several women who became infatuated. Blank gained a reputation as a playboy because he seemed to appeal to attractive women. But, for him, there was still only one person who mattered, despite the betrayals, the breakups and the traumas. That was the woman he called first when he found himself in deep trouble.

And that's how Di Reynolds came to be with him that bleak morning at John Vorster Square police station.

The feeling of wellbeing inspired by Di's presence was fleeting, replaced almost instantly by an awareness of where he was. He was on a hard bench, drowning in loud noises, overwhelmed by the atmosphere of crisis and anxiety that pervades a busy police station. He was in trouble.

There was plenty of time for introspection as his brother and his legal adviser scurried to and fro attending to the red tape of posting bail. His mind raced. So abrupt had been the transition – only six hours before he had been relaxing in his own king-size bed in contented luxury – that he could hardly believe all this was happening to him. Surely, surely, it must be a nightmare, or at least a mistake. He began to conjure up mental pictures of the lifestyle to which he had become accustomed; the lifestyle that *was* him.

For God's sake, he didn't belong in a police station. He belonged with the high-fliers, the achievers – people who had earned their place in society by dint of talent and hard work. He had devoted his life to turning himself into the kind of person he could admire. Nothing was more important to him than the respect of others. Now a couple of police buffoons were trying to snatch it away. They were trying to snatch his own self-image away too. It couldn't be happening.

Blank's first job after leaving Wits University with his BCom degree in 1981 was with the Standard Merchant Bank. A few months after he started he came across stockbroker Sidney Frankel in a steam bath at the gym and Frankel said: 'Why don't you come and work for me?' He didn't think twice. Here, almost casually offered by one of the really big wheels of the Johannesburg Stock Exchange, was access to the world of big money, big deals, big gambles – all the things he loved. It was irresistible.

At the beginning of November 1982 the boyish-looking 24-year-old presented himself at the offices of Simpson, Frankel, Kruger, trading as stockbrokers on the Johannesburg Stock Exchange. Before he turned 25, he passed the examination that entitled him to become a broking member of the JSE, one of the youngest ever admitted. At the age of 25, he became a director of Frankel's. Two years later he assumed responsibility for all the firm's dealers on the exchange.

He had stormed a citadel that was occupied, in part, by mean-spirited, resentful stockbrokers in their forties and fifties. Grudgingly, they had to admit they had never seen such a meteoric rise. But then the boy was good, damned good. He knew the market. He could pull deals out of a hat better than any magician. Despite his boyishness, his air of fresh-faced innocence, clients seemed to respect him as well as like him. He clearly had potential and he worked like a demon. The legend of Greg Blank had been born. The old hands seethed.

On his bench at John Vorster Square, Blank considered how far he had come since the day he first set foot in the offices of Simpson, Frankel, Kruger – subsequently renamed Frankel, Max Pollak, Vinderine Inc., but usually referred to as Frankel's. It had taken him less than nine years to reach the top, to achieve nearly all the goals he had set for himself. How ironic that it had taken less than nine hours for him to tumble from that pinnacle into his present pit.

Almost masochistically, he assessed the balance sheet of his life, as if it might help him gauge how far, and how suddenly, he had fallen. He loved his job, the thrill of multi-million deals, the god-like sense of power. He could move markets and he was respected by his peers (and, secretly, his superiors). He had won back the girl he wanted to marry. And he was rich beyond even his own dreams of wealth. Over the last four years his commission from Frankel's had amounted to more than R1 million a year, rising to R1,5 million in the financial year that had just passed.

His eye for a bargain was impeccable. He had bought his spacious cluster house, which newspapers were later to call a mansion, for a mere R300 000; today it was worth at least treble that. But the value of the bricks and mortar was nothing compared to the value of the treasures they contained. He had bought, amongst others, a Jim Dine painting, a Chadwick piece, a William Russell Flint and antique silver pieces. In all, he had poured nearly R1,4 million into beautifying his home. He thought it money well spent.

In the garage he had a Ferrari 328 GTS, which was appreciating, a BMW 535i, a Harley-Davidson motorbike. He was a partner in a racehorse syndicate and a horse-breeding company; he participated in a share investment partnership that had tied up more than R400 000 of his money; and he had a modest sum in shares on his own account. He owned a stake in an aircraft and a R50 000 watch. Best of all, he thought, was that he had R1,3 million on call at the bank. Instant, available money.

Of course, he had a few debts too, which were a nuisance because he hated being in debt. His house was bonded for more than R660 000, and he had borrowed pin money – R50 000 from his brother, R225 000 from friends. Oh yes, and he owed the Transvaal Totalisator Board and three bookmakers a little over R100 000. Gambling was in his blood. His father loved it and so did he. He could afford the indulgence. His assets had cost him nearly R6 million and, even in the unthinkable event of a fire sale, they would fetch at least R5 million. His liabilities were a mere R1,5 million. All in all, he was happily, gloriously solvent.

He could afford to live any way he liked. But, apart from the almost compulsive need to possess good things, he favoured simple pleasures. Because work was his great passion, he didn't bother much with holidays, preferring a break at a friend's home in Cape Town to a lavish holiday abroad. He'd tried an overseas holiday once, staying with Di in a R1 200-a-day hotel in the South of France. He'd spent a fortune.

'Di apart, I had just as good a time in Cape Town, staying with a friend, running along the promenade,' he would tell me later. 'My life was basically boring to other people. I like simple things and I don't normally drink. An evening out for me is supper at a Longhorn steakhouse, or chicken from Nando's. I'm not one for cocktail parties or fancy dinners. If I went to a club, I had to be very circumspect. I couldn't let my hair down. None of this dancing on tables after a couple of tequilas. I really worried about what people would think. I was sure they would say: "Hey, here's this guy that's handling all our money and he's acting like a drunken idiot."

'My social life was almost a disaster. Work was everything. I didn't socialise with the guys, just did my job and went home. For relaxation, I used to give gym classes in my father's garden, make sure I exercised every day, play tennis at weekends. After that, I was just too tired to do anything else. I liked girls but I simply didn't seem to have the time to give to them.

'And then I met Di…'

Together at John Vorster Square, the young couple waited, incongruous in this world of cops and criminals. A policeman, new on duty, came and asked him what he was doing there. 'Waiting for the general,' replied Blank.

'Go home,' said the policeman.

'I don't think that would be such a good idea,' suggested Blank. And he carried on waiting.

Soon after 9 a.m. on Monday, 11 March 1991, Blank's brother, Vaughan, arrived with the bank-guaranteed cheque to cover his bail. Not long after that, he was allowed to go, no longer in custody but not free either. Blank, Vaughan and the lawyer got into a waiting car. With the ignition, the radio came on. It was a news bulletin. Numbed, he heard only some of the words: 'Greg Blank…stockbroker…arrested…'

Full realisation struck home at last, battering its way through his defences. It was true after all, not just a bad dream. The police had come for him, and now the whole world knew. The indignity, the humiliation of it was yet another hurdle he would have to overcome. Of course, nothing would come of it. The police, anxious for a scapegoat, had grossly over-reacted. How long would it take them to realise that?

He hoped that Di Reynolds would remain in his life because he really needed her now. But that would mean that she would have to share the limelight, the humiliation, too. Could he ask that of her?

3

The Love Child

'You know, of course, that Gregory is a love child.'

A love child. The words have a quaint Victorian ring to them. The woman who speaks them so matter-of-factly is Blank's mother, Gail Dunkley. She is a trim woman in comfortable, no-nonsense jersey and slacks. Only the naughty, smiling eyes speak of a life well lived. Married three times, and in her sixties, she lives alone, apparently content, in a neat flat next door to the Wanderers golf course in Johannesburg. Her sons phone often; her daughters come to play cards. She is not lonely.

Right now there is an impish look on her face, defiant, challenging.

I venture: 'A love child? That must have been embarrassing for you in those days?'

It seems to be the very question she wants. She deals with it briskly, clearing the air to her own satisfaction. 'Not at all,' she replies. 'It wasn't embarrassing at all. We were very happy about it. We loved him. Of course, we told him about it as soon as he was old enough to understand. He didn't mind it.

'He thought it made him somebody rather special.'

Somewhere in his past, perhaps, there is a key to understanding Gregory Lex Blank, born on 20 September 1958 in Johannesburg. The answers can't be found in glib pop psychology or Freudian nuances. He is a complicated man and unplumbed depths lie hidden in layers of defences. Events and circumstances and genes shaped him, just as they shape us all; gave him his unique self, his soaring ambitions, his secret insecurities, his flawed pretensions.

Somewhere, somehow, there must be explanations for why a gifted, loved child would grow up to put at risk, deliberately and methodically, the thing he valued more than anything else – his reputation, his public persona – to make a packet of money he didn't really need. In time, his sternest critics would find one answer that satisfied them completely: greed. The man was simply greedy. But can it really be as simple as that? Is greed not a pathology of a kind too? Does it not arise in some dark corner of a man's soul, nurtured by lacks and wants he sometimes doesn't even understand?

The 'love child' remembers being brought up in a home filled with affection. Parents Robby and Gail believe – and are almost certainly right – that they are good at giving love. Greg describes Robby as his closest friend. The parents will tell you that, as each child came along, they opened their hearts a shade wider, finding equal room alongside Greg for Tracy, and then Daryl, and then Vaughan. They knew it might be harmful to have favourites, and so they studiously avoided doing so.

Early on in her relationship with Robby Blank, Gail converted to Judaism. She had no profound conviction and it was not a Damascus Road experience. All she wanted to do was give her family a solid religious base. With a gentile mother, the children could not be Jewish, like their father. So she happily converted, harbouring no regrets about the change.

Gail watched her family grow with loving pride, making little entries for herself and each of them in her diary when she thought about it. In January 1969 she recorded: 'Gregory now ten years old and in Standard Four at Houghton Primary. Captain of the under-10 cricket team, vice-captain of the soccer team, has been swimming for the school's A team since he was seven. Nice boy, a bit chubby. Weighs 94 lbs. Vaughan is the image of his daddy.'

More than 20 years later, after Greg's downfall, Gail recorded her uncritical loyalty to her four children in her spasmodic diary. 'I love all my children equally,' she wrote. 'And I think they are all wonderful. United, we will stand together.'

Uncritical affection had its limits, however. Twice young Gregory transgressed his mother's standards of domestic honesty. Twice he learnt to regret it. Neither mother nor son has ever forgotten those incidents. When he was about five or six years old, Greg was due to spend the night at the home of family friends who had a daughter about his age. His mother had left the maid's wages out on a table, and he took about R5. Later his mother forced him to admit to taking the money. 'I got the hiding of my life, but you know what young boys are like. I just wanted to impress the girl.' On the other occasion he desperately wanted a silver bracelet with his name engraved on it. He took about R10 from a pile of money his father had left in the bedroom, thinking it would not be noticed. It was. His mother spotted the unfamiliar bracelet on his wrist and put two and two together. Result: another good hiding.

If Mother played the warm-hearted matriarch, Father played role model for his impressionable son. Greg Blank's addiction to physical fitness; his enthusiasm for running and, indeed, all sports; his love of art; his hunger for visible wealth; his pleasure in fine cars; even some of his mannerisms – all these and more he got from the sprightly, articulate person he calls Robby or Dad, according to his mood.

Robby Blank was the son of an Irish Jew who emigrated to South Africa and set up home in Doornfontein, Johannesburg. Even then it was an unfashionable, poor area. They knew what it was to be short of money. Money, or the lack of it, was a compelling subject. Money provided not only comfort but an easy yardstick for measuring success in the world. Without money, fzzzt! – you were nothing.

Robby remembers moving to Bez Valley, another poor area. Later he and his family found themselves in a boarding house in Berea that was little more than a gambling den. Little Robby loved it.

He played snooker all day long and learnt to understand the horses. At the age of 12 he was taken to the dog races at Wembley and discovered how to bet. Dog-racing was still legal in those days. 'Looking back, I think that all I knew was gambling – chemmy, dogs, horses. My father made millions acting as an agent for cement makers and timber interests, then lost it during the war.' That was an ugly time.

One day Robby made an amazing discovery: not everybody lived like the immigrant Blanks. A school friend took him to his home, and young Robby discovered a new world. It was called Houghton, and it was a glamorous, wealthy suburb to be desired more than any other in the world. 'I didn't even know Houghton existed,' he says now. 'I remember saying to myself: "This is how to live!" I made up my mind at that moment that I would get there.'

He did. Young Robby was a determined soul. Later, when he married Gail at age 27, he decided he would go round the world by the time he was 29. He did that too, in the days when such an odyssey was not lightly undertaken.

He brought almost a surfeit of determination to everything he tackled. He instituted two major civil actions to defend his interests and began to believe he knew more about the law than his lawyers. He got a friend released early from jail by digging so hard into the evidence of the chief witness that he effectively discredited him. He overextended himself in business several times. Business, for him, meant anything he cared to turn a hand to, provided it showed prospects of making a profit. Once he thought he was on the verge of the big-time, and persuaded his friends to invest with him in an oil venture. It came to nothing.

He made up for a scanty education by exploiting his lively and enquiring mind. He was shrewd and he made money as easily as he lost it. People liked him, for he was easy-going and amiable, a good host and an excellent sportsman. He liked people, company, crowds.

In his teens he developed a fondness for big, flashy cars, especially if they were something of a novelty in the neighbourhood. He liked the attention they attracted. One day he and ten friends were playing cards in a Lincoln V12 belonging to a parent. Robby won. 'If there was one thing I knew how to do, it was to gamble.' He decided to celebrate. The 11 youngsters – none of them old enough to have a driver's licence – set off in the Lincoln for the tearoom at John Orr's, a central city department store. Robby remembers the whole celebration cost him 2s 6d. He enjoyed the style of it.

He never forgot that he was going to live in Houghton one day. In the early Sixties he achieved his dream. The family moved into a large house in Central Avenue, Houghton, complete with swimming pool. It wasn't so much that he hankered after conspicuous wealth for its own sake, just that he knew – in the circles in which he moved – he would be judged by such material standards.

He was determinedly honest himself, but accepted that, in business, it was sometimes necessary to sweeten a deal if he wanted to get a contract. 'What else can you do?' he says. 'That's the way business works. I remember when I was supplying something to OK Bazaars. My price was R4 a piece. Their guy comes to me and says: "You want the order; make sure, when you put in your bill, that there's something in there for me." I say sure, and I put in a bill for R4,50 a piece, and he gets his 50 cents and everybody's happy. Anyway, OK Bazaars paid so badly, I think the guy deserved an extra R300 or so a month.'

Robby Blank discovered art and photography. 'I didn't get it from my father. He couldn't tell a Da Vinci from a photograph. It was something I found for myself. Maybe that's where Greg got his love of art.'

He liked to think of himself as something of an art patron. Young black artists would bring their work round to the home in Houghton. One in particular seemed extraordinarily promising, and Robby would help him through bad financial patches by buying his paintings. The artist's name was Ephraim Ngatane. Today he is an established figure whose work commands high sums. Some of his early paintings – dark, brooding, vital – still hang in the family home, a tribute as much to Robby's generosity as to his acumen.

Robby Blank was just as staunch as Gail when it came to uncritical loyalty to his children. He recalls a friend who, when he discovered his son was gay, abandoned him. Robby couldn't understand that. 'Good God, man,' he said to his friend. 'He's your son! What would you do if he had leprosy? Abandon him too?'

Greg Blank's need to achieve evolved early. It was accompanied by another compelling need – to be seen to achieve. Not for him the solitary satisfactions of hidden endeavours; there had to be monuments.

When he started his art collection – the Henry Moores, the Marc Chagalls, the Joan Mirós, the William Russell Flints – two things prompted him. The first was that he genuinely loved beautiful things. He can remember, as a child of nine or ten, seeing a Michael Fleischer statue called *The Whistler*. It was for sale at R300. He wanted it, for itself. He was ready to spend all his pocket money on it, but he did not have enough. Resourcefully, he persuaded his mother to go halves with him, and he had his first artwork. He has it still. But Blank admits to another reason for his compulsion.

His art collection, thoughtfully and knowledgeably acquired over years at a cost of more than R1,3 million, makes a statement about him. It says: 'Hey look, I've arrived.' That's important to him too.

Schooldays at Houghton Primary School and King Edward VII High School were notable for his sporting achievements. Young Greg was not particularly fond of rugby but he excelled at tennis. At 14 he was chosen for an overseas tour and, by 16, he was ranked sixteenth in South Africa. In his matriculation year of 1975 he had to make a choice between a sporting career and a business one. He was offered a tennis scholarship to the University of California, Los Angeles. One great interest – sport – came into conflict with another – money. He opted to do a Bachelor of Commerce degree at the University of the Witwatersrand instead. His father was vaguely surprised; he hadn't thought of himself as having scholarly children. (Younger brother Vaughan was to surprise him again by passing his Chartered Accountancy finals at his first attempt.)

Greg became a tennis professional of a different kind, helping to pay his way through Wits by giving tennis lessons. After university he spent two years doing national service, during which time he achieved the rank of full lieutenant, the highest rank possible for a national serviceman. Now he was ready to take on the world. He knew exactly what he wanted to do. He wanted to deal with money. He wanted to make lots of it too. Only when he had money would he feel truly secure.

The picture is too perfect. The newspapers could put it in headlines: 'Near-perfect Boy from Near-perfect Home Commits…' Commits what? Near-perfect crime? There must be more to it than that. There must be undercurrents. Otherwise, why did he have that sense of insecurity in the first place? Small clues emerge.

The fear of being poor was never far away in the Blank household. 'I was always expanding, always battling,' Robby remembers. 'Once I got sequestrated. I battled for money, but my children never had to. I always saw to that.' Or so he believes. It was important to him to feel that setbacks to his own fortunes didn't impinge on his family. Life had taught him that, somehow, it would reflect badly on him if they went short of the one thing that mattered – money.

Gail recorded in her diary: '1968 has been a disastrous year. Robby's business was placed in provisional liquidation. We live at 101 Central Avenue, Lower Houghton – for how long, I don't know.'

Greg discovered the shame of being poor. He remembers being taken, aged ten, to Houghton Primary School in a borrowed and battered jalopy. 'I used to ask my mother to drop me around the corner so my friends wouldn't see me. I think I learnt to care about money from the time when my father lost his. Since then, money's always been important to me.'

Like father, like son. As a boy, Robby Blank learnt to gamble for money, or else go short of the little things all his friends seemed to have. It happened to him in adulthood too. 'Yes, I had some bad times in business, but,' he insists again, 'we never lacked for money and we always had a car.' Either way, in this family, vehicles were status symbols. They sent a signal to the world.

Greg learnt to play cards for money as a teenager, klaberjas and rummy. It gave him a sense of security. Unconsciously, his father had taught him well.

Caring too much about money has a stigma attached to it. Yet society is inconsistent in its views. Money is surely as good a yardstick as any to measure success. Is there anything wrong, then, with weighing up success and revealing the results? Athletes measure their strength, fitness and agility in public and are admired for it. Writers and artists are considered worthless if they do not display the results of their work for public judgment. Why should success in business be any different?

The entire Western world – and most of the Eastern world too – is dedicated to the concept of free enterprise. Implicit is the notion of competitiveness, and competitiveness requires measurement. Large companies are expected to boast about their profits and business know-how; it's called transparency. Businesses that seek listings on the JSE revel publicly in their capital appreciation. Stock exchanges are places where people make fortunes overnight and are applauded for their acumen and flair. There is no convention there that making large sums of money is reprehensible.

And yet there are double standards. The view persists that there is something indecent about achieving wealth. It is fostered by the professionally poor, who have become society's moralisers. People who hoard money are called thrifty, yet those who flaunt it are called greedy. Ours is a curious society which applauds a man as rich as, say, Harry Oppenheimer, while finding it wrong for anyone to want to be as rich as that.

By 1969, the instability in the Blank home had worsened. 'Caught up in a young swinging crowd,' Gail recorded. 'The whole world seems to be changing and morals relaxing. Greg has grown his hair, gets mistaken for a girl very often.'

The brief entry contains its own unconscious revelations. Whose 'whole world' was changing? Whose morals were deteriorating? Greg Blank's parents liked to think they had an open relationship in which fidelity wasn't essential but having a good time was. The parties at the Blank home were famous. Drink flowed with the good vibrations. Sometimes young Greg would creep from his bedroom to the balustrades at the top of the stairs to watch the 'young swinging crowd' enjoying themselves in the lounge-cum-bar below. There was a frenetic feel to the dancing and singing, to the flirtatious flitting among the guests.

To the boy, it was all fascinating but slightly disturbing. This was his 'happy home', yet somehow he felt apart from it, uneasily alien on such occasions. The flirtations made him uncomfortable.

In 1972, when Greg was 14, the marriage of Robby and Gail finally fell apart and they separated. The parents tried to manage it in a way that would minimise the shock to the children. Robby moved out of the Houghton home to which he had so long aspired because he didn't want the children to be uprooted. He endured a legal separation for eight years because someone told him a divorce might damage the youngsters. He visited his children virtually every day and tried to make sure they wanted for nothing that money could buy – even when he was running short himself. He made, and thinks he mostly kept, a resolution that, whatever arguments he and Gail might have, the children would never know about them.

'After the separation I made it a policy that I would take the boys to the gym in the school holidays,' remembers Robby. 'We'd work out and have a sauna. On Sundays, I would take them running. Greg was about 16. We did four laps at the Wanderers, the last half-lap flat out. For the first three months I beat him. After that he was lapping me.'

For Gail too the interests of the children took precedence, as she remembers it. It was only when they were grown and Greg had moved into his own flat that she asked Robby for a divorce so that she could marry another man. Ironically, breaking up seemed to make Gail and Robby better friends. 'We liked each other, we just couldn't live together,' they both say. Friends who meet them today are often amazed at the good relations that exist between Gail and Robby and his new wife when they all get together for family meals. These occasions were, and are, highlights for Greg.

Nevertheless, 14-year marriages don't just break up without consequence. When families fall apart, it is inconceivable that there is no emotional fall-out. It is also unlikely that early deprivations leave no scars. But some memories have been hidden deep, and it is almost cruel to resurrect them.

The Blanks – father, mother, sons, daughters – remain very good friends. Greg Blank remembers his home life as being exceptionally happy and the separation of his parents was a relief rather than a sadness. Gail can recall no moments of trauma or high tension. The waters have closed over the past.

Greg's memory is revealing for what it doesn't contain. If the atmosphere at home improved after Robby and Gail parted, then what was it like before? Clearly, some of the marital stress had communicated itself to the boy, otherwise he could not have noticed the change. The sisters betray signs of youthful insecurity too. One works for her father in the shelter of the Houghton home. The other has retreated into a 'safe', non-confrontational world of kindergartens and undemanding art-dabblers. Blank helps to support her.

None of this is to suggest that Blank came from a tormented household. Affection within the family is too visible for that. Neither can it be suggested that the lifestyles were uniquely or even unusually fraught. There can be few families from which domestic stress is absent. On the Richter scale of domestic trauma, the pressures in the Blank household were closer to a mild tremor than an earthquake. The worst that one can say is that the Blank family members, driven by their different needs, still feel compelled by who-knows-what forces to romanticise their old family life. It is no big deal. Lots of children survive much worse without apparent ill-effect.

It may begin to explain, however, why the family history – the concern for money, the occasional lack of it, the hunger for social acceptance, the 'swinging days', the matrimonial breakup, the sense of rootlessness – contrived to feed the insecurity of a once-chubby 'love child' who, one day, would value wealth and social position too highly.

Two questions remain. The first is this. It is said that eldest sons commonly and unconsciously compete with fathers and younger brothers. Is there something in this? In a family and a community where, for generations, the measure of success has been money, what other family contest is possible? There is no such thing as easy come, easy go when it comes to family fortunes made and lost. Could that have been a driving force? The second question is if unalloyed greed drove Blank to crime in the business world, then what drove him to do so much apparently selfless good in prison? Could it be two sides of a single coin?

There are no glib answers to the Blank enigma. Just questions.

4

Power and Fear

Sidney Frankel drove a hard bargain. Blank might be bright and enthusiastic, but he was going to have to earn his keep with the firm.

His starting salary was R1 400 a month, and that's where it stayed during all his time at Frankel's. If he wanted more, he would have to make it from commission. In the early days, there was precious little of that to be had. Aspiring stockbrokers who look appealingly boyish tend not to inspire great confidence among the investing community. Blank's first two or three years with the firm were simply a slog, 16-hour working days with little to show for it, and he began to wonder whether he would ever get anywhere. Pickings were very slim.

Then, quite suddenly it seemed, his hard work began to pay off and, within four years of joining Frankel's, he was put in charge of the institutional desk, by far the firm's main money-spinner. By then he had already established the frantic, productive routine that was to dominate his life. The appointment to the institutional desk meant that he had a few more duties and responsibilities to crowd into his over-full day. He'd be at work by seven o'clock, to go through his notes and check that the deals of the previous day had been properly processed and read the newspapers, especially the business pages.

By eight o'clock he was ready to start calling a growing list of institutional and corporate clients, confirming orders, seeking new business. At 8.45 the firm's daily meeting took place – half an hour of slightly frenetic exchanges of goals, gossip and information. Blank, not yet 30, was responsible for about 70 per cent of the firm's business. He would tell the meeting what he was doing and what was happening. No one questioned his decisions.

Just after 9.15 there was time for a quick cup of coffee before appearing on the floor a few minutes early for the first trading session of the day. When the bell rang, pandemonium began. Blank sat before a bank of phones, handling calls from eight institutional and several corporate clients. The din was nerve-racking. Shouting voices competed for attention, creating a cacophony that was somehow decoded and translated into action. The fact that, in many cases, huge sums of money were involved created its own adrenalin surge.

By the time the first trading session drew to a close, many of the participants on the floor felt drained, but there was always the next session to come, new resources of energy and concentration to be conjured up.

Blank recalls: 'When I was put in charge of the institutional desk, I had a team of about 40 people on the JSE floor. I had like a switchboard in front of me with four direct lines and about 16 extensions. I'd pick up the phone to get a financial institution and the next moment I'd see another light flashing. Hang on please, I've got another call. And another. And another. Dealers come and say: "We can get this stock…we can get that stock." I'm trying to listen to four conversations at once. I'm also listening to the people working next to me, to see that they're doing it right. The place is like a lunatic asylum. You work flat out until the first break at 11 o'clock. You book your deals during the break and the market starts again. Sometimes I was on the phone for the entire day. It's different now, of course, but those were the days before screen trading.'

At 4.45 p.m. he would call a temporary halt and go off to the gym for an hour's exercise. Then it was back home to work again, catching up with his reading, preparing himself for the next day, making his 10.30 p.m. contact calls to New York, where the Wall Street market was just winding down for the day.

Two years after joining Frankel's, Blank was offered a commission deal. On the face of it, it looked generous and he was thrilled. He would get 50 per cent of the brokerage earned from any private clients he might develop, as well as 5 per cent of the institutional brokerage generated by himself and, subsequently, the institutional desk he headed. But Sidney Frankel wasn't the kind of person who liked to throw money around, so there were two small catches to the offer. One was that Blank's institutional commission would be calculated only after he had achieved a breakeven figure of R80 000 a month in brokerage earned. The second was that expenses incurred in earning the brokerage had first to be deducted. Blank did some mental arithmetic.

Frankel's had earned about R750 000 from institutional brokerage in 1982, the year Blank joined, and just over a million rands in each of the two succeeding years. The breakeven figure for the year – R80 000 a month for 12 months – amounted to R960 000. And then there were the expenses: three or four dealers, office staff, messengers, administration, rent, telephones. If he had been on a commission scheme like that when he first joined, the total earnings would not even have covered the breakeven figure. Five per cent of nothing would have been nothing. Even on the million rands earned in the next two years, there would be nothing left over after deducting expenses.

Commission? he thought wryly. *As things stand I'll be lucky if my bosses don't ask me to put money in the kitty for them.*

There was only one thing to be done. He would have to earn more for Frankel's if he wanted to earn more for himself. He couldn't live on a paltry R1 400 a month. Over the next six years, the firm's institutional brokerage soared. In the financial year 1984/85 it rose to R1,6 million, climbed to R2,4 million the next year, R3,9 million the year after that, and peaked at R6,5 million in 1989/90. That was the year in which Greg Blank took home R1,5 million in commission from his employers.

'When I started I was just a Jewish boy trying to make money,' he explains. 'I used to get on the phone every day and call around. I think it was two years before I got my first order. Then, when I started making money for Frankel's and myself, I had another problem. The clients had never seen me. They didn't know how young I was. It was hard for men of 40 and 50 to take me seriously at first. Besides, I was just a King Edward's boy so I couldn't exchange reminiscences with them about the good old days at schools like Hilton or Michaelhouse. But when I made money for them, they came to respect me.

'I used to have lunch with these older people. No deal was ever completed without a good lunch. It was hard for me because I didn't usually drink. I remember once having lunch with an Old Mutual contact and we finished three bottles of wine. I had about one bottle and he must have had the other two. When I got back to the office I was too drunk to do anything, and I made a resolution never to drink at lunch again. I never have.'

But there was more to his work than simply making big money. Blank had discovered something else, more rewarding than money, more potent than drugs, more heady than liquor – an elixir of life itself. What he had discovered was a mixture of power and fear, to which he became addicted.

He felt the power and fear each time he embarked on a big deal. People gambled fortunes and made millions because of his knowledge and skill. Sometimes, very rarely, they lost too, putting all the blame on him, but that just made the game more heady. They depended on him; they knew he was smarter, quicker, foxier than they were. 'I've made lots of money for people. I used to study the market very carefully. You can't make lots of money with a spread of shares. Some will always go down while the others go up. That's the nature of the market. I concentrated on a likely sector and went for that.'

But there was even more to it than that. He discovered that he could move the very markets themselves. He was a demi-god in the wonderful world of money.

'It's the mixture of power and fear that gets to you,' he says. 'It's an incredible combination. If you've never been on the floor of the exchange with the adrenalin pumping, knowing that you have the ability to make shares go up and down because you're playing with really big sums...it's hard to imagine the feeling. You feel almost...almost...invincible.

'And yet it's really so easy. Lots of people were doing it. Say somebody's shares were at R40, and they wanted to place shares at that price. I would advise them to get the share price up first. So I would buy enough to start the price rising, and keep on buying and selling as it rose. You don't need a lot of shares to do that; a few hundred will do. Once the price had risen, I would go to select clients and tell them I could get them a parcel of, say, a million shares at R40, its original price. And of course they were delighted. Once the first client had bought, everyone wanted to follow suit.'

On the Johannesburg Stock Exchange, dog eats dog. Hungrily. Blank discovered that quite quickly. Some of the older brokers at the JSE resented the young upstart with a university degree – imagine that, a floor trader with a university degree! – who was snatching deals from under their noses. It was in 1986 that some disaffected members devised a simple way to discredit him.

Information is the currency that keeps the stock exchange rolling. The place is invariably a hive of rumour and gossip. But one secret is carefully guarded. If a client, say a financial institution, informs its stockbroker of a major deal it is planning – perhaps to buy or sell a large block of shares, or to launch a rights issue – that stockbroker is honour-bound to keep it confidential. No client wishes its plans to leak out in advance. By and large, stockbrokers observe this principle meticulously because they would lose clients if they did not. But, of course, news does leak out all the same. The rumour machine commands formidable resources. Here, thought Blank's enemies, was a weapon that could be exploited.

One day the young stockbroker received a phone call that disturbed him deeply. Even now, he can feel the outrage in the voice of his caller, the despair he himself felt. 'This guy phones screaming: "You'll never get another deal from me again." I say: "What are you talking about?" He says: "You told so-and-so that we were planning to sell. He told me himself that you had given him the information."'

Blank was almost speechless. He had done no such thing, but, even to himself, his spluttered denials sounded increasingly lame and unconvincing. How do you challenge the power of a malicious rumour? Soon there were more calls like that. 'I had all the institutions phoning up and telling me, you know, I'd betrayed their confidence. They said to me: "Listen, we've been dealing with this other guy for a long time, he wouldn't lie to us."' Blank felt beaten, despondent. He was not being believed. His enemies would stop at nothing to destroy him. He thought about quitting 'the most cutthroat business in the world' and starting another career. But his own tenacious nature wouldn't let him.

Fortunately for Blank, his ability to inspire confidence, his track record of trustworthiness and the undoubted fact of his trading skills won back the Doubting Thomases. After a time he was on his way up again, but it had been a close shave and he was more wary now. Besides, he had learnt a trick or two from the old hands at Frankel's.

Soon after he joined, the firm had been asked by an insurance giant to help it gain control of a company it coveted. The company's shares were trading at about R6 at the time. Because market forces would naturally push the share price up when buying began, the insurance firm agreed to pay up to R9 a share.

'The trick here,' an old hand explained to his young colleague Blank gravely, 'is to get to a situation where the seller is getting more than he expected and the buyer is paying less than he anticipated. Then you've got two happy parties.'

The old hand sat down in his office and refined the strategy. Apprentice Blank looked on in wonder at the simplicity of it all. Soon old hand and apprentice were phoning financial institutions with an attractive and unexpected offer.

'Listen,' one or other of them would say, 'we're looking to buy your stake in Company X. The shares are standing at R6, we are prepared to give you R7,50.' The inevitable happened. Discovering that someone was prepared to pay a R1,50 premium, the would-be seller responded: 'Since you are so keen to have my stake, you're going to have to pay R8.' Done!

As soon as the sorcerer and his apprentice got a bite, other institutions started sniffing at the bait. A rise of R2 on a share priced at R6 represented an instant profit of 33 per cent. What a bargain! Some accepted the R8 offer without quibbling; others demanded more and got R8,50.

The deals took place without the JSE reflecting the slightest quiver of activity because the old hand had quite forgotten, and apprentice Blank didn't know, that JSE rules required that deals handled outside the market, just like those within the market, had to be shown on the board. The old hand's 'oversight' proved helpful. Anyone watching the great board of the stock exchange would have picked up no significant movement in the shares at all. A responsive board, on the other hand, might have made the market far too volatile for the games they were playing.

The insurance firm acquired its coveted company at a share price below the limit of R9 it had been prepared to pay, and the buyers, noting that the board still showed the shares at R6, congratulated themselves on getting a price higher than the prevailing one.

Blank thought silence had indeed proved golden. But he was left wondering at the ethics of the operation. Because his firm was acting as an agent for both buyers and sellers – bringing the parties together in what was termed a 'bookover deal' – it had to be fair to both. The buyer had been willing to pay up to R9 to acquire the shares. Should the firm have fought harder to get a better deal for the sellers? On the other hand, the buyer had initiated the transactions and was the primary client if you like. Should Frankel's have held out for a lower selling price? It was a nice point to debate. But, then, it was an even nicer deal, whichever way the judgment went.

Who was apprentice Blank to challenge the ways of the old hands? Besides, he believed everyone was doing it. It was part of the culture, the morality, of the JSE. Even so, he wondered sometimes whether it was true that power corrupts. He thought it might be true for some, if not many, of the big wheels at the JSE.

As time went by, Blank grew in confidence and style. It seemed he could do nothing wrong. What the hell, power might be dangerous but he could handle it. Wasn't he invincible?

When he finally came to trial for the Old Mutual affair, his advocate, Clive Z. Cohen, SC, paid an impassioned tribute to Blank's skills. 'My Lord,' Cohen told Mr Justice Tom Cloete, the presiding judge, 'as a dealer, he was unsurpassed. He was a specialist with an ability to accumulate large blocks of shares for the benefit both of the institutions and of companies which wanted to place them. We know that there were other firms of stockbrokers who employed dealers to watch Blank to see what he was buying and what he was doing. He became a leading dealer with an enormous amount of influence and ability. And there were numerous occasions when a bookover transaction was recorded – Blank was the dealer who both bought and sold – when he was applauded on the floor of the exchange.'

Blank himself remembers: 'I used to stick my neck out for the institutions. I would do what they wanted, which was to get them the best prices. They weren't interested in how I got them, just so long as I did. I would create a market around the shares, become a buyer, become a seller. And the end result was that they got what they wanted – the best prices. And I got what I wanted. I started getting the business, and the respect and the power.

'I got so good that I could phone up an institution and say: "I want you to buy this stock for this and this reason." And they would say: "Fine, go right ahead." Or I would say: "I don't like the look of this," and they would say: "Okay." It's difficult to explain to anyone what that power does to you, how good you feel. But there's fear too. If you are buying, someone is selling – and they must feel they're doing the right thing. Can both sides be right? At the end of the day, your job as a broker actually becomes that of a mediator.

'You're convincing one guy to sell because the quoted price is too high, and you're convincing another guy to buy before it's too late. It's like walking on a swaying tightrope, exciting and dangerous.'

Blank did it superlatively, and addictively. But he was moving into a greyer area of JSE activity and saw with cynicism the manoeuvres some clients got up to.

'You know, I never used to go away in December, I didn't want to leave the markets. The Big Deals all seemed to make their way down to the Cape, and they would phone from their beach houses and mention a share they held and say: "Jack the price up, jack the price up." So I'd jack the price up and they would sell the shares to their friends on the beach.'

In the secretive, sometimes furtive, world of the stock exchange, curious things could happen. One day a friend who had invested heavily in a company, only to see the shares fall to 95 cents, came to Blank and said he would like the share to be selling at R1,80 or R2 within three months. Fine, said Blank. All it took was a signed buying order from the investor and a bit of ingenuity. The shares were tightly held, but Blank bought what was available at a price of R1 and waited for other sellers to appear. If they didn't bite, he'd go scavenging himself until he winkled out another seller, and buy what the seller had to sell at R1,10. If he couldn't find any shares, he would persuade his investor to turn seller and thus keep a momentum going.

And so the shares were seen to be rising by small, incremental bites, nothing to raise suspicions. Soon, other brokers noticed what he was buying and said to themselves: 'Blank must know something.' So they bought too and, lo and behold, after three months the shares were indeed trading at R2 and the original investor was able to heave a sigh of relief at his good sense in enlisting the services of Gregory Blank, arch manipulator.

On a Friday afternoon around this time, Sidney Frankel came down to the floor of the exchange, his face beaming. He had just finalised a deal in which he had acted for both buyer and seller. He told Blank: 'I've just done this magnificent deal. We are booking over 32 million shares at R1,90 a share.'

'Gee!' said Blank. 'That's fantastic.'

'Yes,' said Frankel, 'I've bought this company for a corporate client.'

Something about the details of the deal made Blank feel a prickle of apprehension. At Frankel's, the rule was that when the corporate department was working on a deal, the dealing department was kept in ignorance of it. It prevented conflicts of interest, but it also meant that the left hand often didn't know what the right hand was doing. What if he and Frankel had been independently involved on opposite sides? His fears were quickly realised. Sure enough, Frankel – in honourable innocence – had purchased the company whose shares Blank – in equal innocence – had been 'jacking up'. The corporate client had paid nearly R30 million more than it need have done. Still, the client was obviously happy that it had got value for money, reckoned Blank. So no harm done.

The game of manipulating share prices is one of the oldest in the stock exchange book. It is not considered improper, let alone dishonest, though of course no one calls it manipulation. The rules of the JSE seek to control and minimise it, but there are just too many loopholes. Indeed, as any investor in unit trusts should know, share prices are manipulated openly by some of the most respectable organisations in the country – the financial institutions and the insurance giants. They call it 'window-dressing'.

Every so often, half-yearly or quarterly, these august entities report publicly on the total value of the share portfolios that underpin the unit-trust investments of the little folk. The figures run into billions of rands, and are entirely meaningless in themselves. But if the institution can show that the portfolio has grown in value, the little folk who lent it their money will conclude that they have invested wisely.

Sometimes it is not all that easy to show portfolio growth in a volatile or declining market and this is where window-dressing comes in. Some time before the institution is due to report, it will send a message to its brokers. 'We would like the following shares to be trading at the following prices on 30 September,' they will say. The list may not be very long, perhaps just three or four key shares in their portfolio, but the message to the brokers is plain enough: do what you have to do, but jack up these prices so that our portfolio looks better at quarter end. The fact that the shares may go down again on 1 October is of little concern.

The procedure is called window-dressing because if it was called 'share manipulation', it would have a negative connotation and the institutions wouldn't like that. Window-dressing is better. It has a fine, fuzzy ring which conjures up images of enchanting department stores with enticing wares.

Buying and selling shares is essentially a legal gamble between willing participants. The market is presumed to set its own values. If there are more buyers than sellers, the price of a share will generally go up. More sellers than buyers, the price goes down. No one can force another to buy a share – or sell it. Each must back his or her own judgment as to value. The simple fact is that nearly every time a sale takes place, conflicting judgments are made.

There is a maze of regulations to prevent dishonesty and shady dealing. But, at the core, the JSE authorities (like those in markets round the world) believe it is a self-regulating process, and that their task is to ensure that no deliberate misinformation about a company and its prospects is purveyed, and that everything is as transparent as it can be. After that, *caveat emptor*. Let the buyer beware.

Buyers were not as wary as they might have been when Company Y, a large public company, decided to have a rights issue. Blank, watching from the sidelines, he and his firm uninvolved, noted how Company Y's shares went from R4 to R8 in a short time. Was Company Y buying its own shares ahead of the rights issue? he wondered. It was not improbable. It happened all the time.

The rights issue came to the market at R5,50 – a discount of R2,50 to the ruling share price. Shareholders scurried to follow their rights. Behind them, running and panting, were the institutions, seeking to pick up bigger parcels of the bargain rights-issue shares. Blank wondered idly which price was correct: the R8 for ordinary shares or the R5,50 for rights-issue shares. Or even the R4 that had been deemed to be correct before the flurry began. The market decided that quite quickly. Company Y's shares dropped to R5,50. But the company remained apparently unperturbed. After all, hadn't something – or someone – created avid buyers at R5,50 by pushing the share price to R8 for a while?

Again, Blank contemplated the ethics. He didn't know whether Company Y itself had 'encouraged' the share price to grow ahead of the rights issue. But he did know that many big companies did that sort of thing. So it must be all right. Mustn't it?

'You know,' Blank muses now, 'the stock market has its own culture, its own way of operating. You can't explain it to anyone else. Some of the things that happen are so wrong you sometimes wonder whether they ought to lock everybody up. But that's the way it works. It's like a little club. You do something wrong, maybe they rap you over the knuckles, but they don't make too much of a fuss of it. Nobody wants to damage the momentum of the market.'

Least of all, the JSE itself.

5
Into the Trap

Invincible! It was hard not to let success go to his head after the years of battling. The young bachelor-about-town began to parade himself a bit, nothing too ostentatious, but then not too self-deprecating either. Blank discovered in himself a natural gift for attracting attention.

He had always loved racehorses, and now that he was a co-owner of 60 of the magnificent creatures he could indulge himself on two fronts. He liked being recognised as someone of stature in the world of the Sport of Kings. Look, people would say, there's that stockbroker fellow, he's a whiz on the JSE. And doesn't he look so young? Newspapers and magazines began to photograph him at Turffontein and other racecourses, preening with his horses in the parade ring.

But if he liked recognition, he loved gambling. It was in his blood, which is why he took to the JSE with such alacrity. It was as if he had been indoctrinated almost from birth with a passion for gambling. Both his mother and his father were, and are, inveterate gamblers. His father played the horses with serious intent and rummy and klaberjas for fun and money with his friends. So did his mother. It seemed as natural a part of family life as breathing. There were always card games at the house and visits to card-playing friends.

When he was about 14, Blank got admitted to his father's regular Saturday afternoon rummy games, the only youngster at the table. He could not afford the stakes – 'You could lose up to R2 000 in an afternoon, a lot of money in those days' – so he 'syndicated' himself among his school friends. They would contribute to the stake money and share in the profits, if any. The teenager won rather more often than he lost, for a simple reason. The older men enjoyed a drink or two before the game, topped up occasionally during it. Friends all, banter across the table was commonplace. But the earnest, almost solemn, non-drinking youngster kept his mind firmly on the game. He had to. After all, he was gambling with his friends' money as well. He was known as a cautious, deliberate player.

From an early age Greg Blank shared his father's love of horses and horse-racing. He studied form like any seasoned punter and liked to have a little flutter. The passion for the sport stayed with him into adulthood. He did not mind spending money on it. His interest in the racehorse-owning consortium cost him nearly half-a-million rands. Feed alone ate up R20 000 a month. On top of that he had a R218 000 interest in a breeding company, and maintaining those horses cost R10 000 a month. The racehorses didn't run fast enough or often enough, so the consortium was not a great success. Neither was the breeding company, which was operating at a loss. But so what? It gave him pleasure and he could afford it. Besides, every now and then he would win a Pick Six, strike it lucky with a jackpot. He preferred the exotic bets, which provided more of a test of his all-round knowledge and paid handsomely when his selections proved sound.

When he won, he would buy himself a little present, some *objet d'art* or collectible for his home. Looking around at the works of art that abound in his house, he says expansively: 'Racing paid for all this.'

Once he got a R500 000 payout from a R600 investment in a Pick Six. At the time when his accounts were being scrutinised by the court, he owed R75 000 to three bookmakers and R32 000 to the Transvaal Totalisator Board. For him, it was a pretty average sort of gambling bill; nothing to be concerned about. Blank finds the thrill of gambling almost irresistible, but the precise size of the stake is important to him. It must be large enough to hold his interest, but not so large that he feels out of his depth. Before his arrest, he was comfortable risking R5 000 or R10 000.

But, in reality, horses and cards were just hobbies. He kept his real flair for the stock market. He didn't much enjoy the social events that seemed an integral part of his job – the lunches, dinners and trips – but he couldn't avoid all of them, nor did he want to offend the people who brought him business. Besides, he rather liked this new circle of good companions – 'friends' would perhaps be too strong a word – that he was making. There were those two nice guys in Cape Town, David Schapiro and Marco Celotti, fund managers for Old Mutual. And then there was Colin Harper, an older man who was Old Mutual's head trader. Blank had no direct dealings with him, but he seemed a friendly enough soul.

These guys had a lot of money and understood that money was made for spending. They knew how to have fun. And they seemed to want to include their new stockbroker friend in some of their outings. He couldn't help but be flattered. He learnt to call them by their first names. Every couple of months he would go down to Cape Town and take them and their wives out to supper. Wine would flow, but Blank hardly touched it. Neither did he care much for the endless snooker sessions they seemed to enjoy.

Of course, he was not so naïve as to believe they liked him simply for his charming personality. There was a steely business motive underpinning the relationship. Part of the fellowship was easily explained: they had discovered young Blank, he was their protégé. If he did well by Old Mutual, why, they looked good too. All of them liked the fact that business had brought them together. It was an understandable bonding agent. They would have suspected an acquaintanceship founded on sentiment alone.

Blank was confident in such an association. He knew he had served them well. He could point to several great deals that had cemented his reputation, and one in particular.

Now, that had been some deal. It had helped Old Mutual to make a gain of about R200 million. He liked to bask in the memory of it. That's what he called a real gamble, except that it wasn't a proper gamble. He had done his homework far too well for that. The element of risk had been reduced to virtually nil.

It began in 1987, when a chemicals company was listed on the JSE. Blank knew the top men. He had seen the managing director's business acumen in operation, and he thought the company was bound to be a runaway success.

The board wanted an institutional investor; could their young stockbroker friend help? Of course he could. Blank thought immediately of Old Mutual, not only the biggest single investor on the JSE but also his largest client, so he brought the parties together. It turned out to be one of those marriages made in heaven.

The company did indeed prosper, and over the next three years Old Mutual bought up more shares, increasing its stake until it owned a quarter of the business. Then came the events that transformed a good investment into a brilliant one. A food product company divested from South Africa in 1989, leaving behind a remnant, which was scooped up by the chemicals company and ultimately tranformed into a major food giant. The new company, as Blank had anticipated, quickly found favour with the investing public and the share price soared. Old Mutual found, to its delight, that it had made a windfall profit of R200 million almost overnight. The figure was astronomical. And Blank had been the one to make it happen.

David Schapiro came to Johannesburg in the late summer of 1989 and Blank put him up, giving him the downstairs bedroom in the Khyber Rock cluster house. They went to the Longhorn steakhouse in Corlett Drive for supper. It was all very congenial. In April Schapiro returned the compliment. He said that he and a couple of 'the guys' from Old Mutual were going to the Comores. Would Blank like to join them?

Blank said: 'Great! I'll check with Sidney Frankel.'

Frankel thought it a great idea too. Blank reported back to Schapiro: 'The firm will even pay for my ticket.'

They had an idyllic week on the tropical islands. Blank shared a room with his new mate Schapiro and went for a 10-kilometre run every morning with Chris Logan, another of the bright young men on the Old Mutual dealing team. The days passed in swimming, scuba-diving, eating, making merry. Schapiro talked about the money he was making, the million-rand home he was building in Hout Bay. Blank thought he must be a very clever man: he was a lecturer at the University of Cape Town Business School and had won an award for being Old Mutual's top performer of the year.

The others all seemed to be rich too. For Blank, who had seen himself as a poor boy for so many years, it was truly a heady experience. This was how people lived.

He tried not to think about the little cloud that had appeared on his horizon. It was nothing. Nothing! Life was too sunny for a single cloud to matter. But it got bigger, and one day it was to blot out the sun for him.

The little cloud first appeared when he had dinner with Schapiro at the Longhorn steakhouse.

'Listen, Greg,' said Schapiro. 'I've got a business proposition for you.' He had Blank's instant attention. There was nothing vague about the proposition he outlined. He, Schapiro, was part of an Old Mutual syndicate that had been working with two brokers from the stockbroking firm of Ed Hern, Rudolph – Kenny Fouche and André Coetzee. Between them, they had created what was dubbed a 'stopover' or 'way-lay station'. This was no more than a special broking account in which could be accumulated parcels of a particular share that Old Mutual had expressed a wish to buy.

'We're saving Old Mutual a lot of trouble,' explained Schapiro. 'They want the shares, but they don't want the burden of having to assemble a large block themselves. So we do it for them. Okay, it costs them a little more this way, but they have the convenience.'

Blank understood instantly, having seen the phenomenon so often at the JSE. When consistent buying started, share prices rose. Old Mutual would be buying at the ruling price on the day it took possession. But the syndicate would have had the benefit of buying earlier, when prices were lower. It promised a tidy profit. But, then, that's what share-dealing was all about, wasn't it?

Schapiro said that relations with the Ed Hern, Rudolph brokers had become strained and the syndicate was looking for a new partner. They wanted an account at Frankel's and they wanted Blank to handle it. 'We've been operating the scheme for five years, there's nothing wrong with it,' Schapiro reassured him. But Blank could see that there was.

'Look, David,' he said, 'I've just started earning real money and I can't get involved. As you know, a broker can't have an undisclosed account. But thanks very much for thinking of me.'

Schapiro said: 'Fine, Greg. I understand.'

And that was that. No more was said. They finished their steaks and went back to Khyber Rock.

The next time the cloud appeared was in the Comores. Schapiro again raised the subject of Blank creating a way-lay station.

'Really, Greg, there's nothing to it. You know how to do it. You're good at getting large lines of shares, you've got the contacts for it. Those guys at Ed Hern are taking us for a ride, they're taking too big a cut. We have to find someone else.'

'Sorry,' said Blank, 'but count me out.'

The refusal didn't mar the holiday, however. They all had fun, just the same. Blank went back to work to find the markets were very quiet. June, July and August 1989 were terrible trading months for the JSE. Every day he would come back from the floor of the exchange to find Frankel waiting for him. 'How much money have you made today? What business have you done?' He was very conscious that he was responsible for 70 per cent of the firm's business. There were 250 employees who depended heavily on him. He felt the pressure.

Schapiro didn't make things easier; he seemed to have this fixation about Blank joining the syndicate, and kept insisting that it was untenable for the syndicate to be dependent on the Ed Hern, Rudolph stockbrokers.

One fateful day in August 1989, Blank cracked. The scene, the words spoken, are etched in his mind with ghastly clarity, though he can't remember the precise day on which it happened. Frankel's had organised a lunch for clients in their boardroom. Because the market was so quiet, there was more drinking than usual. David Schapiro was among the guests. Some time during the lunch he whispered urgently to Blank: 'I must see you afterwards.' Blank lingered behind when the other guests left.

Schapiro came up and offered him a chocolate-coated after-dinner mint.

'Greg,' he said, 'I'm sorry, but we are now insisting that you come in with us. We're breaking away from the Ed Hern guys. If you don't come in, you will lose our business. Remember Martin & Co? They took a chance, and lost a whack of business with us.' He said it gently, as if it pained him to put an ultimatum to a friend.

Yes, Blank did remember the Martin affair. A. Martin & Co., very upright stockbrokers, slightly snooty. Thought themselves a cut above their colleagues. Old Mutual employees had apparently approached them with a dubious proposition, and the firm had gone straight over the heads of the employees to complain to the top brass of the insurance company. The grapevine at the JSE had it that their representations had been successful – but that they had lost an unquantified amount of business anyway.

Blank put the chocolate in his mouth, took a bite and said: 'Yes, okay.'

He had paved the way for his own downfall. He couldn't quite believe that he had agreed. Typically, he began almost instantly to rationalise his decision to himself, a decision that had blurted from his mouth almost of its own volition, taking him by surprise as if someone else had said it. The market was bad. He couldn't ignore the Martin & Co. episode. Frankel's might not survive without the Old Mutual business. In just one year Old Mutual had paid R6 million to the firm in brokerage alone. And, of course, he did have special skills when it came to accumulating large blocks of shares; that was what he enjoyed most.

What if he did have an undisclosed account? How serious could that be? What could the JSE do to him – smack his wrists? He knew other brokers had such accounts; one, for example, had been running an undisclosed account for 20 years on behalf of a major institution. Everyone knew it. He might be committing a breach of the JSE rules, but a crime? Never.

The rationalisation, the tortuous justification, was to prove to be a big mistake. It made him complacent and cost him dear.

6

The Magic Circle

One brief post-lunch conversation and Blank was hooked. He was part of the conspiracy now. He knew what to do. The plan was beautifully simple. It was to exploit their insider's knowledge. Because the Old Mutual conspirators knew in advance precisely which shares their institution proposed to buy in time to come, their illegal syndicate could accumulate those shares in a secret account ahead of the Old Mutual buying order. Then, when the order came, Blank could sell the secret stock to Old Mutual at the current ruling price, which would, of course, be higher than the price prevailing when the syndicate first began to buy. Result: a handsome profit for the conspirators.

Once Colin Harper, Old Mutual's head trader, had identified the loopholes in the insurance giant's procedures, the mechanics of the operation were straightforward. Whatever problems there might have been had been ironed out over the previous five years with the Ed Hern, Rudolph brokers. The scam was airtight.

Marco Celotti and David Schapiro, as investment portfolio managers, were empowered by Old Mutual to invest the firm's funds. In deciding where to invest they had absolute discretion, but certain procedures had to be followed. Before an investment could be made in a JSE-listed company, they were required to identify the company, specify the size of the investment and state the price per share they were prepared to pay. Equity analysts helped to guide them.

Once their decisions were approved, it was over to the traders on Old Mutual's equity desk. Their job was to negotiate the acquisition with stockbrokers while ensuring that the fund managers' directives were carried out to the letter. Presiding over the traders was that wily old fox, Colin Harper. All the traders operated under his direct control and supervision – until November 1990, when he parted company with Old Mutual of his own volition four months before Blank was arrested.

Business deals could arise in one of two ways: at the behest of the financial institution; or on the suggestion of a broker who had access to a block of shares that he felt might interest the institution. In the ordinary course of business, brokers would often contact a portfolio manager to offer him shares that were available. If the portfolio manager decided to go ahead, he would naturally enough instruct the institution's trader to deal with the broker who had made the offer, as that broker had the shares available.

This provided a heaven-sent opening for the conspirators. Nobody would think twice if they specified Blank as the broker of choice in some of the bigger deals.

Blank's initial role on joining the conspiracy was to arrange a discreet account, and the necessary finance, through which shares could be bought and sold and in which profits could accumulate before they were shared. The account had to be suitably disguised to avoid linking it in any way to the conspirators. For the Old Mutual employees, exposure would have opened them to criminal charges arising from a gross betrayal of trust. For Blank, exposure would mean facing disciplinary measures from the JSE for failing to disclose an account. Or so he imagined.

Arranging the account proved easy. Blank approached an old friend and business associate, Joe Z., with a plausible proposal that skirted the truth. He and a group of friends, he said, wanted to speculate on the JSE. If Joe Z. would agree to open an account in his own name and raise a R3,5 million line of revolving credit, then he could join the act. He would have the benefit of Blank's demonstrable expertise, and be entitled to a one-sixth share of the profits. In the unlikely event of there being no profits, Joe Z. would not suffer disproportionately. His liability would be limited to one-sixth. Blank and his cronies would cover the rest.

Blank was careful not to reveal the real scheme to Joe. He didn't want to implicate him if, heaven forbid, things went wrong. Looked at another way, he reasoned, he was actually doing an old friend a favour by involving him but keeping him in ignorance. The profits were guaranteed, courtesy of Old Mutual. Joe Z. would be the innocent recipient of a windfall.

The next step was for Joe and Blank to pay a visit to another old friend, Jeffrey Rubenstein, who was chairman of Rubenstein Finance (Pty.) Ltd. Rubenstein was told no more than Joe. He agreed to open an account at his company and provide the required revolving credit at market-related rates. The account would be in Joe Z.'s name and only he would be allowed to operate it. As far as Rubenstein was concerned, his new client was the only person involved.

Blank's role was easily explained. He was the broker. His firm would open a trading account in the name of Rubenstein Client Account No. 2 to deal with the buying and selling of the chosen shares.

Blank had now made doubly certain that his tracks were covered. No one could trace things back to the conspirators. In fact, he had done even better than that. He had turned a profit of his own.

But that was a side issue. The real game was ready to begin.

It really was ridiculously easy. Celotti, Schapiro and Harper would get together and decide among themselves on a suitable share for purchasing. That effectively bucked a control system of checks and balances which had one flaw: it assumed there could be no collusion between trusted senior employees operating in separate departments. Once the purchase decision was made, and before it was formally ratified, the conspirators would tell their tame stockbroker Blank to go ahead and buy as many shares as he could at ruling market prices. These shares would be bought for an account in which they all had an interest. They would also be bought for friends and colleagues whom Blank wished to favour.

Sometimes the purchases would be made over a month or more, and the shares would nestle in this joint account while their market price rose, and rose again, in response to continuing demand. When an agreed number of shares had accumulated in the Rubenstein No. 2 account and were trading at a suitably higher price, either Celotti or Schapiro would relay the instruction from Old Mutual to buy. If the instruction was conveyed to Blank as broker, he would simply sell from the Rubenstein No. 2 account and buy for Old Mutual.

On those occasions where another broker got the business, Celotti or Schapiro would let Blank know, and he would sell his stock to the broker concerned.

It was as easy as that, and the buying strategy was well-nigh perfect. Although the risk was always there that some extraneous event might send the price tumbling, only once in the 45 deals that Blank was involved in did the share price fall before sale to Old Mutual. That was when they bought Publico shares and, after brokerage and tax, incurred a final loss to themselves of R111,02. As their net profits eventually amounted to nearly R3,5 million over 19 months, the partners felt they could wear that setback.

Once they got a brief scare. They had bought more than a million Consolidated Mining ordinary shares at 45 cents each over six days between March and April 1990, but they were nowhere to be found in their Rubenstein No. 2 account when the Old Mutual order came. Where on earth could they be? There was more than R60 000 profit to be made in this deal. It turned out that a clerk had erroneously booked the shares to Joe Z.'s personal account at Frankel's, so no harm was done. The profit could be shared as easily from that account. But, Blank wondered, what would have happened if the mistake had involved an account with an outsider? Would questions have been asked? Might they have become vulnerable? He didn't like to think about the implications.

Then the syndicate took its first small risk: the members agreed that all profits would be converted into Krugerrands. Joe Z. would take his one-sixth share, as agreed, and hand the rest to Blank for distribution. By this time, the conspirators had co-opted a new recruit – Allan Greyling, another portfolio manager at Old Mutual. The remaining Krugerrands were to be equally divided. The beneficiaries were Blank, Celotti, Schapiro, Harper, Greyling and Logan.

Now it is quite true that Krugerrands in themselves are safe and convenient instruments for holding cash. Nevertheless, the decision to buy them involved risk. The mere act of purchase creates a money trail, something that the conspirators had been anxious not to do. By their decision they had created a path down which a dedicated detective might travel if he felt so inclined. They all agreed that the risk was minimal and the eventuality too remote for concern. They were the only ones who knew about the scheme, and they all had a vested interest in keeping their mouths shut. What could go wrong?

In taking the small risk, they could not conceive of the bigger one – that one of the conspirators might decide to open his mouth. Then the Krugerrand trail would become an aid to detection.

In February 1990, about six months after Blank's recruitment into the scheme, Old Mutual's three wise crooks decided it was time to introduce him to their partner in another illicit operation.

They arranged a lunch for Blank to meet a man who revelled in the name of Walter Harry Peter Paxton Rawson, a Zimbabwean financial adventurer. Rawson ran a business called A. W. Bradshaw & Co. Ltd., registered in Guernsey in the Channel Islands, a well-known haven for business adventurers. His company was also being used as a conduit for routing shares to Old Mutual and creaming a profit. Blank remembers that lunch vividly.

'Peter left Zimbabwe under a bit of a cloud, foreign currency irregularities, that kind of thing. He had 24 hours to get out. He did a lot of business with South African broking firms. David and Marco asked if I would like to meet him. I said of course, I like to meet anyone I can do business with.

'I had lunch with him at a restaurant called Between the Chains at the JSE. We only had half an hour. The guy had two bottles of wine in that time. I couldn't believe it. We hardly talked about business. All he said was: "I believe you can get large lines of shares, place large lines. I'm in the business of moving large lines."'

Rawson told Blank he would like to use him. 'Fantastic,' said Blank. But each time he phoned Rawson overseas there was no business – until the day in March 1990 when Rawson called and asked him if he could get hold of a large line of Consolidated Mining shares for him.

'That's funny,' said Blank, 'I had 25 million Cons Mining three months ago and tried to sell them to Old Mutual, but they weren't interested.'

'Try to get them again. I'll take them,' urged Rawson.

The deal that Bradshaw did with the 25 million Consolidated Mining shares that Blank was able to acquire for him netted a profit of R2,75 million in just five days. Bradshaw bought at prices ranging up to 34 cents. He said he had a client who was very interested and he wanted to sell to the insurance giant quickly – at 45 cents. That's where Blank came into the act again. It was his next job to ensure that the market price rose to the higher figure. Blank had to use initiative. When the price seemed to be moving too slowly, he went to another stockbroker and struck a side-deal. If that stockbroker would buy everything he could find, Blank would guarantee to buy it back from him at a higher price. Eventually the price of 45 cents was reached and Rawson realised a minimum profit of 10 cents a share on 25 million shares.

And that marked the beginning of Greg Blank's involvement with a new 'magic circle'.

He insists that he didn't know at first what he was getting into. He thought he was simply doing an honest job as a legitimate broker. Rawson wanted specified shares. Blank had a genius for finding them. His Old Mutual mates had been kind enough to introduce them, and now they had a good business going. Yes, he sometimes had an uneasy feeling he could not define, but for a while he didn't want to believe there might be something wrong, so he didn't. He preferred to believe that he was a genius of a broker.

One day Rawson phoned and asked Blank to buy him as many Furnicor shares as he could. Blank thought to himself: *Great, I've got a client who's got a big line. He wants to sell a million.*

Rawson was prepared to pay up to 490 cents a share. The client wanted a higher price but Blank kept on nagging at him and eventually got them at 490 cents. Blank remembers: 'Five days later Rawson comes to me and says he doesn't like Furnicor any more, and will I get rid of them. Oh yes, and don't record the volume. We didn't record it last time, don't record it now. I phone the institutions. No takers. I phone a friend at Old Mutual and tell them I know the Furnicor owners, the shares are doing well. I suggest that I leave the line with them. Four hours later Old Mutual says it wants the shares. I phone Peter. Everyone is very happy.

'I think: I am an absolute genius. That's brokerage! That's fantastic! But the alarm bells are ringing too. There's something fishy here.'

It was the next phone call from Rawson, a week later, that forced Blank to confront reality. Rawson said: 'I just want to thank you for all the business we've been doing. Your share of the profits, where do you want me to put it?'

'What do you mean, my share of the profits?'

'No listen, I've done very well out of this. I'm giving you 10 per cent.'

'You know, Pete, you don't have to do this.'

'Ah, but I do. For all the deals we've done so far.'

'That's fantastic.'

Blank thought about the political turmoil in the country, the fact that money he had earned was now piling up in an account at Barclays Bank plc, Angel Court, London. It was time to try the Swiss bank route, just like so many South Africans he knew. A fellow broker on the JSE said he could open such an account for him, no trouble. He had done it before, for others. It seemed a fairly uncomplicated procedure, and Blank never even got a secret bank account number. He used a codeword for deposits. The codeword was 'cheese'. His first deposit amounted to R530 000 – just under $133 000. From then on, when he said the word 'cheese' he really was smiling.

Not long after his rewarding conversation with the Guernsey go-between, Schapiro came up to him and said: 'Has Pete Rawson spoken to you? Are you happy with the arrangement?' Then the penny dropped. Rawson was also being tipped off by the Old Mutual conspirators as to what the insurance giant was planning to buy. Blank felt deceived. He thought: *Oh yes, here we go again. I've been played for a sucker again. I knew, but I didn't want to know. I thought something could be going on, but I'm benefitting from it.*

Today he admits: 'It's a weak side of me.' However he adds quickly: 'But I don't know how many people would say: "It's very kind of you, but no thanks. I don't want $125 000".'

Blank came close to discussing the illicit operation with his boss, Sidney Frankel. So close. But in the end he backed away. He told the media much later that Frankel would have been outraged at the idea. He recalls the conversation at the time.

'Sidney, what would you say if we were offered a deal like Martin & Co. were offered? What would you do?'

Frankel said: 'Don't even ask me that question.'

'Yes, but what would you say?'

'You know exactly what I would say.' And that was where their conversation ended.

In essence, the new scheme that Blank was sucked into was little different from the one he was already involved in, except that now the shares would be accumulated in an offshore company and the profits taken there. This meant that the conspirators could make use of the financial rand and keep their money in a foreign account. While they readily recognised that both activities were illegal for South Africans, it was the kind of crime that had become almost socially acceptable in some circles. People actually boasted about having a nest-egg abroad. They said it would be irresponsible not to protect themselves and their families if things were to go badly wrong in South Africa.

Now the conspirators would be joining that exclusive coterie. If only they could talk about it, they would surely be the envy of some of their colleagues. What a pity they couldn't.

The account they established at Bradshaw was given the title of Capital International Trust No. 2. They thought the 'No. 2' was a clever touch. It implied that there was a No. 1 account already operating, which created an aura of respectability. Rawson handled the administration of the account from his UK base and the Bradshaw company charged an administration fee of 15 per cent on all capital gains. The rest of the profit was divided between Celotti, Schapiro, Harper and Blank. The fifth conspirator on the local front, Allan Greyling, was not included. He would be grateful for that one day.

For the overseas operation, it didn't matter much to the syndicate which broker handled the sale of the shares to Old Mutual. It didn't have to be Blank; indeed, it was sometimes better that it was not, because then there was nothing to link the sale to any of the conspirators back in South Africa. All Old Mutual would ever know was that there was a legitimate seller (Rawson, for Bradshaw & Co.) who just happened to be holding large quantities of the very share it desired. How convenient!

For safety's sake, a further wrinkle was added to the operation. The deals were not recorded. That was easy to arrange. When Blank was buying for Capital International Trust No. 2, he simply omitted to report the deals in the way required by the JSE. When he was the broker handling the sale to Old Mutual he also omitted to report it. And when other brokers were acting for Old Mutual – why, Blank or Rawson simply urged them to break the rules too. It was no big deal. Brokers were doing it all the time.

In fact, it was Blank who was asked not to report the deal the first time he acted for Rawson. The 25 million Consolidated Mining shares were in the possession of a man who shall be nameless. He and Blank haggled for two days to reach agreement. Finally, Mr X brought his price down from 37 cents a share to 34 cents, on one condition. Blank had to agree that the volumes would not be recorded.

Ironically, this secrecy kept Blank himself in ignorance of the fact that Rawson was selling the Consolidated Mining shares back to Old Mutual. That deal was done through a different broker. As it wasn't recorded either, Blank had no way of knowing it had happened. No official way, anyway. As for the practice of suppressing information – well, it was commonplace.

'I had no problem,' says Blank. 'I asked this stock exchange official if he minded if the volume didn't reflect. He didn't care. It was very simple in those days. When you booked volume overseas you recorded it as a foreign sale. But when you did that, you put two XXs in the remarks column, which meant that it did not go through the clearing house. If you omitted the XXs, the volume didn't reflect. If anyone queried it, it was a mistake, right? You forgot to do it, okay?'

A number of fairly large transactions were never officially recorded, and did not reflect in the price and volume statistics published by the JSE. This may have been rough on the investing public but, for the syndicate, it was an eminently sensible precaution. The Bradshaw company was a big buyer. Deals like the Consolidated Mining one attract attention. In the space of a mere nine months, such brisk transactions generated a profit of more than six million in financial rands. Might that not have raised eyebrows somewhere? Surely it was better to avoid speculation by omitting to record some things.

As time went by, the syndicate's manipulation of the market became more sophisticated. One of Blank's last deals provides a case study. Over five days in August 1990 Blank – with a little help from his stockbroking friends – was able to increase the price of Utico Holdings shares by nearly 20 per cent, generating a profit to the syndicate of 500 000 financial rands. He thought it was so easy a child could do it.

First, Blank bought 125 000 Utico shares at the ruling market price of R22 a share. That was his stakeholding for Rawson. The transaction was not reflected in the JSE statistics and the ruling price remained static.

Now he needed a lever for manipulation so he bought 300 Uticos at R24. It was his seed investment. The transaction was not recorded. By arrangement, he sold the 300 shares to a stockbroking firm called Michiel du Toit for the same price – R24 per share. The sale was not recorded. Michiel du Toit sold 100 of its shares to yet another stockbroking firm, Turner Patterson, for R25, which became the ruling price on the JSE board. Blank bought another 200 shares and sold them to Michiel du Toit for R26. Later the same day he bought them all back – 400 from Michiel du Toit, 100 from Turner Patterson. All at R26. Then Blank booked over his original block of 125 000 shares to Old Mutual, which accepted them gratefully at R26 a share.

The ruling price had been firmly established, and there had been enough activity in the share to prevent suspicion. Rawson made a profit of R500 000.

For Blank, 1990 was one hell of a year. At last, he felt, he was making money beyond his wildest dreams, at home and abroad. The local operation provided for all his needs – and more – in South Africa. The account at the Pictet et Cie bank in Geneva was mounting nicely. By September of that year his balance showed that, after four deposits in five months, he was the proud possessor of just under $300 000. The way the South African currency was going, that would be a million rands in no time, he reckoned.

He had his safety net. And nobody could find out – Swiss banking security was legendary, wasn't it?

In a state of exhilaration, Blank flew to Switzerland in June 1990 to complete the formalities for his bank account. He thought to himself: *How wrong can it be, having money overseas? I mean, everybody wants to get money out of the country. You walk around the northern suburbs of Johannesburg, everyone you meet tells you they've got money overseas.*

An official from Pictet et Cie met him at Geneva airport to give him the papers to sign. For God's sake, he had never even been to Switzerland before. Now he was playing a cloak-and-dagger game at an international airport, laying formal claim to a small fortune before flying off to the South of France for a well-earned holiday.

He recalls: 'I needed money overseas. It was a back door in case something went wrong. The government of the day forced you into doing it. Look what happened in Zimbabwe. What would happen if I suddenly had to get on a plane overnight? I knew it was wrong, but when something is taboo, what do you do? You find a way to do it. I might not even use the money, but it was there just in case. A comfort zone. It felt fantastic. Everything I wanted at home, and half-a-million dollars overseas. That's what life was about.'

Some of the money in the account came from the syndicate operations and some from his own earnings in South Africa. For a while, he let himself believe that the golden days would never end. But he was wrong, of course. Wrong about everything, especially about the security of his Swiss nest-egg.

7

Money Makes Enemies

In December 1990 Greg Blank forced himself to confront what he was doing. It frightened him.

Peter Rawson phoned from London and asked him to buy Da Gama, a share trading in the clothing sector of the JSE. He didn't need to be told; he knew by now. Old Mutual would eventually want Da Gama and – oh happy chance – Rawson was just going to have a line available.

Blank sprang into action but, for once, the market became capricious, erratic and unpredictable. The more stock he bought, the more became available and the price, instead of rising, kept on dropping. Now he had to prop the share up. Over six frantic days of trading, it would fall to 650 cents, he would chase it back up to 700 cents by buying more, then it would fall again. As his acquisitions grew in volume – 300 000 shares, 400 000, 500 000 – the price seemed to become ever more volatile. The Master of the Universe had lost control. The market was fighting back, demonstrating that it could only be manipulated so far before it rebelled. It was scary.

He finally bought 527 300 Da Gama shares for his client Rawson at prices ranging from 652 cents a share to 701 cents. But his job was not over. He still had to push the share up because Rawson wanted it higher before he sold to Old Mutual. When the right day came Rawson sold for 720 cents.

At last, Blank was truly alarmed. Sure, the exercise had put more than 300 000 financial rands in the syndicate's kitty. But at what price? Even today, Blank feels that same shiver of apprehension. 'I knew we were playing with fire. We were going totally against the market.' Whether the deals were recorded or not, someone would surely notice the curious price fluctuations in Da Gama and the extraordinary fact that, when supply exceeded demand, the price still rose, albeit erratically. Old Mutual, at least, would have to smell a rat.

Blank went to Schapiro, saying: 'David, I want out. I can't handle this any more. It's putting enormous pressure on me. I've got other work to do.'

'Sure,' said Schapiro, 'but we'll have to phase you out slowly.'

'Yes, but what is slow?'

Slow could be a year. That was far too long for him. He had a feeling that, now that he was in their grip, his co-conspirators would never let go, never stop. They had all become too greedy, the money was too good. As it happens, he was wrong. The Da Gama deal was the last one he handled. Unfortunately for him, it was one deal too many. The net was closing.

Frankel's was attracting attention on the Johannesburg Stock Exchange in that heady year of 1990. People were noticing that it was doing more business and was thriving. Some estimated that it was responsible for about 25 per cent of the entire turnover of the JSE. That bright young stockbroker Gregory Blank seemed to have a magic touch. He was obviously the kingpin of the firm, the man to watch. Aided by his massive contribution, Frankel's was expanding, swallowing competitors.

Not everybody wished it well. Money makes enemies as well as friends. Some people were looking critically rather than admiringly at what was going on. Retribution was sharpening its knife. Some time in the first month of the new year of 1991 someone went to the General Purposes Committee of the JSE – responsible for day-to-day administration and control – and reported that there was something odd happening in the Frankel's account known as Rubenstein Client Account No. 2. There were too many peculiar entries that seemed to make no sense. Only someone with access to Frankel's accounts could have had the information to make a report like that.

Sidney Frankel later told the world that it was he who went to the then president of the JSE, Tony Norton, to ask for an investigation. He had, he said, become suspicious of Blank's activities – but not so suspicious that he rejected the brokerage generated by the movements in the Rubenstein account. Norton confirmed that he had had a visit from Frankel about the account. But others questioned the sequence of events; had Frankel been preceded by someone else?

Blank thought so. In fact, he was sure he knew who first blew the whistle. Every deal he had ever done through the Rubenstein account was meticulously recorded and brokerage was paid. That was the strength of the scam. Everything looked so normal. Frankel had been living with the Rubenstein account for nearly a year. Why would he suddenly get suspicious about it?

No, the man who had blown the whistle had to be someone inside the firm with a score to settle. He thought about likely candidates. Frankel, a difficult person, had had his squabbles with staff. But one employee, in particular, had been at loggerheads with the boss for weeks on end. It had to be him. He had motive and access to the firm's accounts. In Blank's mind, his suspicions were confirmed when an indiscreet secretary showed him a copy of a letter from his prime suspect to the internal control department of the JSE. The letter pointed out the oddities in the Rubenstein account and suggested an official inquiry.

Blank remembers: 'The man I believe tipped off the JSE checked all our deals every day…all those shares being accumulated and then sold off. In itself, no one could pick up that anything was wrong. The institutions did it all the time. They called it front-running. If they wanted a particular line of shares, they kept on buying, buying, buying. And as they bought, the price went up. That's all anyone could see in the Rubenstein account.'

But, thought Blank, the man must have twigged what was really going on, and saw an opportunity to give his boss, Frankel, a shot in the eye. That's how it must have happened, Blank told himself. Did it matter, anyway? Who dunnit wasn't the real issue. The real issue was whether the JSE authorities could unravel what was going on – at home and abroad.

Blank remained quite sure that they would not be able to. No matter how they probed, all they would find was a legitimate account in the name of a legitimate account holder featuring a string of apparently legitimate buys and sells. There was no link to him – except that he had been the broker in most instances – and no link to any of the other conspirators. If he was questioned, he would tell them what, by now, he half-believed himself: these were perfectly above-board transactions done on behalf of the account holder. No, he didn't know why Old Mutual featured so heavily, but it was the biggest player on the JSE, wasn't it? Old Mutual was his client too. Wasn't it reasonable that he would go to Old Mutual first when he had something worthwhile to sell?

Once again he reminded himself: the only danger was if a member of the syndicate spilt the beans. But that wasn't going to happen. He certainly was not about to talk, and the others had too much to lose. If they all held their tongues, mere suspicion could never be hardened into evidence.

Back at Old Mutual, meanwhile, puzzlement was hardening into suspicion. When the JSE authorities had first pointed out on Thursday, 31 January that there were 'unusual' features involving six deals, the general manager in charge of investments asked an internal audit inspection team to provide as much information as it could about the deals without awakening suspicions. Old Mutual wanted to take no chances that a guilty party might become aware of the inquiry and then try to frustrate it. For a few intensive days and nights, team members followed the clues in the JSE report, which dealt with transactions only and did not mention names. Soon it became clear that Celotti and Schapiro were the portfolio managers who decided on the deals on behalf of Old Mutual. Gradually, it became apparent that Colin Harper might be involved. If indeed something was fishy, then the possibility existed that the interests of one or more of its major clients could be prejudiced. Perhaps a major pension fund that the company administered was being cheated. This was something the top executives could not ignore.

On 7 February Old Mutual issued a public statement announcing that Celotti and Schapiro had been suspended with immediate effect. 'Some investment transactions which require investigation have come to our notice,' the announcement said. 'An internal investigation into these transactions is under way.' The two suspended employees were told very little more; all they knew was that 'suspicious deals' were being probed. But Old Mutual needed them out of the way for a fuller, more intensive investigation to begin.

Colin Harper was already out of the way. He had resigned the previous November. He was known as a man for the high life; someone who had once enjoyed the trappings of wealth and had spent prodigiously. He had been a stockbroker, but had lost everything when he invested in an ill-starred game venture and property development in Hermanus. Down on his luck, he had successfully approached Old Mutual for a job in its equities department. Quite quickly his talents had enabled him to rise to the position of head dealer, and to celebrate, as it were, he had acquired a Mercedes-Benz 500 sports car to go with his lavish home in Hermanus. No one seemed to think there was anything odd about his sudden return to riches; they simply assumed that the substantial Harper family trust had come to his aid. But now – for better or worse – he was beyond the clutches of his erstwhile employers and unable to impede the investigation.

Quickly, and confidentially, a more formidable task force was set up to conduct a full-time investigation. Its members included the institution's chief accountant, its chief legal adviser and two external auditors. The team was to operate as if on a military exercise. Ordinary office hours went by the board, and meetings took place in secret, away from the prying eyes of staff.

Three alarming situations began to emerge: there appeared to be crimes involving fraud and currency control regulations; similar fraudulent schemes involving other financial institutions were apparently in operation; and the market had been defrauded through unreported transactions. It was time to act.

The necessarily incomplete picture that began to emerge caused alarm in the executive corridors of Old Mutual. Something was amiss. The unthinkable had happened: trusted senior employees whose functions had been so designed that they would provide checks and balances on one another were in fact colluding to defraud the institution. That was bad enough. Worse was the fact that Old Mutual could take its investigation only so far.

The firm considered its position. Its investigation had confirmed wrongdoing in its own ranks but, lacking the powers of a government agency, it could go no further. It could not establish the full ramifications of the conspiracy. It could not say for certain that no trust funds had been violated; no clients disadvantaged. What should it do?

The decision Old Mutual took has become a case study in business ethics at some business schools in South Africa. The easy way out – the way many companies might have taken – would have been to get rid of the erring employees, devise new systems to prevent similar malpractices and sweep the whole sorry affair under the carpet. That way, public confidence in the institution would not take a knock. But that was not how Old Mutual decided to deal with it. Investments that pension funds had entrusted to Old Mutual were involved. Old Mutual had a fiduciary duty to determine if, and to what extent, these funds were prejudiced. It reasoned that only a full-scale, empowered investigation could ensure that.

The day after the internal investigators had completed their report, an Old Mutual delegation went across Cape Town to present its findings to the ministers of justice and of finance, and shortly after that, Attorney-General Frank Kahn was appointed to lead an in-depth investigation. Old Mutual had decided that its first concern had to be for its members and clients and not its short-term reputation.

In an ideal world, that should perhaps have been enough to protect it from further criticism. In the real world, however, it was not. Many asked whether the insurance giant had been lax in some way, not vigilant enough with public money. How could rogue employees get away with scams – month after month, year after year – without detection? I put the question to Old Mutual's chief legal adviser, Koos Stassen, who replied: 'The investments division had rigorous procedures to prevent abuse. The participants to the scheme ensured that they played by these rules. The only sure way to pick up this type of collusion is to look at both sides of transactions – in other words, the buyer and the seller. Since the other side was not accessible to Old Mutual, fully effective monitoring to prevent collusion of this kind can only be done by the JSE.

'The Old Mutual investigation showed that other institutions had been drawn into collusive deals with brokers. This tends to show that the industry as a whole did not have better or more effective preventative measures than Old Mutual at the time. The difference between the scam in which Blank was involved and the other scams was mainly in scale and sophistication. When suspicious indications did come to light, Old Mutual did not hesitate to act swiftly and decisively.'

Celotti and Schapiro did not hang around to see what Old Mutual would do next. In late February 1991, some two weeks after their suspension, they fled. Perhaps they heard that Harper was going to spill the beans; perhaps it was a five-line report in the *Saturday Star* that said, blandly, that the Old Mutual investigation was making good progress and that arrests were expected soon.

Nobody tried to stop Celotti and Schapiro at the airport or queried their going. They left no goodbye notes for their former employers. They didn't even say cheerio to their old buddy Blank. On 22 March – 12 days after Blank's arrest – Old Mutual completed a formal disciplinary hearing and fired both men in their absence.

Blank was getting anxious. He had read about the suspension of Celotti and Schapiro in the newspapers, but there seemed to be no hard information. The rumour mill was churning out scare stories. The suspension was just the tip of an iceberg, said the usual 'anonymous sources' so beloved of newspapers. The authorities were hot on the trail of a massive fraud and some stockbrokers might be implicated. As far as Blank could see, it was all sound and fury, nothing to get panicky about. Still, he had better phone Schapiro, find out what was going on.

He called for a week. Once, Schapiro's wife answered. 'David's not here… he's just gone round the corner to the shops,' she told him.

'Ask him to call me, please.'

'Okay. Bye.'

No call came. Blank began to wonder: was his friend being interrogated? Had he been kidnapped? His thoughts were too fanciful. He put them out of his mind. February was the busiest month ever for Frankel's at the JSE – Blank alone had done R3 million of brokerage – and he had a lot to keep him occupied. Besides, he had this ability to concentrate on the job at hand to the exclusion of all else. He actually forgot about Schapiro and thought about nothing but the dazzling prospects that lay ahead in the market. He felt like a Master of the Universe again.

He was distracted but not perturbed when four heavyweights from the Reserve Bank of South Africa arrived at the JSE on 27 February 1991. Charles van Staden, a senior bank official, was the leader and he seemed quite a decent guy. Van Staden wanted to know about the overseas deals Blank had been involved in.

Blank's face never altered, his eyes never flickered. He was utterly convinced of his invincibility. 'It's quite simple, gentlemen. I'm a broker, I act as an agent. My client phones from overseas and says he wants these shares. If I can get these shares, I sell them to him. That's all I'm doing.' He took them through the deals one by one, Consolidated Mining, Utico, the lot. He thought he handled his questioners well for they seemed satisfied. He was 11 days away from arrest.

A few days later, the phone rang.

'Greg? It's David [Schapiro].'

'David, where are you? I've been worried. I thought…'

'I'm in Guernsey, with Marco. We've…'

'Guernsey! What the hell are you doing in Guernsey?'

'Don't worry, Greg. We're just fixing up a few things. Sorting things out. We'll be back at the weekend.'

Blank felt an overwhelming sense of relief. They were fixing things up. They would be back. The crisis was over. He was eight days away from arrest.

Five days before the policemen finally came to his home for him, he met Attorney-General Frank Kahn. Kahn was a pushover. Blank's explanations had been accepted. He had nothing to fear from him; indeed, he'd quite enjoyed the mind games. Sure, Celotti and Shapiro hadn't come home, but that meant they were out of the country, not available to give evidence. He didn't give Colin Harper a second thought. Harper was a weak man, and in any case, he was no longer employed by Old Mutual, so the company would have got nothing out of him. Harper wasn't going to talk, not now that he had had so narrow an escape.

How could Blank be expected to know that Kahn had outwitted him? He had only seen one side of the man, his ruffled appearance and brusque manner. He hadn't had a chance to see the keen intellect and the deeply suspicious nature in action. How could he have known that Kahn would quickly decide to conduct his own investigations without the aid of the officers of the Johannesburg Stock Exchange?

Petrus Marais, seconded to the Office for Serious Economic Offences and ultimately to be the prosecutor in the Blank case, remembers: 'That's one thing you've got to give Frank credit for. He trusted no one, and quite rightly so. He didn't trust the JSE either. And so, after the first week or so of trying to work with the JSE he told them upfront: "Forget it. I'm taking over. I don't report to the president of the stock exchange and I don't report to the executive committee of the stock exchange." And I think it was largely that decision that enabled us to get the information we needed without there being any leaks.

'Frank was very conscious of the danger of leaks. Even when we met Old Mutual people we would see them only on Saturdays and Sundays at secret and neutral venues so that the office staff couldn't see who was coming and going.'

All of which begins to explain why Gregory Lex Blank got such a shock when his two midnight visitors brought an arrest warrant to his home on that traumatic night in March 1991. There was another shock lying in wait for him two days later.

Realising that the authorities might discover not only that he had a nest-egg in Switzerland but even which bank it was in, he thought it wiser to shift the money. He phoned the Pictet et Cie bank on Tuesday, 12 March, and asked to speak to the manager. An official came on the line.

'It's Gregory Blank here,' said Blank. 'The "cheese" account. I want to move my money.'

'Oh,' said the official. 'We have a little problem. But don't worry. It's all okay.'

'Problem? What do you mean "problem"? I want to move my money.'

'You can't. The magistrate has frozen the account.'

'But how can you let them into my account?'

From the bank official's laboured explanation, Blank realised one thing: he had been wrong about the security of Swiss banks. The South African authorities had stolen a march on him. In normal circumstances, Swiss banks will disclose nothing about a client's account, especially not in cases of suspected foreign currency contraventions. But where a recognised crime is suspected, provision exists for a Swiss court to order that activity on a particular account be suspended. A member of Kahn's team had gained such an order, saying that they were investigating fraud charges against Blank. So now the foreign nest-egg that had meant so much to him had been snatched from Blank's grasp. He was never to see it again.

8

Out on Bail

For a few weeks after the arrest of Blank and Kenny Fouche, the newspapers had a wonderful time. 'Breakthrough in JSE/Old Mutual fraud investigation,' said the headline in the country's leading daily, *The Star*, on Monday, 11 March 1991. Its report began:

> Last night's arrest of two leading JSE stockbrokers represents a major breakthrough in the Government investigation into irregular investment transactions involving JSE brokers and the Old Mutual. The arrests stunned the broking community. It had been thought that the transactions being investigated were of such a complex nature that establishing sufficient evidence even to bring a charge against any parties would be extremely difficult. Already there were rumours circulating the JSE this morning of further arrests being on the cards, and other stockbroking firms being brought into the investigation.
>
> JSE president Tony Norton stressed that the investigation would be continued and 'no stone left unturned' until all the ramifications had been thoroughly investigated.

Sidney Frankel told the media that Blank had been suspended, and stressed that his firm was fully supportive of the investigation and was keen to establish the integrity of the JSE as an institution.

Ed Hern of the firm Ed Hern, Rudolph said that the arrest of Kenny Fouche had come as a surprise to him. His firm was 'fully behind' the government investigation.

The police issued warrants of arrest for Marco Celotti, David Schapiro and Peter Rawson. *The Star* reported on 12 March: 'There is now speculation that one informed source is providing considerable assistance to the investigating team. This may be sufficient to compensate for the difficulties that are expected to arise as a result of the departures of Mr Celotti and Mr Schapiro.' Colin Harper, as befits an informed source, kept his head down at his Hermanus retreat.

The notion that Blank was some kind of playboy fanned media interest. *Finance Week*, a business publication, reported on 14 March that his wealth supported a flamboyant lifestyle.

> While he's only travelled abroad three times in the past ten years, he drives a Ferrari, owns an art collection said to be worth a small fortune and lives in a townhouse in an upmarket Khyber Rock complex. A gregarious bachelor and fitness fanatic, he is to be seen as regularly at the Sandton Health and Racquet Club as he is at the horse-races. Blank, immensely charming and widely popular as one of the boys, was role model for many younger dealers. On the floor, he built a circle of admirers because of his ability to swing big deals.

Not to be outdone, the mass-circulation *Sunday Times* took up the playboy cry on 17 March and burrowed into Blank's social life. 'Beautiful women, luxury cars and race horses dominate the life of high-flying stockbroker Greg Blank,' it breathed. 'Asked about his pending trial, he said coolly: "Look at me, I'm cruising."'

More soberly, the *Financial Mail*, the country's most influential financial weekly, reported on 22 March, under the headline 'Diagonal Street Blues': 'Members of the investment community say they're gratified Diagonal Street is being cleaned up, chagrined that the broom had to sweep up some of the nicer guys in the business, and also nervous about who will be next.' It quoted a former stock analyst as saying: 'People are happy something is being done. But this is just a small bit of what is going on. All sorts of fiddles are being pulled. Some practise it, and some don't.' A JSE broker confidently predicted that 'dozens of people will be put on Frank Kahn's hit list. There's no question they'll get some convictions.'

'The JSE is built on mutual trust between its members and also between its members and the public,' pronounced *The Star*. 'Stockbrokers boast that their word is their bond. They are extremely angry because it appears that a number of trusted people have resorted to practices which could damage the reputation and standing of its members.'

In all the hullabaloo and turmoil, one thing was noticeable. Not even the most loyal supporters of the JSE believed that two arrests and three warrants of arrest would be enough to clean up the stock exchange. No one seemed to have any doubt whatsoever that malpractices were commonplace and even fairly widespread. All seemed to subscribe to the 'tip of the iceberg' theory. If there was surprise at the arrests, it was surprise that they had happened at all.

On 10 June, three months after their arrest, Greg Blank and Kenny Fouche made their first appearance in court on allegations of fraud. No indictment was ready and they were not asked to plead. Fouche, whose bail had already been reduced from the original R500 000 to R250 000, asked for it to be reduced still further. 'I have nothing in the bank,' he told Johannesburg

Magistrate J. Moolman. 'All my accounts have been frozen. While this case continues, no one will employ me. I am not allowed to trade on the JSE and it is the only game I know.' He was 43 years old, had a family, lived a life of quiet respectability outside the office and had worked as a broker's clerk for virtually all his adult life. His home in suburban Florida, valued at R250 000, had been put up as surety for the bail. He wanted to sell his property to repay Ed Hern, whose firm had put up the bail money in the first place. The prosecutor objected to any reduction in bail because Fouche, like Celotti and Schapiro, might flee the country. The trials of Fouche and Blank were formally separated. Neither had any inkling then how different their futures would be.

Blank remained stoically silent in court. The size of the bail was the least of his worries. Magistrate Moolman kept his bail at R500 000 and told him the next hearing would be in Cape Town in October of that year. He set about living as near normal a life as he could. It was difficult, near impossible, at first.

One of his bail conditions was that he had to report to Sandton police station twice a day, between seven and nine o'clock in the morning and between five and seven o'clock in the evening. He reported for the first time on Tuesday, 12 March. The policeman on duty said: 'Who are you?' He said: 'I'm Gregory Blank, I've come to sign in. What must I do?' But no one knew. The papers had not yet arrived from the court and would not appear for another four days. So for those four days he didn't really exist at all as far as the Sandton police station was concerned. The policemen thought he was a bit of a nuisance, wanting to report in without documentation.

After that, it was a matter of establishing a routine. He would check in at the police station in the morning, go on to Sandton Health and Racquet Club for a workout, go home, have a shower, get into his dressing gown and watch videos. After lunch and, possibly, a doze, the routine would be reversed. Back to the gym, back to the police station for the evening sign-in, then home. But the lure of the JSE remained irresistible.

'I *wasn't* suspended from the firm. I'd make a few calls to the market – I was still putting deals together, still earning brokerage from my clients. Sidney Frankel said it would be better if I worked from home. Later, he ended the arrangement.'

Blank didn't mind all that much. His heart wasn't really in it anyway. He felt as if he was in limbo. He didn't feel much like going out. When he went to a restaurant where he was known, someone would say: 'Look, there's Greg Blank,' and eyes would turn towards him and the place would fall silent as he walked to a table. He tried to look nonchalant and walk naturally, but his legs would suddenly feel heavy. Once, at a Longhorn steakhouse, he overheard a conversation at a nearby table. Somebody said: 'I wonder what happened to Greg Blank,' and a loud voice replied: 'That dirty crook, he should be in jail.' He heard a murmur of assent, and cringed. He thought to himself: *Should I walk over there and tell them I'm Greg Blank, and bang the guy's head down on the table?* But, of course, he didn't. Instead he consoled himself with the thought that people liked to see a big man pulled down. They got pleasure out of it.

At first, reporting to the police station was an agony of embarrassment. It was the contrast that struck home. Yesterday he had been riding the crest of a wave, the world at his feet. Today he was a suspected criminal. 'You walk in, you try to hide, you know, in case someone recognises you. If there's a member of the public there, you hope they'll think you're a plainclothes policeman or something.'

He learnt who his real friends were. Most of the people he knew seemed to stand by him, offering support; even old workmates, until management stopped them from associating with him. But he was painfully conscious that some people appeared to be holding back. When he asked for business, they would say: 'Well, things aren't going so well now. Another time, perhaps.' They didn't seem to be saying to themselves: 'This guy helped us to make lots of money, so what can we do to help him now?' Oh yes, they were friendly enough. 'They would shake my hand, and then they would...sort of...count their fingers.' He found an easy formula for assessing friendship: 'The people who stood by me were my friends. The people who fell by the wayside were not my friends.'

Everybody assumed his guilt so he felt he had been firmly placed in the category called 'criminal'. The worst kind of people took to phoning him, asking him how to make money and whether they could join him in an illegal money-making scheme.

One man did offer practical help. Meeting Blank at the Sandton Sun hotel for tea, the man produced a false passport for him, complete with new name and photograph. He would put a private plane at the stockbroker's disposal any time he wished. Blank could flee and go free. All the stranger asked in return was that Blank should take a substantial sum of money out of the country on his behalf.

'I'm not going anywhere,' Blank said coldly.

One day another stranger came to see him, waving a cheque for R20 million. 'See this cheque?' said the man. 'It's from the Swaziland government. No one will know it's gone missing for at least three months. Now, how do we launder it?'

Blank could hardly believe his ears. Did people really think he was willing to do anything? Was it a trap?

'Do you know what kind of person I am?' he asked.

'Yes, I think so.'

'Do you know I'm helping the Office for Serious Economic Offences with their investigations?'

'So what? I just want to know how to wash this money. I'll cut you in.'

'Have you ever been arrested?'

'No.'

'Well, I have. And I don't intend to have it happen ever again. Now get out, and if you're lucky, I'll pretend this conversation never took place.'

About three months after his arrest, Blank made up his mind. He could not ask Di Reynolds to share this burden with him; it was too much. He told the girl he loved: 'I can't see you any more. You must get on with your life.' She tried again and again to make him change his mind, but he was adamant. Di was devastated. 'I couldn't understand why, if he loved me, he didn't want to be with me. I would have stuck by him, even if he had to go to jail. I was in love with Greg, but I felt I was banging my head against a brick wall. You know, when you get pushed away and pushed away so many times, eventually you go.' But they stayed friends.

Blank analyses the breakup now. 'It was very hard for me to really maintain a relationship. I'm a practical sort of guy. At the end of the day, if the worst came to the worst and I ended up in jail, I didn't want to have any ties. It would have made things harder. I used to go out and try not to have too good a time. I would hold myself back. I didn't want to have too many happy memories if they locked me up. It was surreal. You want to go on as if nothing has happened, but something *has* happened!'

Living in limbo and cutting ties became, in his own words, 'a dangerous lifestyle'. He was beginning to wallow in his own misery. One day, after about six months, he took a hard look at himself. *Gregory!* he said. *You can't go on like this. You have to get out of this rut.* So he changed.

By the time of his third court appearance – in Cape Town in January 1992 – he had developed a coping philosophy, regaining his equilibrium and optimism. He had mastered anew the trick of compartmentalising his mind. *Right,* he told himself, *that's my arrest. I'll go back to it when I have to. This is my life, let me carry on.*

He began to count his blessings while rationalising his problems. His family were warmly supportive. There had been no recriminations from them. 'I thought he had been greedy, but I never once lost faith in Gregory,' says his mother, Gail. 'There is nothing in the world that would make me admire him less.' And his father, Robby, reasons: 'I think he was a bit of a fool. I wish he had talked to me, I would've told him not to get involved. He made a mistake but he's still my son.'

What sort of crime was he accused of anyway? Blank wondered. He knew the market, knew what was condoned – or ignored. The worst thing that could happen, he told himself, would be that the JSE authorities would give him a ticking-off. 'I'm the smallest player in the syndicate. I thought: They've only got a little fish. I sort of felt,' he says now, 'what I had done wasn't the most terrible thing in the world.'

He knew he would have to break the pattern of solitude, of hiding himself. It was time to get back to business again. In September 1991 he went to share offices in Illovo, Johannesburg, with his friend David Hirschowitz, an entrepreneur. He began to manage money for a small circle of clients. Over the next two years or so he would give this circle of blessed clients a return of something like 170 per cent on their investments.

'When I went back into business, that's when I began to come right,' Blank recalls. 'It was like being back at work. It was great. In fact, I was looking after more money in this new business than I had been at the exchange. That was quite uplifting. It meant that people's faith and trust in me hadn't gone. If a client came to me, he knew all about me. I didn't want to hide anything.'

What he did was perfectly legal. The JSE might not permit him to act as a broker, but there was no law to stop him giving financial advice. Even so, nothing could be completely straightforward. He knew that some of his clients were embarrassed at still having dealings with him, preferring to be more circumspect. So when Blank phoned these sensitive souls, he would tell the secretary: 'It's Lennox Brown speaking. May I speak to your boss?'

Not everything was rosy all the time. There were days when he woke up thinking that the waiting for trial was almost worse than prison could be. He was in a prison of another kind, living a half-life. Days turned to months as the law plodded along the path of due process. Tuesday, 28 January 1992 was a particularly bad day. That's when the prosecutor produced the 57-page indictment, listing 49 charges of fraud. It was filled with the portentous language of the law, designed to inspire in laymen dread and mystification.

It began with a ringing statement:

> The Attorney-General for the Witwatersrand Local Division, who prosecutes in the name and on behalf of the State, presents and gives the court to be informed that GREGORY LEX BLANK, an adult male (hereinafter referred to as the accused) is guilty of the crimes of:
>
> Counts 1–6: Fraud
> Counts 7–30: Fraud
> Counts 31–35: Fraud
> Counts 36–48: Fraud
> Count 49: Fraud.

Each little cluster of fraud charges was accompanied by an alternative charge, a litany that read something like this: 'Alternatively Contravention of Section 2 (a), alternatively Section 2 (c) read with Sections 1 and 9 of the Financial Institutions Act 39 of 1984, alternatively contravention of Section 3 read with Sections 1 and 9 of the Financial Institutions Act 39 of 1984...' And so on.

These guys are serious, thought Blank. *They're throwing the legal book at me. They're not going to let the JSE rap me over the knuckles. They've actually set a trial date: 5 October 1992, in the Rand Supreme Court.*

But then, mere weeks before that time, Blank was able to breathe a massive sigh of relief. *Sanity,* he thought, *has prevailed.* Witwatersrand Attorney-General Klaus von Lieres und Wilkau announced that he had decided to allow Kenny Fouche, the stockbroker arrested on the same night as Blank, to pay admission of guilt fines. The same dispensation was to be offered to André 'Stompie' Coetzee, another stockbroker from Ed Hern, Rudolph. When the Fouche/Blank trial was separated, Fouche had found himself bracketed with a new alleged accomplice, Coetzee. Both men had originally been charged with 570 counts of fraud arising from irregularities in institutional share dealings. The charges against the two men were to be reduced to 200, and they would be allowed to pay admission of guilt fines amounting to R1 000 per count, for each of them. In exchange, the fraud charges would be withdrawn.

The attorney-general seemed delighted at the outcome. In a press release, he explained: 'It is a case which should more appropriately be brought in the Regional Court. Then I was approached by defence counsel to explore the possibilities of paying admission of guilt fines. According to my calculations, not more than R650 000 had been made by the two defendants in illegal operations. I am entitled to impose admission of guilt fines of up to R1 500, and decided on balance that I could live with this.'

The reduction in the number of charges and the imposing of a fine of R1 000 per charge meant that the total paid by each of the two men was R200 000, a figure well within the rights and authority of the A-G to set. The men, duly grateful, promised to assist with the prosecution of other people involved in the scams.

Von Lieres offered further motivation for his act of grace. His job, he said, required him to apply his mind to ensuring that the whole procedure was as cost-effective as possible. A trial might have lasted six to nine months and would have occupied at least three counsel and a judge. 'Whatever profits these two people might have made, the size of the fine will mean that there will be no profit left and that they will have to dig deeper into their pockets,' said his press release.

The decision outraged observers within and outside legal circles. So this is how seriously the government took white-collar crime, they cried. It seemed to the critics that the comfort of the courts was the criterion. If the State could save time and money by making a deal, why then, deal with criminals. Treat them with kid gloves, especially if the money defrauded was not monstrously large.

Some of the observers more skilled in arithmetic than the attorney-general did their own calculations. If the men had got away with R650 000 in illegal transactions, and they were required to pay only R200 000 each in fines, that left them with an estimated R250 000 of illicit money in the kitty with which to start their new lives. Truly, crime seemed to have paid.

On the other hand, the attorney-general's decision was greeted with delight by Greg Blank. The authorities could hardly treat him differently, he reckoned. He was quite prepared to pay a fine, so as to get rid of this burden hanging over his head. Perhaps this whole nasty business could be laid to rest at last.

As would happen so often, Blank was destined to be disappointed.

As the days ticked by to his trial in October, it became apparent that he was not to get the dispensation offered to Fouche and Coetzee. His trial would take place as planned. There was to be no mercy, no leniency, for him.

Nevertheless, he found himself smiling secretly to himself. His parents didn't know it, his friends didn't know it, but he had one last big ace up his sleeve. It would be played on the opening day of his trial. It would be a surefire winner.

9

The Secret Deal

Sometimes, not often, in the 19 months between Blank's arrest in March 1991 and his trial in October 1992, he would spare a thought for his two conspirators on the run. Apart from the one phone call from Schapiro in Guernsey, he had heard nothing from them directly. But from time to time he would get news of the fugitives from the newspapers, from mutual friends, from his lawyers and from the investigation team that was bent on tightening the noose around the neck of the only suspect they had been able to nab – Greg Blank himself.

Blank felt nothing for Marco Celotti, the man with everything. Celotti looked like everyone's image of a Latin playboy – lean face, dark hair, rakish moustache, warm smile, bright white teeth. He had an MSc and an MBA, a loving wife called Margaret and a successful career (until the bubble burst). A female acquaintance said of him: 'He was sweet. One of the nicest people in the business.' Celotti was 34 when he fled. He went first to Israel and then, cavalier as ever, bounced out of that sanctuary and into nowhere. Blank, at least, had not heard from him again and he thought, with the sad wisdom of hindsight, that Celotti would certainly not be worrying about the predicament of former co-conspirators. Celotti was nothing if not self-centred.

Celotti's would-be captors had reason to believe their prey had finally gone to ground in the fastnesses of Italy, where he was said to be running a financial consultancy. Their warrant of arrest was never executed and no extradition attempts were made. As Celotti was an Italian citizen with an Italian passport, extradition was virtually impossible anyway. Italian law provided for a trial in Italy, but the South African authorities didn't much care for that option. They wanted to do the job themselves.

On the other hand, Blank felt only pity for poor, tortured David Schapiro. Schapiro had been a 'golden boy' too. He had been an above-average lecturer in economics at the University of Cape Town before he joined Old Mutual. He was mad about sailing, and had bought a yacht which was later wrecked at sea. Colleagues said he was an ordinary guy who liked the good life. He was putting the finishing touches to what people described as a 'palace' at Hermanus when he ran away.

For all his money, Schapiro became a forlorn figure – homesick, harassed, remorseful – while he was on the run. He had scuttled around Europe for several months, forever frightened, dodging arrest, drinking himself into nightly stupors. His wife was seeking a legal separation; his two young children were with her in South Africa. He was alone and rootless. Finally, he had ended up in Israel. Gone was the happy-go-lucky spirit who loved people, the engaging freckle-faced, mop-haired yachtsman who liked nothing better than a convivial party. In its place was a tormented soul.

From time to time, he would contact his lawyer in South Africa to ask if there was any way he could come home, do a deal. His lawyer, Cyril Prisman of Cape Town, contacted Frank Kahn, who went to London for a secret meeting with Schapiro and Celotti. It started inauspiciously. Schapiro had to be given a few stiff drinks before he could talk coherently and participate in the discussions. It ended inauspiciously too. Kahn had been adamant: he had his gaggle of tell-tales, of turncoats; he needed no more witnesses. What he needed was another accused. The only way Schapiro or Celotti could come home was if they were ready to face the music.

Schapiro brooded and boozed himself into an Israeli mental hospital. Eventually he could bear it no longer. He phoned Kahn and said he was coming back. On the morning of 28 May 1991 – two months after Blank's arrest – Schapiro flew into Johannesburg. The journey home was a nightmare for him. He was beset by doubts and fears. Was he doing the right thing? Could he face the humiliation of an airport arrest, the ordeal of a trial, the terror of a jail sentence? Would he ever be able to hold his head up again? He was dirty and partly drunk when the police picked him up at what was then called Jan Smuts Airport outside Johannesburg. His fuzzy hair stood on end. He looked to be close to the end of his tether.

They took him first to Kempton Park police station, and later transferred him to Sea Point police station in Cape Town. Twenty-four hours after that a psychiatrist found him to be clinically depressed and had him admitted to Valkenberg mental hospital.

Within a few days he seemed to be better and the psychiatrist reported that he could find no trace of mental illness. Schapiro was fit to stand trial. They put him back in a cell at Sea Point.

On 8 July Schapiro escaped – although 'escaped' is perhaps too dramatic a word for it. He had to get away, collect his thoughts. So he simply walked out of the cells during an unguarded moment and made for the one place where he thought he might find peace. He circled his home in Hout Bay and took a familiar path up Table Mountain. He spent two nights in the open, at an isolated spot from which he could look out over the sea he so loved. Then he climbed down again and went to hide at his mother's home. He had no plan, no objective, no sense of purpose. He just wanted to hide. There didn't seem to be anything else to do.

They came for him on Tuesday, 10 July, and took him back to Sea Point police station. That afternoon, he wrote several notes and posted them to local papers. They were burning with hatred and self-loathing. Everybody, especially his wife, had betrayed him, he claimed. His life had been empty. He made a pathetic little disclosure. His world had been so meaningless for so long that, many years ago, he had turned to shoplifting for his thrills.

The next morning he was found hanging from his cell bars. He was dead.

Every now and then, Blank would think with sadness of the mess his friend Schapiro had made of his life. He, Blank, was not going to fall into that trap. He had a plan for the future, a card up his sleeve. In the month before his trial he found himself in buoyant mood.

He would sit in the pre-trial meetings with his lawyers – Clive Cohen, SC; Gilbert Marcus, SC; Raymond Blank, his uncle and attorney – wondering what they were doing there, why they were bothering. The ritual of pre-trial planning seemed pointless. Something had come up that would make it all unnecessary. That something was 'the deal'. In his mind's eye, he could see the words in bold capital letters.

The deal was a stroke of genius. Soon, very soon, he would be free again. He would be able to go to a health resort and put all the trauma behind him. Okay, so he couldn't be a stockbroker any more. That was history. But his new business was going well. *When one door closes,* he thought, *another one opens.*

It was hard for Blank to keep his mouth shut about the deal, to keep it from his family and friends, but he had to. Advocate Cohen had warned him that if anything leaked, the arrangement could backfire. He didn't dare take that chance.

Of course, the lawyers didn't call it a 'deal', because that would sound too much like plea bargaining, a common procedure in the United States but frowned on in South Africa. Plea bargaining means exactly what it says. An accused can try to reduce his sentence by offering to co-operate with the prosecutor, by pleading guilty or fingering some third party or whatever. If they can reach agreement, this will be presented to the court for ratification. South African judges would not countenance such an agreement, but they might be persuaded by cogent argument that some or other course of action agreed to by State and defence was reasonable, equitable and in the interests of justice.

Which is exactly what Blank expected to happen.

Negotiations began in a curious and roundabout way about a month before the trial was due to start. A Cape Town attorney representing some Old

Mutual conspirators let Blank's defence team know that counsel for the State would 'entertain discussions concerning the settlement of the case'. The parties got together and the cautious jockeying began.

Defence Advocate Clive Cohen set the process in motion in classic style. Clean-shaven with gnome-like features, he was a smallish man with a commanding presence. He gave a false impression of slow-wittedness because he liked to draw thoughtfully on his pipe before speaking. 'Look,' he said, 'I have no mandate from my client. He has not indicated to me whether he has any intention to plead guilty or not. But were he to plead guilty, what would the State be arguing for by way of sentence?'

This hypothetical situation was taken to the attorney-general who, after consideration, declared that if Blank did plead guilty it could be interpreted as an indication of remorse and would certainly save court time. The State was not prepared to bargain, he said, but it thought a jail sentence was not indicated and would accordingly not ask for one.

Finally, with the trial due to start in a mere two weeks, a high-level private meeting was called. It was attended by the attorney-general for the Witwatersrand, Klaus von Lieres und Wilkau, his deputy, and the counsel for the State, Petrus Marais. Advocates Clive Cohen and Gilbert Marcus were there for the defence. At this gathering the parties established a meeting of minds on the question of sentence. By happy chance, both sides had an Achilles heel that could be exploited.

Cohen and Marcus were adamant. There could be no 'arrangement' if it entailed a term of direct imprisonment. The defendant would rather take his chances and plead not guilty if the alternative was a jail sentence. For Blank, going to jail was the ultimate horror. Using his compartmentalised style of thinking, he had faced up to the prospect, and for five months he had been 'practising' for jail, making his lifestyle rigid, regimented. He accepted, intellectually, that a trial might logically lead to a prison sentence and he knew he had the mental strength to survive the experience. Emotionally, however, the prospect was unthinkable. It couldn't possibly happen that Greg Blank, northern suburbs socialite, would end up in a prison. The indignity, the shame. Sometimes his imagination would run wild. He had seen those movies about what happens in jails. He thought of the violence, the sexual assaults, the brutality. No, no, that couldn't happen to him.

The State, for its part, was hungry for a conviction. It needed to redeem the image of effective justice that had taken such a knock in the débâcle of the Fouche/Coetzee affair. The public had been outraged over what was seen to be a travesty of justice. If the State failed to secure a conviction now, it would make a public ass of itself. But it faced a daunting task. Each of the 49 charges would have to be separately proved. The summary of substantial facts was 74 pages long and covered complicated transactions. Its list of potential witnesses ran to 79 names. Included on it were no fewer than 23 stockbrokers or employees of stockbrokers, all deemed to have information of value to the court. If the State was forced to call them all, the case could run for months. The costs, to both sides, would be horrendous.

That apart, the State did not regard the offences as requiring a prison sentence. It had no problem with not asking for one. Its bottom line was simple. It would drop one charge – relating to foreign currency contraventions – if Blank would agree to repatriate his Swiss nest-egg to the Reserve Bank, which would impose an additional fine of R250 000. He would then plead guilty to the remaining 48 fraud charges and undertake to reimburse Old Mutual in full for its estimated losses, plus interest. Blank had made an illicit profit of roughly R1,4 million. Damages and interest amounted to just over R521 000. The total to be paid would be just under R2 million. The State and defence would then prepare a document which they would call the 'agreed factual submissions in mitigation'. That would save a lot of argument.

It seemed like a perfect resolution. The case could be disposed of within days, not months, and justice would be seen to be done. Each side would make submissions as to an appropriate punishment. Here, however, there was no meeting of minds.

Marais felt strongly that Blank should be heavily fined and also sentenced to a spell of correctional supervision. This was a new form of punishment, about to be introduced on the Witwatersrand on 1 October 1992.

Correctional supervision was no picnic for an offender. It was like house-arrest under stringent conditions. It enabled offenders to remain in the community and continue working, but that was about all. It limited heavily their social life and activities. It kept them pinned at home after dark. It made them subject to unexpected phone calls or visits from Department of Correctional Services officers at any time of the day or night. It obliged them to do community service. Some experts believed that, though correctional supervision seemed more lenient than prison, it was a slow-acting punishment that grew more onerous and unpleasant as the days went by. But at least the victim wasn't incarcerated in a state institution. It wasn't jail.

Blank's defence team thought that the State should be satisfied with reparation and a stiff fine, but no matter, they could argue that point in court and let the judge decide.

Marais's offer not to ask for a prison sentence was not as magnanimous as it sounded. He didn't believe any judge would consider a jail sentence in this sort of case, especially if the accused had made full reparation. Besides, the fact that Fouche and Coetzee had been allowed to pay admission of guilt fines stuck in his mind. The news about that deal had come out while the negotiations were in progress. Legally, that episode wasn't relevant, Marais would argue in court. What an attorney-general did administratively could not possibly have a bearing on what a judge should do in his own court. It established no precedent. In the privacy of his own thoughts, however, it was nevertheless hard to disregard the Fouche/Coetzee episode entirely. There was such a thing as common fairness.

Blank's defence team, on the other hand, wanted to make maximum use of the attorney-general's decision on Fouche and Coetzee. This, they considered, was a bull point for their client. The crimes were basically the same, but the degree of culpability was surely not, they argued. Fouche and Coetzee had actually instigated their scam and seduced institutional buyers into joining it. Blank had merely been sucked into his scam by others. Fouche and Coetzee had been doing it for years. Blank had been involved for only 17 months and was the newest recruit to an existing syndicate. If there was a scale of criminality, Fouche and Coetzee were way up there, while Blank was way down here. Yes, the defence team would certainly want to run with that argument. They thought they had a winner.

As the pre-trial conference broke up, Petrus Marais reminded everyone again that there could be no talk of a deal. There had been no quid pro quo. The prosecution had reached an independent decision on sentence. In any case, judges would react badly to any suggestion that they were merely rubber stamps. All agreed that no court would send an accused to jail when even the prosecutor thought it inappropriate.

As a courtesy, prosecution and defence decided to tell Judge Tom Cloete about their discussions. Blank would plead guilty, they informed the judge, and make arrangements to reimburse Old Mutual in full for its estimated losses. The State would not ask for a prison sentence, but would recommend correctional supervision and a substantial fine. The whole business could be over in a day, or two at the most.

Sitting in chambers about a fortnight before the trial was due to start, the judge nodded gravely. He would, he said, advise the judge-president that the trial would now be considerably shorter than the several months that had been set down for it on the rolls. Oh yes, and he had a problem in making the trial date of 5 October. Did they want another judge or could they wait until 13 October? Both State and defence chose to accept the week's delay. The defence thought another judge might not be nearly so sympathetic to the pre-trial agreement. Judge Cloete said: 'Thank you, gentlemen, for keeping me informed. I shall see you in court on 13 October.'

In time to come, Judge Cloete would feel obliged to rebut angrily an implication that he had somehow agreed to the State's submission that Blank should not be jailed. But it remains an undisputed fact that defence

Advocates Cohen and Marcus left chambers after the meeting with a feeling of elation. True, the judge had offered no comment on the arrangement as it was outlined. That was to be expected. The purpose of the meeting was to keep him in the picture so that he would not be taken unawares by developments when the trial started. But His Lordship had offered no objection! That, surely, was significant, thought Cohen. Read with everything else, that was hugely significant. Decisive, in fact.

The defence team went to tell Blank the good news. Everything was on track. It might be premature to celebrate, but he would not be going to jail. He could afford the fine and he would survive correctional supervision if the worst came to the worst. He felt a load lift from his shoulders. At last, this ordeal would be over.

Gregory Blank entered the courtroom on 13 October 1992 with a jaunty step. The place was crowded. There was a full turn-out of the press, his mother and father, his brothers and sisters, Di Reynolds, a scattering of female friends, a few old colleagues, some well-wishers and the inevitable curiosity seekers drawn by a high-profile trial. Observers were struck by his composure. Everyone seemed in high spirits. The light-hearted banter at counsel's tables seemed to communicate itself to the courtroom at large.

Petrus Marais turned to Clive Cohen and his client and said: 'Imagine if the judge doesn't go along with us...' They all laughed. 'I suppose then that I will have to give your client an appeal.' It seemed like a rich joke.

Just then the judge appeared and all rose. Blank took a last, fleeting look around the courtroom and tried to look as grave as the judge himself. Inwardly, he was smiling. Boy, were they all going to be surprised when they heard how he was going to plead! That would bowl them over.

When the moment came for him to respond to the traditional question of 'How do you plead?', Blank said: 'Guilty, My Lord' in a loud, confident voice.

There was a moment of stunned silence, followed by gasps. The spectators and the media were indeed caught by surprise. For weeks, months, Blank had cut a confident figure in public, apparently unconcerned about the consequences of his impending trial. The aura of invincibility had convinced many that he had no reason to be fearful. Those who believed him innocent were sure he would be acquitted. Those who believed him guilty were confident he would wriggle off the hook. And now this: a guilty plea. What could he be doing?

They had no way of knowing that Blank's worst fear had been laid to rest. By pleading guilty, he would avoid going to jail. He was certain of that.

PART TWO

10

Weaving the Argument

Within a matter of minutes, Mr Justice Cloete was able to pass judgment on Gregory Lex Blank. Finding the right sentence was going to take a lot longer.

At the start of the proceedings, the judge raised in public an issue he had raised in private with counsel for both sides. 'Before the matter goes any further,' he said, 'I would like to place on record that I had and still have investments in the Mutual consisting of insurance policies and retirement annuities, and neither the State nor the defence has any objection to me hearing this matter.'

Cohen replied: 'Yes, My Lord, that is so and as it unfolds, Your Lordship will hear that the investment is a good one.'

It seemed a cordial beginning.

Petrus Marais withdrew Count 49 of the indictment, the charge relating to fraud against the Reserve Bank, explaining that Blank had repatriated the money and paid an administrative fine of R250 000. Then Clive Cohen for the defence explained precisely what Blank had pleaded guilty to and summed it up for the court.

COHEN:	And so, My Lord, in essence the accused is pleading guilty to having failed to disclose that he had a personal interest in the transactions which he was conducting on the stock exchange for the Old Mutual.
JUDGE:	Thank you, Mr Cohen. Mr Prosecutor?
MARAIS:	It is accepted as such by the State, My Lord.
JUDGE:	The accused is then found guilty of the crime of fraud on counts one to 48 of the indictment on the basis of his plea and statement.

The clamour in court over the guilty plea was as nothing compared to the consternation outside when the implications struck home. Suddenly the gossip-mongers had a new angle. 'Aha!' they said. 'Blank must have got millions to take the rap for all the others.' Today, Blank laughs bitterly at the mere thought. 'There wasn't enough money in the world to make me spend one night in jail, let alone years,' he says. At the time almost anything went. The wilder the story, the better. But what was true was that, by pleading guilty to the charge of failing to disclose, Blank appeared to achieve two objects. He seemed to minimise the nature of the fraud and – with the willing help of the State and intentionally or not – he ensured that the full details of the crimes would never be explored. True, his admission constituted an admission of fraud. Equally true, the formal summary of substantial facts together with the further particulars – two documents before the court – provided the bare bones of the tale. But now no one would ever hear from the 79 prosecution witnesses who could have put meat on those bones. Most of the witnesses worked at the stock exchange, some of them were known to be co-conspirators and others had information about malpractices at the JSE. Now none of them would be required to speak. No one would ever know the extent of the corruption in the JSE. Deliberately or not, the whole bag of potentially sleazy tricks had been sealed up.

If ever there was an opportunity to dig deep and come clean, it was provided by the Blank case. The JSE realised that. It wanted something to stop the flood of gossip and malicious rumour that was undermining its name; something to clear the air. The media realised that. So when revelations were not forthcoming, the newspapers were full of misgivings.

After all, in the public mind, what the event was really about was not so much the trial for fraud of an individual stockbroker as the public parade of the ability, or otherwise, of the Johannesburg Stock Exchange to regulate itself and its members in such a manner as to retain the confidence of investors.

As *The Sunday Star* reported on 25 October: 'The full extent of the irregular transactions and the efficiency or otherwise of institutional controls and the JSE's own surveillance system may never be told. Stockbrokers interviewed this week said they had hoped that cross-examination of key players in the multi-million rand scam might have forced further revelations.'

As chance would have it, it was not simply the guilty plea that fuelled public misgivings. It was the inherent structure of the trial itself; the fact that the severity of the sentence was the only remaining issue. Both the defence and the State, for very different reasons, wanted to emphasise the prevalence of malpractice in the JSE.

Blank's legal team wanted to demonstrate that the stock exchange was corrupt in order to support their argument that Blank had been subverted by the culture. The prosecution wanted to emphasise the prevailing level of public mistrust of the activities on the JSE in order to stress the enormity of Blank's crime. As a result, the State's argument amounted to an indictment of a wide range of people connected to the stock exchange, from stockbrokers to investors. Outlining the harm to the JSE's image that Blank had already done, the State proceeded to look at the 'potential prejudice'. The 'mistrust of members and users' had had to be countered by increased systems and surveillance. The mere fact that more surveillance was necessary could 'put at issue the whole nature and continuance of the JSE'. A 'degree of honesty and integrity was always necessary' so that users and operators could have faith in the markets; the JSE might not be able to provide such an environment. The disregard of ethics had reduced the standing of the JSE in the eyes of the government and of local and foreign investors. This could damage the national economy. The JSE could look for government intervention in its affairs if it was perceived to be unable to regulate itself.

'My Lord,' said Petrus Marais in his opening address, 'we have heard from our learned friend [Cohen] that abuse of their positions by fund managers appears to be widespread. We have heard that the accused as a stockbroker indulged in illegal activities and we have heard of the activities of Coetzee and Fouche. Your Lordship might already have taken note of the events subsequent to the accused's arrest where at least four other stockbrokers have lost their licences for irregular trading activities.

'We are dealing with a fast-moving and dynamic business environment where a high degree of trust and confidence is necessary. Surveillance is difficult and appears to a large extent to have been insufficient. It is therefore my respectful submission that when considering a sentence, one should look to deterring others, not merely the accused.'

The argument was effectively, if obliquely, reinforced in the summary of substantial facts, which distilled some telling facts. Celotti and Schapiro had been employees of Old Mutual. They had an absolute discretion in making investments on behalf of their employer. They didn't tell Old Mutual that they had a 'personal interest' in where the investment money went or that they had a tame stockbroker to connive with them; several, in fact. Blank was a johnny-come-lately in that area. And so on, and so on.

Once explained, the ingenious deals were simple to grasp. It became evident to observers just how easy it was to skirt the JSE regulations and get away with it. Why, it seemed mere child's play to ensure that dubious deals were not reflected on the big accounting board at the market. The trick was not unusual, nor invented by Blank.

It confirmed a growing public view that the Blank case was unlikely to be a single, isolated incident, a mere aberration at the JSE. And so it came about that in the absence of a full-scale hearing into Blank's offences – which might have produced hard evidence as to the prevalence or otherwise of general malpractice – both State and defence unwittingly fed the rumours of widespread corruption while doing nothing to prove or disprove them.

Back in the courtroom, with Blank's guilt formally established, the issue now was to find an appropriate punishment. The time had come for the defence team to work their magic, put the offence in such a perspective as would incline the court to leniency. What would they say in mitigation? Speculation was rife. Would Blank have instructed his defence team to finger accomplices, name names of other offenders, try to bring the whole castle down? Denizens of the JSE waited tensely.

The Blank team smiled a quiet smile. They had the deal. All they had to do was provide the court with effective arguments that would validate a decision not to send Blank to jail. They were confident they could do that easily enough. Indeed, they thought their case would win the day, even without a deal. They had marshalled at least four powerful, nay, irresistible, arguments, four golden threads. Each, they thought, was a winner. Besides, they had the State's agreement that, come what may, it would not ask for a jail sentence. On top of all that, the judge had once been Cohen's junior and would surely be disposed to give his old colleague a sympathetic hearing.

Painstakingly, the defence team proceeded to weave their four threads into a single, cohesive fabric. How could they have guessed that, before the case was over, the fabric would be rent apart, the four threads broken and useless?

There were no intimations of disaster as Clive Cohen got to his feet to address the court. The first issue was the master thread, the central strand that gave strength to the whole. The issue was fairness: fairness and equality of sentence. It rested on the precedent established when the attorney-general allowed Kenny Fouche and Stompie Coetzee to pay admission of guilt fines.

COHEN: Your Lordship might have seen the press publicity with the objection that the stock exchange raised to the fact that an admission of guilt fine was allowed to Fouche and Coetzee.

JUDGE: I did not, but I will take notice of it now that you mention it, Mr Cohen.

COHEN: We are going to show Your Lordship some of the press publicity by leading, reputable financial journals and newspapers, talking of unequal justice. Why is Blank required to go to trial when Fouche and Coetzee were not? We are going to submit, My Lord, that viewed objectively Blank's offence and participation is much less – morally, legally, in every way – much less than Fouche and Coetzee…

JUDGE: Is the situation then going to be that I should treat the accused in this matter as the attorney-general treated the other two?

COHEN: My Lord, I am going to suggest that one of the cornerstones of justice is that there must be equal justice and I do not suggest that Your Lordship is bound to impose the same sentence, but Your Lordship will be seen to be fair. And to use the words of Mr Justice Conradie [a fellow judge delivering a precedent-setting judgment in an earlier case], it is vital to the administration of justice that there should be equality of sentence.

JUDGE: Provided the sentence with which one is being asked to equate the matter is not startlingly inappropriate or totally unacceptable.

COHEN: Absolutely, My Lord, but nobody suggests that it is. The attorney-general has given sound reasons why the sentence which he fixed was an appropriate sentence, and the State has agreed that those factors apply to Blank.

So, My Lord, my first task is to persuade Your Lordship to view the Blank case in its correct light and not in the light that some newspapers try to pose, that this was the more serious case. It was not. It was the less serious case.

I cannot submit and I do not submit that because there was a thousand rands [fine] on each of 200 counts imposed on Fouche and Coetzee, that Your Lordship is now bound to impose a thousand rands on 48 counts. But what I will submit is that Your Lordship will, above all else, be seen to be fair and to be applying equal justice.

Point by point, Cohen built up his argument. Fouche and Coetzee actually proposed the fraud to Old Mutual. They were in positions of influence at the stockbroking firm of Ed Hern, Rudolph – Coetzee in charge and Fouche second in charge of the dealing desk. They had been involved in their fraud far longer than Blank. Their scheme was so designed that they couldn't lose. They had defrauded five financial institutions in all. They had risked not their own money but money from the institutions. They hadn't made restitution. They had misused the backdating system provided for in the JSE rules for their own advantage. They had misrepresented their activities, whereas Blank had merely failed to disclose his.

'The submission I am making,' said Cohen, 'is that Your Lordship will regard the moral blameworthiness of Fouche and Coetzee as far more serious.'

And then, back to the nub: 'As Mr Justice Smalberger [another precedent-setting judge] said, if people are placed in the same position and one can draw comparisons between their moral complicity or guilt, and the other circumstances, unless the sentence is wrong, and there is no suggestion that the sentence of Fouche and Coetzee is wrong, one should seek to do equal justice.'

Cunningly, Cohen started to weave his three other threads into the tapestry of the defence, so that the finished cloth in all its splendour would become visible to all.

The second thread made its appearance. Guilty though he was, Greg Blank was also a victim. He had been blackmailed into crime. The ugly word hung in the still court air.

COHEN:	I cannot say he was brought in kicking and screaming…
JUDGE:	Hardly.
COHEN:	Although he did turn it down once.
JUDGE:	Yes.
COHEN:	But he was blackmailed. I use the word, My Lord, which most clearly is appropriate to the circumstances. And I will be returning to this.

And so he did later.

'Blank was in fact approached, and this is an important point I wish to make,' stressed Cohen, 'Blank was in fact approached in approximately March 1989 by Schapiro, who invited him to participate in the syndicate, and Blank declined. I do wish to emphasise that, because this gives the force to my naming the conduct as actually blackmail.

'In approximately August 1989 Blank was again approached. This time, however, Schapiro was more insistent. It was made perfectly clear to Blank that, should he refuse to participate, the Old Mutual would take much of its work elsewhere. Blank was aware that this was the course of conduct when another firm of stockbrokers, Martin & Co., fell out of favour. A delegation from Martin to the Old Mutual at senior level averted this consequence.'

The judge asked for clarification of a point in the written submissions on the issue of blackmail. It was an awkward moment for the Blank defence, a little stumble.

JUDGE:	I don't understand it. You called it blackmail. You say Blank was aware that this was the course of conduct

when another firm, Martin & Co., fell out of favour. That is, that the Old Mutual was going to take its work elsewhere.

COHEN: Yes.

JUDGE: But then it says a delegation from Martin to Old Mutual averted this consequence. So they did not take the work elsewhere?

COHEN: Well, My Lord, it might be that it was restored... I am dependent on my learned friend for precisely what happened.

JUDGE: Yes, I would be grateful if you would just obtain clarity on that with the State.

COHEN: I do not mind if my learned friend wants to tell Your Lordship now.

JUDGE: Yes, perhaps you could just agree on the wording here, because what it suggests, your thesis as I understand it, is that the accused in this matter was blackmailed by Schapiro, Schapiro saying that if you do not do what I want you to do, the same will happen to your firm as happened to Martin.

COHEN: As happened to Martin, yes.

JUDGE: But the question is whether anything happened to Martin.

Hammering away, Cohen pointed out that Old Mutual had provided 10 per cent of Frankel's brokerage and Blank had felt compromised. To resist participation could have drastic consequences for himself and the firm. Blank had known what he was doing was wrong, but had rationalised it. It might actually have been an advantage to Old Mutual to be able to buy large blocks rather than acquire shares piecemeal.

Towards the end of the trial, Cohen returned to the subject of blackmail to try to rebut the prosecutor. He referred to the statement of agreed facts, a consensus between State and defence. 'The agreed fact is that he was blackmailed into joining. True, as Your Lordship puts, there were other ways that he could have handled the situation, but he believed that he could deal in the syndicate to the advantage of the Old Mutual. The evidence is that he was compelled, as he saw it, to go into the syndicate. If he had withdrawn at any stage, the threat of withdrawal of business from Frankel's] was still there.'

The third thread began to emerge in the tapestry of the defence. Blank believed himself to be a scapegoat, a victim of the culture of the stock exchange. What he had done had been a practice engaged in by many others.

Blank himself believed that up to 90 per cent of stockbrokers engaged in sharp practice. Why was he being singled out?

COHEN: From what Your Lordship knows in relation to Coetzee and Fouche, this is not a view which is without merit.

JUDGE: Well, I think as you have read from the agreed facts of submissions in mitigation this morning, there is a paragraph that says that the accused knew, as everybody ought to know, that the people were indulging in this sort of thing. It is a widespread practice in the stock exchange.

COHEN: That is so, My Lord. So one understands his view that he knows it is wrong, he will not do it again, but really he has been victimised. He has been treated differently from everybody else. I submit that Your Lordship will share that view.

And then the fourth thread. It came in the form of a report from Nicro, the South African National Institute for Crime Prevention and Rehabilitation of Offenders. Nicro is a voluntary organisation of high repute. Its opinions have often carried great weight in the courts. The defence had made Blank available to a Nicro panel so that it could assess his suitability for a sentence involving community service. Its report was prepared only days before the trial began and it was a godsend to the defence.

In essence its findings were these. Firstly, as Blank was willing to make full restitution and to pay a significant fine, imprisonment was not an appropriate option. Secondly, correctional supervision – effectively, house arrest – while seen by Nicro as an important and valued addition to the sentencing options, would not be suitable because Blank did not require supervision of any degree to prevent him from committing a similar offence. A period of house arrest would only serve as undue punishment. He was not in need of any rehabilitation treatment programme. Thirdly, community service was recommended for these reasons: Blank would be seen by the community to be making retribution, and could not be perceived as simply having 'bought' himself out; he would be able to use his skills to serve the community; community service would remind him of the consequences of his behaviour and would be an active deterrent; and he would be able to continue his job.

The Nicro committee went further. It had consulted Operation Hunger – a non-governmental organisation set up to feed starving black children, predominantly in rural areas – and that charity had been willing to place Blank in its programme for the full duration of the community-service sentence.

One thousand hours spread over three years was the recommended length of the service. There it was then, from the mouth of an authoritative, independent organisation. Sending Blank to jail was not 'appropriate'. A deterrent sentence of community service was.

There was just one small snarl in this fourth golden thread. For all that Blank had come across as a confident person who had been able to relate to Nicro's full panel; that he had forfeited his career; that his personal relationships had suffered; that once he had been considered a success and now he was stigmatised as a criminal...for all that, there was something that ought to be mentioned. 'In detailing the offence and reasons for committing the offence,' the panel reported, 'it is apparent that the client is not particularly remorseful about having transgressed the law in this manner.'

This was precisely the kind of statement that might niggle away at a court. The defence decided that it ought to address the point lest it loom too large in the judge's mind. 'Whilst he feels,' Cohen explained, 'that he would avoid in every way coming into conflict with the law again, he views his offence as part of the stock exchange culture. A practice engaged in by many others. He expresses the feeling that whilst he recognised the wrongness of his actions, he felt unduly victimised. But one actually understands that when one looks at what happened to Fouche and Coetzee with 580 counts, and what happened to the people who instigated this scheme.'

The four strands had come together beautifully, the tapestry of Blank's defence was a little masterpiece, thought his counsel. Nor had the team omitted to give the finishing touches. The essential worthiness of Blank's character had been discussed at length: his sporting prowess, his leadership qualities, his appointment to the highest possible commissioned rank for a civilian doing national service, his phenomenal success in his chosen career.

All that was left was to bring in the only mitigation witness the defence wanted. He was a man of unimpeachable reputation and integrity; a partner in one of the country's top legal firms and a legal practitioner for 35 years; a loving father who was ready, even now, to embrace the accused as his son-in-law. His name was Peter Edward Blaine Reynolds, father of Dianne.

COHEN:	For how long have you known Mr Blank?
REYNOLDS:	About six years.
COHEN:	How did you become acquainted?
REYNOLDS:	He is a friend of one of my daughters.
COHEN:	Now, can you tell His Lordship, was this a very close relationship?
REYNOLDS:	As far as I know, it was a very close relationship over quite a long period of time.

COHEN: In consequence of Mr Blank's arrest, was there a change in that relationship?

REYNOLDS: Yes, there was.

COHEN: How was that explained to you?

REYNOLDS: As I understand, there were discussions with regard to the possibility of the accused and my one daughter becoming engaged. Because of the arrest and pending prosecution, the accused felt it would be unfair or improper for him to seek to continue with the close relationship. In the event of the prosecution succeeding, he felt it would bring my daughter down.

Reynolds told the court he found it strange that Nicro had concluded that Blank did not seem particularly remorseful. 'He is remorseful, he is contrite. He, I think, is very sorry for the crime which he has committed.' Cohen asked him how he thought Blank would react to a prison sentence. 'I think he would be treated as a pariah. The effect on him would be devastating.' And what sort of a person was Blank anyway?

REYNOLDS: He is what I would describe as a gentleman. He is kind, he is considerate, he is helpful. There is a degree of naïvety about him. He is moderate in his habits. He never over-eats. He is a non-drinker of alcohol. He is gentle, he is kind, he is everything which one would embrace within the context of a person who is a gentle person…

JUDGE: Or as a son-in-law, sir?

REYNOLDS: He would be very acceptable as a son-in-law. Seeing My Lord raises that point, the accused is still very welcome in my home. There are some people of my acquaintance who I would not trust and there are others that I do trust. My Lord, he falls in the latter category. Notwithstanding the crime for which he stands convicted, he still has my complete trust.

COHEN: Do you believe there is any prospect of Blank committing a crime of dishonesty again?

REYNOLDS: I would very much doubt it. Since the time of his arrest, he has lived through a nightmare. As also his family.

JUDGE: You said that he is contrite. How does that manifest itself?

REYNOLDS: I cannot put it into words, but if I may paraphrase it. He wishes that he had not committed this offence, he wishes that he was not in this predicament, he wishes that the crime he committed had not resulted in the destruction of his career, he wishes that the crime had not resulted in the destruction of personal relationships.

That, surely, would be the clincher, thought the defence team. They could not have asked for a more unequivocal endorsement for their client. And, of course, the judge and Reynolds knew each other professionally. It would have to count when it came to assessing how much weight to give to Reynolds's testimony. The Blank entourage could barely hide their satisfaction. They did not put their client on the stand and they didn't mention the issue of the pre-trial deal. These omissions didn't seem to be serious.

11

The Argument Unravels

Prosecutor Petrus Marais listened attentively to Cohen's argument about sentence. After all, that was the only issue left alive. Cohen was replying to a statement made earlier by Judge Cloete.

COHEN:	We are going to submit that it would be wholly inappropriate to consider any term of imprisonment, and the State is not asking for it.
JUDGE:	Yes.
COHEN:	But yes, Your Lordship is correct, theoretically there could be a 480-year imprisonment.
JUDGE:	I think only 48, Mr Cohen.
COHEN:	Oh, is it not ten years [per offence]?
JUDGE:	It is 10 years times 48...that makes 480.
COHEN:	It could be 480 years in prison. If there could be a guarantee to Mr Blank that he could serve that, I am sure he would want it.

The little joke fell on deaf ears.

JUDGE:	Yes.
COHEN:	My Lord, in regard to the maximum fine of R10 000 [per offence], this is not the most serious case under the Financial Services Act. Now, in regard to Fouche and Coetzee, the attorney-general considered R1 000 to be an adequate fine for each count. I do not suggest that where, on 200 counts a fine of R1 000 is fixed, by parity of reason there must be R1 000 on each of 48 counts. I may make a suggestion of something of the order of R5 000 on each count, which would come to R240 000 in total, which would be approximately half of the estate, of the net assets which Blank has left to him after satisfying the Reserve Bank and making full restitution to the Old Mutual.

Suddenly, Marais pricked up his ears. He had detected a change of tone in the defence argument, something akin to the harsh note a sports car engine emits when it is being pushed to the limit. He didn't like what he was hearing. It seemed as if Cohen was going further than had been agreed at the pre-trial meeting by suggesting to the court that even the mild punishment of community service was unnecessary. Blank would be punished enough, he was arguing, by a court-imposed fine of R240 000.

If that's the way Cohen wants to play it, thought Marais, then we will show that the State has teeth too. Agreeing not to ask for a jail sentence didn't mean that he was about to minimise or make light of the crime.

He didn't agree at all that Blank's offences were of a lesser order than those committed by Fouche and Coetzee. In fact, his reason for not recommending jail was based on practicalities, not sympathy. He thought that the judge was unlikely to impose a prison sentence. The prisons were overcrowded anyway and if Blank did indeed go to jail, he would in all probability be released in short order. That would be a travesty. So would letting him off with a relatively mild fine. The State's approach toughened perceptibly.

Marais recalls: 'Clive was so confident of success that he wanted to get even more clever. He seemed to decide that he had conceded too much to the State, and he now wanted to argue for even less of a punishment. When he went in there asking for a R240 000 fine only, I thought to myself: I'm going to have to fight just to get correctional supervision. So I put everything I had into the arguments. Clive was extremely peed off with that. He phoned me and said he was very angry. But I told him: "Look, it was your decision. You chose to try to reduce the sentence to a simple fine." So I argued as vehemently as I could for the sentence that I thought appropriate, which was correctional supervision.'

First of all, Marais had to vanquish the spectres of Fouche and Coetzee.

'My Lord,' he said, 'my learned friend has dealt at great length with the decision taken by the attorney-general. I must stress that these were allegations made by the State. They have not been found to be so by any court of law. Neither were they specifically admitted to by either of the parties who were charged. No indictment containing 570 counts was ever served on any accused. The only form of indictment ever served on any party dealt with the 200 counts on which their admissions of guilt had been paid.'

The point was a telling one. People can sign admissions of guilt for reasons – convenience, expediency – other than the fact they are guilty. But then, of course, the opposite argument would be pertinent too. Why would anyone who was innocent voluntarily plead guilty to anti-social criminal actions and accept the contumely of an angry public? The questions neutralised each other.

Marais proceeded to try to unravel the rest of the defence tapestry. Blank had not been more at risk than Fouche and Coetzee. 'The only risk that he had to take was the risk that he might be betrayed by his co-conspirators. For as long as he was confident that Celotti, Schapiro et al would keep their side of the bargain, the risk to the accused was absolutely minimal.'

The Blank case was not an extension of the other one. 'An entirely new mechanism was set in place when the accused agreed to participate.' There was a change in *modus operandi* to earn a higher profit from fewer transactions. Blank had taken the initiative in drawing a friend and business associate into the offences unwittingly. He took a leading role in the day-to-day administration of the account, participated fully in all the frauds. He had manipulated the volume statistics at the JSE in an 'iniquitous' way. He had only repatriated his foreign assets after the State had discovered that they existed.

Marais ran through the names of some of the co-conspirators on the witness list, arguing that they bore lesser guilt for one reason or another. Colin Harper, David Cox and Philip Thompson were merely Old Mutual traders; they had no executive decision-making powers. Chris Logan was involved only in the Fouche/Coetzee matter. Allan Greyling was involved in the Blank conspiracy to a lesser degree, but had the grace to pull out. Both Logan and Greyling 'voluntarily came forward when an investigation commenced to offer their services'. The names were largely unknown to the audience in the courtroom. The people behind the names might have had their brief moment in the spotlight if there had been a need to call them as witnesses, but there wasn't. And so the names simply surfaced and submerged again. No one was ever going to charge them, or make them talk in public.

'To sum up,' Marais told the court, 'we see that the accused colluded with the Old Mutual employees. He participated actively in the opening of the accounts. He participated with the prior knowledge that the shares would all be off-loaded to Old Mutual at higher prices. He participated in the distribution of profits. It is my respectful submission that it should be clear to the court that the accused was a willing and enthusiastic participant.

'The accused had a phenomenal earning capacity and wanted for nothing. And yet there is no indication from the defence that he had reached saturation point or that he intended to scale down his activities. It appears that his greed remained unsatisfied.'

There were other aggravating factors, according to Marais. Blank had been guilty of 'persistent dishonest premeditated conduct'; he had betrayed a position of trust; he had no lofty motives.

Marais went on to argue what he called 'one of the most fundamental principles of the stock exchange'. It was that a broker could act only as an

Photo: Blank family album

Robby and Gail Blank with Greg on North Beach, Durban

Greg Blank, aged ten, captain of the Houghton Primary School soccer team

Photo: Blank family album

Clockwise from top: Greg Blank, Tracy, Vaughan and Daryl

Photo: Blank family album

Greg Blank (far right, front) in the King Edward VII High School tennis team

Photo: Akkersdyk Studios

Greg Blank receiving his degree at Wits, 1979

Photo: Blank family album

Greg Blank and Dianne Reynolds at the Houghton family home, 1990

Photo: Blank family album

Greg Blank and Dianne Reynolds at a donkey derby in aid of Operation Hunger, 1990

Photo: Blank family album

Greg Blank leads in one of his jointly-owned racehorses

Colonel Nico Lotter, commander, and Lieutenant-Colonel 'Nollie' Nolte, head of prison, in the Krugersdorp prisoners' health club, 1995

Greg Blank by the outer door of his cell, February 1996

Photo: Dennis Gordon

Krugersdorp inmates during computer training, February 1996

Greg Blank in his cell at Krugersdorp prison, February 1996

Photos: Dennis Gordon

Greg Blank using a new prisoners' phone, with a prison officer

Photo: Blank family album

Vaughan and Greg Blank with their mother, Gail Dunkley, 1994

Photo: FAIR LADY

Greg Blank at home, March 1997

agent, not a principal. If he wished to deal with personal shares, it had to be done through his own stockbroker. 'One of the reasons for that is that the client – the user, the investor – is then given the protection afforded him by the common law of agency. Where, unbeknown to the buyer, the seller is his own broker, the buyer has absolutely no protection whatsoever. It is for this reason that the principle of agency is so well entrenched in the stock exchange.'

There it was again, the precise nature of Greg Blank's offence, just as Cohen had outlined it in his opening address. Blank had violated the principle of agency, acted on his own behalf – and he had failed to disclose it.

What Petrus Marais could not know was that this 'fundamental principle' was soon to be abolished, and the Johannesburg Stock Exchange today follows the rest of the world in permitting a broker to act as both agent and principal. That change in JSE regulations came after the Blank case, towards the end of 1995.

Just as Cohen thought he saw an opportunity to get his client off with a fine, so Marais became determined to ensure that Blank got nothing less than correctional supervision. It is one of life's ironies that, in the end, neither succeeded.

The last words that the judge and the accused heard before the court adjourned at the end of the first day were these from Marais: 'It is my contention that the interests of society demand the court to impose a sentence that is severe.' For the defence, they were not reassuring words. Not knowing what was in Marais's mind, they wondered for a moment whether the prosecutor was going to renege on their agreement. The next day they were to find out.

Marais began the new day by continuing to pick at the defence tapestry. 'It is my contention that the court cannot start at the Coetzee and Fouche matter. It must look to the underlying principles. I would respectfully urge the court to proceed with caution when trying to attach any weight to a decision by the attorney-general.'

JUDGE:	I have before me a statement by the attorney-general in which he motivated why he did what he did.
MARAIS:	My Lord, that was a statement to the press.
JUDGE:	Should that be dealt with differently from a statement to me?
MARAIS:	I was not aware whether the attorney-general was able to give his full reasons to the press. It is – is it not? – usually

policy not to comment at all or comment to a minimal degree on any decision that has been taken.

JUDGE: Are we talking about Mr Von Lieres?

MARAIS: That is correct.

JUDGE: I see.

MARAIS: But it is my starting point that the appropriateness of the sentence can only be judged in the light of the relevant circumstances.

JUDGE: Yes, what you are saying to me – I'm sorry to keep interrupting, I quite stopped doing that – what you are saying is I should not start with the Fouche case and work from that. I should look at the offence as a whole, and bear in mind what happened in the other matter as one of the factors to be taken into account.

MARAIS: Yes, My Lord. As one of the factors. That is correct.

JUDGE: Do I need to know what the attorney-general did, and all the motivations? If I can accept for the purpose of argument, or for the purposes of my decision, that what the attorney-general did would have been entirely inappropriate in this matter, then I simply put my pen through what he did and ignore it.

MARAIS: It is not my argument that the decision in that matter was wrong.

JUDGE: I understand that.

Marais moved to another tack. He needed to undermine the defence contention that Blank had been subverted by the culture of the stock exchange. He quoted from an article in *Time* magazine which in turn had been quoted by the chief justice of South Africa in another case:

> Many Americans harbour an unwholesome and even dangerous contempt for the justice system. Neither criminals nor victims have much faith in its workings. The one class do not fear it much and the other do not trust it.
>
> A society can be subverted by a system that appears to be not only inconsistent, but almost whimsical in its workings. A huge sense of grievance festers. The injustice of the courts seems to mirror the injustice of the economic system. All the rules of society seem to have changed. You work hard, but inflation destroys your gains. So much for the work ethic. You obey the law, but somehow you get hurt and criminals profit unpunished.

'It is my submission,' declared Marais, 'that the court must guard against a perception such as this developing in South Africa.' He went on to argue that submitting a complaint took courage from an institution like Old Mutual, which had to weigh up the effects of negative publicity. Commercial crimes were difficult to detect and expensive to investigate. Severe sentences were required as a warning to businessmen who might feel inclined to abuse the confidence that must necessarily exist in a civilised state in the field of business and industry.

'While it may be so that unethical or dishonest practices could be rife on the stock exchange or amongst the employees at major institutions, it is my respectful submission that this is no argument for leniency.

'We are dealing with more than just an ethical standard for brokers. The Stock Exchange Act requires a high standard of regulation to protect the investing public. The Act requires that the stock exchange channel the savings of the nation to meet the capital needs of productive enterprise.' This could only be done if there were trust and financial competence.

Finally, there was the question of the character of the accused. Marais readily agreed that there were 'a number of mitigating factors'. But mere talent didn't justify his behaviour; nor could it be claimed that the humiliation and stigma of a fraud conviction constituted a mitigating factor. 'They are disadvantages inherent in the conviction of any criminal whose misdeeds excite the public interest.' Paying back Old Mutual? Well, if he hadn't, then that would have been an aggravating factor, wouldn't it?

Marais dismissed contemptuously the R240 000 fine proposed by the defence. That was roughly half of the present value of Blank's disposable assets. He suggested more than four times that figure, paid in instalments. 'It is not beyond the capabilities of the accused to deal with a fine of R1 million, if it is properly structured by the court and he is given realistic opportunity to realise his assets. The court should not allow the accused to be in a position, now or at any stage in the future, where he can resume his life as a man of means, or even in a position of relative financial comfort.

'We are dealing with a young man of 33, 34 years old. He has got the bulk of his working life ahead of him. All a fine of R50 000, R60 000, would be bringing him to is to breakeven, with his working life ahead. It would be ignoring the punitive and retributive aspects of sentencing.'

On top of that, Blank's commitment to repay Old Mutual needed to be enforceable, perhaps by a suspended prison sentence. 'My Lord, the next point I would like to make is that the accused should also be required to sacrifice his freedom.'

The defence froze. Was Marais going to renege after all? Was he going to recommend jail? No, but he was going to ask for a sentence of three years' correctional supervision, and he was going to make darned sure it didn't seem like a cushy alternative to a cell. As outlined by Marais, the general principles governing the punishment did indeed seem fierce.

An offender was confined to his home, a form of house arrest. He was not allowed to leave without permission. He could work, but had to go straight home afterwards. He was allowed only four hours free time a week – on Saturdays – to shop or do household chores. All alcohol was forbidden. He had to perform a certain number of hours of community service a week. He was required to submit himself to any programmes or treatments deemed necessary by the Department of Correctional Services.

The restrictions were enforced by unannounced and regular checks. Night time raids and phone calls to his home ensured his compliance. Should the offender breach the rules he would be immediately placed in custody for a minimum of 72 hours. With time and co-operation, he could earn slightly more free time.

'It is,' said Marais, 'a severe sentence.' And he called Colonel Johannes Petrus Smit, the officer in charge of implementing the correctional supervision programme, to confirm it. Smit was the 'father' of the concept in South Africa, having studied its efficacy elsewhere and devised the local equivalent. Judge Cloete asked him how tough correctional supervision really was.

'My opinion,' replied Smit, 'is that the longer the sentence endures, the heavier it gets. The first month, the second month, are easy. After three years, I understand, people want to sell their house just to get away from the place.'

The law permitted two forms of correctional supervision. In one, there was a fixed period imposed by the court and, unlike imprisonment, the commissioner of correctional services had no discretion to reduce it. It allowed for a maximum sentence of five years. In its alternative form, correctional supervision could be tagged on to a prison sentence, and the convicted man would go from cell to house-arrest at some point. This option gave more discretion to the commissioner.

The court wished to know a little more about this second option.

JUDGE: Colonel, what is the possibility that this accused, if he is sentenced to correctional supervision, will be set free immediately?

SMIT: If I were handling him?

JUDGE: Yes, or whoever would be supervising him in the Johannesburg area.

SMIT: Your Lordship, I would have a total study of the man done, and I would look at the evidence in the case, and I would probably transform this person very quickly, if I had the right information and there was no contrary information to hand.

JUDGE: And what is 'very quickly', Colonel? Are we talking about hours or days or weeks or months?

SMIT: If we accept that there is no other evidence?

JUDGE: Yes.

SMIT: It can be a question of days or weeks.

That settles it, the defence thought. The court is not going to impose correctional supervision. It leaves too much in the hands of the Department of Correctional Services. So maybe Blank will get community service or, better still, a fine only. Not the outrageous fine suggested by Marais, but something closer to their own assessment.

But, they noticed, the judge wasn't automatically excluding the option of prison. Of course, they thought, he had to explore all avenues. It was nothing to get alarmed about.

Called by the State, Lieutenant Christiaan Jacobus Serfontein of correctional services took the stand. Serfontein was the social worker who had evaluated Blank's suitability for correctional supervision. Yes, he could confirm that Blank was a suitable candidate.

Cohen seized the opportunity to reinforce the opinion that prison for Blank was not a good idea.

COHEN: Lieutenant Serfontein, is it so that, at present, it is impossible to ensure the safety of a person like Blank in prison?

SERFONTEIN: It is difficult. The department is doing its utmost to ensure the safety of every prisoner to the extent it can, but I must add that the possibility exists that his safety could be threatened. It is not possible to have 100 per cent control in a communal cell.

COHEN: Yes, it's a danger.

SERFONTEIN: It's a danger, yes.

COHEN: For a person like Blank?

SERFONTEIN: For a person like Mr Blank, yes.

But the court didn't propose to let Cohen have things all his own way.

JUDGE: Why Blank in particular?

SERFONTEIN: Because he's a first offender. It will be his introduction to the prison. In prison a person must first fit in, and as a consequence of that, it can happen that he is introduced to negative elements, and this could have an influence on him as a person.

JUDGE: I'm speaking specifically on the question that Mr Cohen raised, namely the safety of a person. Is there any greater absence of safety for a person like Mr Blank as opposed to any other prisoner?

SERFONTEIN: No, no.

Defence Counsel Clive Cohen had the final word that day; one last chance to reinforce his original arguments. Again, he concentrated on his four basic threads.

He knew he had to convince the court that Blank had been placed under immense pressure to join the conspiracy, that 'blackmail' was not too strong a word for it. Painstakingly, he retraced the ground. It was heavy going. The judge seemed reluctant to accept the proposition. But even the State had accepted it, in that doughty document submitted to court, the agreed statement of facts. The word 'blackmail' appeared there, accepted by both parties. 'The point I am making, these are not allegations,' said Cohen. 'These are agreed facts and the agreed fact is that he was blackmailed into joining the conspiracy.'

He had to convince the court that the Fouche/Coetzee case was relevant when it came to assessing an appropriate sentence; that a fine would be equitable and just. But not R1 million. That would be outrageous. It was relatively easy to rebut the notion that Blank could somehow raise the money over a number of years if he was required to pay it in instalments.

Cohen didn't believe the court would take much persuading about the inappropriateness of a prison sentence. After all, look at the array of people who had argued against it – Nicro, the correctional services witnesses, Peter Reynolds and, indeed, the State itself. By not calling for imprisonment, the State had implicitly rejected the idea. Nevertheless, Cohen went over the arguments again. New-style community service and correctional supervision sentences had not only been approved by legislators but were finding favour with the courts. The extent of the crime, the fact that Blank had been blackmailed, did not warrant a prison sentence. The State had not asked for a prison sentence and Nicro had positively advised against it.

'We recognise,' said Cohen, 'that Your Lordship will impose a heavy fine which will be felt. It must be a meaningful punishment, so that the community knows that this hurts, that crime is not profitable, that you cannot pay a small fine and get away with it if you are caught. My learned friend submitted R1 million. My Lord, R1 million is just not available, it is not there, it is not there from honest and hard-working earnings over a lifetime. My learned friend's proposition is, with respect, startling.

'It is that you must see to it that in the future Blank cannot rehabilitate himself and build up a new estate. You must, by your sentence, ensure poverty.

'Well, if that is the effect of the submission by the State, then we would submit it is an unknown principle to penal systems.'

Judge Cloete called for more information about correctional supervision and its applications, and adjourned the court, announcing: 'I shall pass sentence in this matter at 10 o'clock on Monday morning.'

The Greg Blank defence team felt quietly confident. They had done all they could. And they had done it without submitting their client to the ordeal of the witness box. Nevertheless, it would be an edgy weekend for all of them. In law, as in life, nothing is certain.

12

Bombshell in Court

Monday, 19 October 1992. Sentencing day. As ever, a buzz of anticipation in the courtroom. Female voices, a giggle. From his position towards the front of the court, Greg Blank turned and smiled at his admirers in the gallery. He looked a picture of serenity.

Today he would close the door of the past, mused Blank. Today would mark the first day of the rest of his life. Oh, of course, the judge would have some harsh things to say about his conduct. Probably he would lay it on a bit thick simply because he was not going to send him to jail. He wouldn't want to seem soft on white-collar crime. And, yes, it would be embarrassing for a person like Blank – proud, but needing the constant reassurance that his pride was justified. If only the judge knew it, public criticism was as harsh a punishment as could be devised for him. It struck at the heart of his insecurity, his sense of self. But he could take it, just as he had taken other knocks in his life. And then it would be over. He resolved to show no emotion, whatever the judge had to say.

The defence didn't have to wait long to discover where Judge Cloete stood.

'Fraud,' said the judge, quoting a colleague, 'is always a grave and ugly offence, and worse when it is fanned by human cupidity over a deliberate period.' And then he took the delicate fabric of the defence tapestry and flayed it mercilessly.

The accused was greedy for money and burning with ambition. He had played an active role, actively concealed his efforts. The claim that he was blackmailed was unjustified hyperbole. 'What should an honest person have done in the face of the threat from Schapiro?' declaimed Judge Cloete rhetorically. 'Surely he should have reported this threat to his partners to enable them to send a delegation to the senior management of Old Mutual – the more so as, to the accused's knowledge, such a delegation had been sent previously and the threat had been averted.'

Snap went the first thread of the defence's argument.

'Even if the consequence were to have been that his firm lost the Old Mutual account altogether, that [reporting the matter] is the course he was obviously obliged to adopt.'

Curious, thought Blank. *He doesn't mention how apparently lax Old Mutual was in plugging loopholes after the Martin & Co episode. He's clearly discounted our point that Celotti and Schapiro could have found ways to get their own back. He doesn't seem to realise how easy it would've been for them…*

Now it was time to deal with defence counsel's plea of equality of justice, particularly as it related to the Coetzee and Fouche affair. Reviewing various authorities, the judge concluded: 'The principle of equality before the law does not necessarily entail the consequence that equal punishment should be imposed for the same, much less similar, crimes. Uniformity of sentence is desirable only to the extent that the sentence imposed by one court for a particular type of offence should not be disturbingly disproportionate.'

As for the decision of the attorney-general to accept admissions of guilt, that was not a court decision and, in any event, he would have been astonished if a court would have imposed 'such apparently lenient sentences' in the absence of compelling reasons. 'In the circumstances, I do not consider that my wide discretion to determine a suitable sentence is in any way affected by the admission of guilt fines fixed by the attorney-general.'

Snap went the second thread in the defence fabric.

The suggestion that Blank deserved leniency because he had fallen victim to the culture of the stock exchange backfired badly. Said Judge Cloete: 'I am appalled to find the following statement in the facts agreed between the defence and the prosecutor: "Blank had reason to believe, as did or should most stockbrokers on the JSE, that certain portfolio managers and dealers of financial institutions, including Old Mutual, dealt secretly for their own account on the JSE."

'I take note of the fact that Advocate Marais is attached to the Office for Serious Economic Offences and of the fact that Advocate Cohen is very experienced in financial matters that come before the courts. I therefore have no hesitation in accepting the accuracy of the statement I have just quoted. I am aware of the fact, and take judicial notice of it, that so-called "white-collar" crime is on the increase.

'I feel fully justified in imposing a sentence which will deter not only the accused and other stockbrokers from committing crimes similar to those of which the accused has been convicted, but also others involved in business who may be tempted to indulge in large-scale crimes of dishonesty.

'The time has already arrived when the severity of punishments imposed for this sort of crime should proclaim that society has had enough and that the courts, who are the mouthpieces of society, will not tolerate such crimes and will severely punish offenders.'

The third thread snapped.

There goes the fine-only option, thought Blank. *It looks as though the court has bought the prosecutor's argument that the 'severe' punishment of correctional supervision was called for. Oh well, it's still better than jail.*

One thread to go, the most powerful thread of all. The deal. That surely would hold. The judge could reject all the defence submissions he liked, but he surely couldn't argue with the combined weight of State and defence urging alternatives to imprisonment.

There seemed almost a note of sympathy in the judge's early words on the subject of sentencing. Or was it irony? Afterwards, the defence thought it *was* irony. 'I am very much aware,' said Judge Cloete, 'that sentence of imprisonment would be harsh for a person who is used to the luxuries which an annual income of more than R1 million enables him to afford, such as a residence in Woodmead, a Ferrari, interests in racehorses and works of art by internationally renowned artists; and that such a sentence would be far harsher in the case of the accused than in the case of a person who does not have a fixed abode and who is not used to three meals a day. I believe I can legitimately take these facts into account in assessing both the nature of an appropriate sentence, as well as the duration of a sentence of imprisonment, should such a sentence be imposed; and I shall do so.'

Judge Cloete listed the other things he would take into account. That Blank's record showed he was a man of glittering potential with leadership qualities. That Old Mutual would not be out of pocket. That Blank's career as a stockbroker had been ignominiously terminated. That he had suffered the humiliation and stigma of a fraud conviction. That he had saved the State considerable trouble and expense by pleading guilty. That the plea of guilty was accepted – 'with some difficulty' – as a sign of remorse.

Blank listened to Judge Cloete with mounting optimism. He was convinced now that he had been over-reacting to what he assumed were early warning signs. Clearly, the judge had been impressed by his record.

On the other hand, continued the judge, Blank had not given evidence, so he had been unable to gauge properly the degree of contrition, if any. That's why he had had difficulty in accepting the guilty plea as a sign of remorse. On top of that, Blank had been in a position of trust, and there were the interests of society to be considered. 'Absolute honesty,' said the judge, 'and nothing less, is required from a broker; and if a broker falls short of this standard he must expect the full rigour of a severe sentence to be visited upon him, both as a punishment and to serve as a deterrent to others.'

It was, however, irrelevant that other guilty parties had been indemnified or were at present beyond the jurisdiction of the courts. 'It may well be that Celotti and Schapiro are even more deserving of censure than the accused. But that is a reason for sentencing them more severely than the accused, if they are ever brought to justice. I shall accordingly be careful not to impose a sentence upon the accused which, on the facts presently available, would be more appropriate for Celotti or Schapiro.'

Where's he going to? thought Blank. *Doesn't the judge know Schapiro is dead? Is he trying to play cat-and-mouse with me? There're ominous undertones here that I don't like. But still, no need for alarm. Not really.*

Now the judge was weighing up the sentencing options. 'Let me say immediately that if I considered a fine with an alternative of imprisonment to be appropriate, I would not hesitate to impose such a sentence. But I am totally unpersuaded by either of Mr Cohen's suggestions. A fine – particularly of the magnitude suggested by Mr Cohen, or even a fine substantially higher – would not serve the interests of society.' The judge paused for a moment, then uttered a sentence that would echo through the country. 'In my view, if the most that an offender could face for defrauding a client of sums approaching R10 million and personally pocketing R1,4 million, was an order to restore his share and a fine of R500 000, potential criminals would be tempted to regard the fine as venture capital.'

Good heavens! thought Blank. *Clive Cohen hasn't won a single point with this judge. He's demolished every argument. Thank goodness I pleaded guilty. Where would we have been without the deal, the arrangement with the State?*

Judge Cloete began to assess the relative merits and demerits of community service and correctional supervision. 'I go so far as to say that in the circumstances of this case a fine coupled with community service would not only fail to serve the interests of the community but would bring the system of the administration of justice into disrepute. Such a sentence would be unbalanced and too lenient. The game would still be worth the candle.

'I now come to the submissions of the prosecutor. I am as little bound by those submissions as I am by the submissions on behalf of the accused, although, as I trust will appear from this judgment, I have considered both carefully.'

Right then, thought Blank, *it's to be corrective supervision. I can bear it.*

'At the outset I record that whilst I shall carefully consider the views placed before me, I am in no way bound by them, as the question of sentence remains a question for the court to determine.'

Meticulously, Judge Cloete dissected corrective supervision: how it could be applied, under what circumstances it was called for, what the law specified, its objectives and intentions, precedents established, appropriate cases. Yes, it was certainly an option he was entitled to consider. No, it was not the only option. A court should not be seduced by the availability of new options to impose a sentence which would be unbalanced and inappropriate when measured against the purposes of judicial punishment. He had also to consider the magnitude of the crime and sentences imposed for lesser crimes like shoplifting and car theft. Sometimes the magnitude of an offence was so great that... And then came the bombshell.

'When I balance the interests of the accused against the interests of the community, I am left in no doubt that the only appropriate sentence in this case is a long period of direct imprisonment. I have already dealt with the effect which imprisonment is likely to have on the accused, but in my view he deserves to go to prison and the requirements of society demand it.

'I have considered the possibility of suspending a portion of the sentence. I have, however, decided not to do so. I will take all the counts together for the purposes of sentence. The accused is sentenced to eight years' imprisonment.'

Greg Blank sat stunned. All he could think of was his resolution to betray no emotion. He hardly heard the turbulence in court as reporters raced for phones. He could see the headlines in his mind's eye – 'Greg Blank gets eight years' – but the voices around him seemed to make no sense. Clive Cohen was telling him that they would appeal, the judge had misdirected himself. Some women were crying. There seemed to be a kind of pandemonium, a numbness of noise.

All that he knew was that he had been promised that he would not go to jail. He had focused all his hopes on that, yet now he was going. It was as if the very foundation of his life had been snatched from under him.

Dianne Reynolds turned to her father with tears in her eyes. 'Daddy,' she pleaded, 'you've got to do something.' But there was nothing anyone could do. The judge had spoken. The shattered defence contingent left the courtroom. Somehow, in the next hour or so, it would have to regroup and devise an appeal against sentence.

13

The Press Speaks Out

On the afternoon of that grim day, Greg Blank and his dispirited band of lawyers and friends made their way back to the Rand Supreme Court in central Johannesburg to try to persuade the same judge who had sentenced him in the morning to allow him to appeal against the sentence. Once again – his hopes of avoiding prison dashed – Blank had to clamber back from a pit of despair. He did so with his usual astonishing resilience, aided by a legal team that had convinced him that Judge Tom Cloete had erred grievously in the judgment that accompanied his sentence.

Blank recalls: 'You've got to understand about these disappointments. Before I go to court I get told: "Don't worry, everything's organised. You can book for the health farm." And then the judge says something else entirely. You must go to jail. You want to die.'

Through sheer effort of will, the Greg Blank who walked into the courtroom that afternoon was sprightly again, looking for all the world like a man without a care. Somehow Advocates Cohen and Marcus, in a matter of a few hours, had cobbled together a document listing the grounds for an appeal against sentence. It was eloquently blunt:

> The sentence was so severe as to induce a sense of shock, and was out of all proportion to the gravity of the offence. The court had failed to give adequate weight to the many factors in mitigation, including the fact that there had been full restitution to Old Mutual; the circumstances giving rise to the accused's involvement; the plea of guilty; the accused's co-operation with the State; and his personal circumstances. The sentence was also contrary to the expert recommendation of State witnesses and to evidence led for the defence. It failed to give due weight to the purpose of correctional supervision and its role in deterrence and punishment. Considering the attorney-general's informed decision not to seek imprisonment, and the strikingly disproportionate punishment imposed on Fouche and Coetzee, the sentence was not in the interests of justice nor its administration. A sentence of direct imprisonment under-emphasised Blank's personal circumstances and the alternatives, and over-emphasised the interests of society.

All in all, concluded the document, 'The sentence was an exemplary sentence not justified by the circumstances of the case, nor supported by the evidence, and constituted a misdirection.'

At the end of that long day, Blank went back to his father's home in Houghton. Friends and well-wishers began to flock in, gathering round the bar counter in the lounge. Blank will never forget that evening. 'It was almost like a wake. Jews are funny that way. When someone dies, or experiences a tragedy, they're not sure what to do. So they wish you long life and they bring you flowers or something to eat. I'd just been sentenced to eight years in jail and there I was, behind the bar, serving them drinks. Everyone walks in with long faces. I say: "Listen, I'm not dead. I haven't died." But they've brought me all this food and they come and say: "I'm so sorry; here, have this kitke."'

The Blank team had to wait 24 hours for the judge's response. When it came, it too was eloquently blunt:

> The grounds on which the accused seeks leave to appeal have been set out in a document entitled 'Notice of Appeal'. I do not propose to quote them, nor do I propose dealing in detail with the arguments advanced by Mr Cohen or his junior, Mr Marcus.
>
> It suffices for me to say that I have had an opportunity of considering the grounds and of considering the arguments advanced; I have utilised that opportunity; I have clinically reconsidered my judgment in the light of the criticisms advanced against it; but I am not persuaded that there is any reasonable prospect that an Appeal Court will adopt a different approach to the approach which I adopted, much less interfere with the sentence which I imposed on any of the established grounds for which interference by a Court of Appeal with a sentence imposed by a lower court is sanctioned.
>
> The application for leave to appeal is accordingly refused.

Still, the legal door had not been fully closed. There was one more avenue for the defence to explore. This was to go over the head of the trial judge and petition the chief justice to allow the appeal.

In the meantime, would Blank have to sit it out in jail? Such are the niceties of the legal system that the judge who sentenced Blank and then refused him leave to appeal would also make the decision as to whether he should get bail while he waited to hear from the chief justice.

With a shared suppressed sigh, the defence team of Cohen and Marcus prepared to apply for bail for their client. The obvious question was now that he was convicted, would he decide that flight was preferable to jail? They had a small problem on that front. Only a few days before, Blank's loyal sister Daryl, angered by what she saw as the unfairness of charging her brother while others went free or got off lightly, was quoted in the media as saying: 'If this is the way justice is done in South Africa, then maybe we should all leave.' Did she know something?

Only one person could answer that. For the first time, at the urging of his junior counsel, Gilbert Marcus, Gregory Lex Blank took the stand. He was totally unprepared, but the showman in him welcomed the opportunity. He hadn't enjoyed being a bystander at his own trial.

For somewhat obscure tactical reasons, counsel had decided not to call Blank to testify during the court case itself. It is a moot point whether he would have been able to sway the court. His charm was legendary, his regret at his actions profound and deep, if the assessment of lawyer Peter Reynolds is to be taken at face value. Perhaps the judge might have been mollified had he heard first-hand from Blank. Perhaps not. Only one thing is certain. When it came to deciding whether Blank was truly sorry for what he had done, the judge had one bit of hard evidence that was damning. That was the sentence in the Nicro report that said: 'It is apparent that the client is not particularly remorseful about having transgressed the law in this manner.' No one will ever know now whether Blank could have dispelled the lasting impression those 18 words left in the mind of the judge during the trial. The fact is he wasn't allowed to try.

Now there was an opportunity to impress the court in another way. Could he persuade Judge Cloete that he would stay to face the music if he was given bail?

The inevitable question came from the prosecutor, Petrus Marais: 'How do we know that you won't leave?' Before he could respond, there was a loud interruption from the spectator gallery. All heads turned. Daryl Blank was on her feet, her hand raised: 'Excuse me, excuse me…'

Spectators gasped. The judge turned coldly to Blank's advocate. 'Mr Cohen, please tell that woman that I will have her removed if she interrupts again.'

But Daryl was determined to have her say. As the judge was speaking she called out: 'Excuse me, but I didn't say that about all of us leaving. I was misquoted. The reporter misquoted me.' Then she sat down again. The little disturbance was over. Proceedings continued.

In the box, addressed by the judge, Blank heard the question that he had been dreading for some time. It had first cropped up all those months, years, ago on the night of his arrest, when his South African passport had been confiscated. General Nollie Hulme, hostile and suspicious, had asked him then where his Portuguese passport was. 'All you Jews have Portuguese passports,' the general had said. And Blank had replied that he had no Portuguese passport and that he didn't know what the general was talking about.

Now was the moment of truth. The judge was asking him: 'How many passports do you have?' Blank felt slightly dizzy. He slipped back into his seat, thoughts racing. *Does he know? Doesn't he know? Does he know? Doesn't he…?*

The truth was that Blank did have a second passport. He had taken advantage of General Hulme's very specific question to keep quiet about it. He didn't have a Portuguese passport, but he did have an Irish one. He had qualified for it because his father was of Irish extraction. He had not taken advantage of it to flee during all the time leading up to his trial because of his determination to see things through.

Now the judge had asked him a penetrating question. If he admitted to a second passport, would the court think the worse of him? But if he denied it and the court knew it to be a lie, would it trust anything else he had to say? He said to himself: *Look, what do you want to lie for?* And the thought cheered him up, made him feel less tense.

'My Lord,' he told Judge Cloete, 'I have two passports. I have an Irish one as well as my South African one. But if I had wanted to leave, I would have left ages ago.'

He looked up and, for the first time since the trial ordeal had begun, he saw the glimmerings of a smile on the judge's face. He also saw the face of one of the policemen who had been involved in investigating his case. Captain Neil Pearson was standing in court with his mouth open, his jaw slack. The lieutenant could hardly believe his ears. All this time, the police team had believed that Blank could not escape because he had no passport.

The defence did not have long to wait for the judge's ruling on bail. As before, it was meticulously reasoned. 'I have,' he intoned, citing references, 'at common law, a discretion to grant bail to the accused in these circumstances. The accused had every opportunity to flee, as others have done, to avoid the consequences of his crime. I found in my judgment on sentence that there must have been an obvious temptation for him to have done so. It is true that circumstances have changed in that he has now been sentenced to unsuspended imprisonment for a lengthy period of time; but he could have fled the country after I imposed sentence, had he been so inclined, as he had a passport in his possession which would have enabled him to do so.

'No doubt bail should be refused where the petition would be frivolous, but that is not the case here. No doubt, too, the maxim "justice delayed is justice denied" applies to the interests of the community, which require that proper sentences should be carried out without delay, but practice has shown that it should be a matter of weeks, not months, before the decision of the chief justice on the petition is known.

'I do not believe there is any reasonable prospect of the accused absconding. Such risk as there might be can be reduced by stringent bail conditions.'

Judge Cloete granted Blank bail of R1 million – double his previous bail figure – to be secured by bank guarantee or suretyship from his attorneys. He was ordered to surrender his second passport and to report to Sandton police station twice a day. He was forbidden to leave the Transvaal or go within a one-kilometre radius of any point of departure from South Africa.

To Blank, the granting of bail was like a reprieve. Well, almost. At least, he would not be going to jail immediately.

Subject to the ruling of the chief justice, the legal technicalities were over. Blank was living on borrowed time again. It would be one month short of two years before the spectre of jail loomed up again for him. But while the legalities of the imprisonment decision remained in limbo, some of the issues didn't go away.

There was, for those who cared to notice it, a bitter irony in it all.

In his judgment, Judge Cloete had emphasised the point that the community had had enough of white-collar crime. It wanted action. It wanted retribution. The fact that Fouche and Coetzee had got away with such lenient penalties did not mean that Blank should be treated accordingly. That wasn't fairness or equality of justice; that was a travesty. And the fact that Blank had been the only one of the conspirators to be charged was irrelevant too. He had been convicted, and he deserved to be punished severely in accordance with the community's desires.

The community, however, was not as certain as the judge of its own desires. The issues of fairness and equality of punishment kept recurring. As far as the media reflected that vengeful community – and this, of course, can be debated endlessly – it reflected also a huge uneasiness at what many had begun to think might well be a distortion of justice. Or, at least, a gross unfairness.

In a leading article on 21 October 1992, *The Star* wrote:

> As it turned out, of 14 identified culprits involved in two fraudulent rackets, two got off lightly, two managed to flee and the rest got off scot-free in exchange for becoming State witnesses, if required. So far, their evidence has not been required. Which means that the public will almost certainly never hear the inside story of what was being

> done, who was doing it and which other parties were implicated. Justice will not be seen to be done.
>
> In the circumstances, Blank's belief that he is a scapegoat, a fall guy, rings true. And, blatant though his behaviour was, it seems unfair to let him carry the can while all other crooks scamper free.

The figure of 14 in this article includes a range of people who were involved, to a greater or lesser degree, in the Blank and Fouche/Coetzee scams. None was prosecuted and one was never even named.

The day before, *Business Day* had commented:

> The Blank case, and other loosely associated cases which preceded it, highlighted the ways in which the course of justice might be inadvertently frustrated. Others involved in similar frauds have escaped a full trial and imprisonment by paying admission of guilt fines, or have won indemnity from prosecution by promising to turn State's evidence. It does not take much commonsense to see the unfairness of this and to realise the bad light it throws on our system of justice.

Business Day's editor, Jim Jones, was even more pungent in an article in the same issue of the paper. Under the headline 'Blank case leaves a murky trail of intriguing questions', he observed: 'The fact that Blank is one of the few people to be brought to trial is scandalous… The guilty plea in the Blank case could mean that the JSE investigation will have to start from scratch, though it will presumably have access to court papers.'

To be fair to the stock exchange authorities, Blank's guilty plea, with all its consequences, was none of their doing and suited them not at all. The then president of the JSE, Tony Norton, had let it be known that he favoured full exposure and his name was on the list of potential witnesses. It seemed likely that, if called, he would do his best to persuade the public that the JSE was aware of problems and was dealing with them. A number of stockbrokers called in public for a full inquiry.

The investigative authorities were also extremely sensitive to any suggestions that they had let share-buyers and the stockbroking community off the hook in the Blank case. Greg Blank himself had regained his old, bullish spirit. On 27 November, the *Financial Mail* published an interview with him in which he said: 'No one seems to want to understand that this is the way the stock exchange is. There's a skeleton in every broker's closet. But right now, of course, they're all pretending to be holier than thou. I recognise that what I did was wrong but I feel I'm being victimised and that I'm being forced to be Jesus Christ for the whole exchange.'

The uneasy climate led to a curious but revealing clash between a major publication and Attorney-General Frank Kahn. This little episode reflected the pervasive feeling of things left undone, of 'unfinished business'.

Immediately after the court case, on 22 October the *Financial Mail* published a strong leading article headlined 'The Greg Blank case: not a man alone'. The article listed what it called 'unsatisfactory' aspects. It was particularly critical of the fact that Celotti and Schapiro had been able to flee the country before criminal investigations were launched: 'They slipped out so easily it was almost as if by design. Who allowed this to happen?'

It was also critical of two other points: the fact that no fewer than six indemnifications were given to convict one man, who was neither the originator nor the main beneficiary of the swindle; and also the suggestion in Attorney-General Von Lieres's press release that the prosecution against Fouche and Coetzee had been dropped because it would have been too time-consuming and costly.

'In the end,' said the newspaper, 'we have been treated to the sad spectacle of one man, alone, pleading guilty in the courts and receiving sentence for the crimes of a sizeable syndicate. This is not to say we carry any brief for him; we do not, and it is right that he has been punished with severity by a judge more sensible than the prosecutor to the seriousness of the crimes.

'Nevertheless, there is a pronounced public perception that Blank is the fall guy for too many others. We are left with the impression that the process of justice has been degraded and debased.'

What delicious irony! The points that the *Financial Mail* found unsatisfactory about the process that saw Blank come to trial were the very points raised by Blank's counsel in mitigation of sentence. If the processes were so grossly unsatisfactory, surely that should have argued for a more lenient punishment, yet the *FM* approved of the harsh eight-year sentence. But that is by the way.

Kahn was outraged by the publication's comments, feeling they reflected on him. He wrote a letter to the editor in response, which was published by the magazine on 6 November:

> Firstly, the criminal investigation started immediately upon my appointment. Six days later five warrants of arrest were issued when it was felt that there was sufficient evidence to justify such warrants. The process of justice which you appear to have felt was degraded and debased would indeed have been brought into disrepute had such a step been taken without sufficient evidence.
>
> Secondly, the innuendo concerning the fleeing of Celotti and Schapiro prior to the criminal investigation is incomprehensible. Was

anyone expected to act against them without sufficient evidence? Why have you ignored the fact that extradition proceedings have been put into motion against these men?

Thirdly, you allege that six 'indemnifications' against prosecutions were provided 'apparently in order to secure certain testimonies leading only to one conviction – and then not of the originator nor main beneficiary of the swindle'. The indemnities granted were not provided to secure apparently only one conviction, as you imply. They were resorted to in order to secure at least five convictions. Others are expected to follow.

The due process of law which you bring into question can hardly be faulted when it leads to:

- Unravelling of conspiracies;
- The seizure of ill-gotten gains amounting to about R11 million in foreign currency which places the Reserve Bank in a position to impose administrative penalties; and
- An investigation that is so thorough that it has already led to three people pleading guilty, let alone the cases still to come.

I do not wish to comment on the view taken by my colleague in the Transvaal [on the Fouche and Coetzee admissions of guilt]. His judgment was an independent exercise of his discretion at a time when my mandate in the matter had ceased.

Unfazed, the *FM* added a laconic footnote to Kahn's letter, notable for its logic and a quirky insistence that Schapiro was still alive:

1. Even before the attorney-general was involved, Old Mutual took its investigation to the point at which the matter was handed over to the police. It is possible, during the course of an investigation of this kind, for the A-G to apply administrative procedures to ensure that people under investigation do not suddenly remove themselves. These men were patently highly intelligent and clever. That they were sufficiently alerted to the degree of the investigation is evidenced by their unimpeded departure from SA.

2. Kahn has not previously revealed that extradition proceedings have begun. Indeed, when we spoke to Petrus Marais (Kahn's man handling the Blank prosecution) at the time of Blank's sentencing we were told that extradition proceedings would be launched soon but there were difficulties. Firstly, there is no extradition treaty with Italy, where Celotti is said to be residing (which doesn't preclude extradi-

tion but makes it problematic). Secondly, Marais said Schapiro had been careful not to put his roots down anywhere. He has moved, according to Marais, at least five or six times.

3. The indemnities: The facts are, according to our count, that the following six persons were indemnified: Colin Harper, Allan Greyling, David Cox, Philip Thompson, Chris Logan and Peter Rawson.

Two alleged felons escaped overseas. Two connected with an asociated series of frauds signed admissions of guilt (Fouche and Coetzee). One was brought to court, found guilty and sentenced (Blank). We know nothing of 'five convictions'. Neither does anyone else.

We did not complain about the indemnities. We reflected on the freedom with which they were used in relation to the dividends earned – one conviction in the courts, two by admissions of guilt. In any language, the A-G's liberality with indemnities has so far showed a poor return.

The A-G says other convictions will follow. That presumes other people will be charged. When the *FM* asked Marais about this, he said he'd heard rumours around the marketplace that charges were shortly to be laid against other people but had no concrete information from his own office about it.

4. The return of stolen money is incidental to justice being done and to have been seen to have been done.

5. Until further convictions have been secured, the *FM* sees no reason to alter its opinion.

There the correspondence seemed to lapse. To the best of anyone's knowledge, no further charges have been brought, nor further convictions secured. The Greg Blank case has been the first, and last, judicial glimpse into the JSE in the last two decades. The 'community', once described as demanding retribution, having got its pound of flesh, sank back into the familiar torpor of acquiescence.

14

Life in Limbo

Waiting for an Appeal Court judgment is like waiting for Godot. Life goes on in a desultory sort of way, directed yet aimless, absorbing yet strangely unreal. Blank went back to his office to do the job he was best at (studying the markets), calling in at Sandton police station on his way to and from home, and then putting his feet up with a cup of tea while the phone rang. And rang. And rang again. He was back in business and, almost of its own volition, his investment advisory service flourished. On the surface, he still had all the old aplomb and style; inwardly, he alternately entertained and suppressed the nagging question: *How long will I be allowed to carry on?*

The passage of time had earned Blank not so much absolution as indifference. In the public mind, the trial and conviction was all but forgotten as month followed month, and eventually year followed year, without apparent development. Those acquaintances who had rejected him had long since gone. Those, and there were many, whose trust in him had not faltered began to see him as a permanent fixture. The threat of imprisonment had been hanging over his head for so long that people no longer seemed to give it much thought. It felt quite odd to him that his sense of his own invincibility had somehow transferred itself to his clients, who seemed to assume he would be around for ever.

Judge Cloete was proved right on one point very quickly. The chief justice did attend to the petition with alacrity. On 25 November 1992, a mere month after the trial, Blank's attorneys received the following letter:

> Sir/Gentlemen
>
> APPLICATION FOR LEAVE TO APPEAL:
>
> GREGORY LEX BLANK vs THE STATE
>
> With reference to the petition lodged in this office on 9 November 1992 I am directed by the Honourable the Chief Justice to inform you that the applicant was granted leave to appeal on 25 November 1992 to the Appellate Division against his sentence.

The letter didn't mean all that much in itself. It certainly didn't mean that the chief justice thought Blank stood a good chance of winning an appeal; rather that the law allowed a serious petitioner every reasonable opportunity. In fact, all the letter signified was that it was time to jump aboard the legal merry-go-round once more.

The higher up the legal ladder one climbs, the more complicated and esoteric the issues become. Documentation arising from the trial and the appeal formed a pile of paper as tall as six large Bibles. The appeal judges would have to read through everything, peruse everything, before they could deliver their final judgment.

Once again, Blank began the increasingly difficult process of cranking up his morale, restoring his courage. Once again, his legal team helped. After studying the documentation, his newly appointed advocate, Schalk Burger, came to him and said: 'Don't worry, Greg. We've studied Cloete's judgment and we've found the misdirections. You only need one misdirection to have the sentence reviewed. We've found five.'

Five misdirections! That meant that on five occasions Judge Cloete had made errors in his judgment that could be reversed on appeal. That was great. If there had been only one misdirection, it would have made him feel insecure. He had seen how easily the trial court had undermined what he had believed to be unassailable arguments. But five misdirections? Now that was surely an insuperable obstacle between him and a jail cell. The Appeal Court could throw out one, two, even four misdirections and still there would be a fifth to protect him.

Cautiously, gingerly, he allowed himself to hope again. Or, at least, he allowed that irrepressibly optimistic part of himself to hope again. The optimist co-existed with an alter ego that needed to prepare for the worst. The alter ego said to Blank: 'Listen, you'd better be ready to go to jail. You'd better be emotionally prepared.'

So he began to play a curious little game with himself. When he went home at night he imagined himself in a prison. The doors were locked, he could not get out.

Mentally, he transformed his luxurious bedroom into a cell. This cell was his whole world. He could not leave it nor could he admit anyone to it. With his eyes closed, he could feel the walls closing in, the room growing smaller and smaller. He pictured the cold eyes of warders staring in on him. He tried not to hear the phone if it rang, and after a while he didn't. He enforced on himself a sense of solitude that others might soon impose on him. He tried to imagine how it might feel to be completely alone and vulnerable in an alien setting.

But, of course, in the morning the sun was shining and he was free, and he could shower and drive away, dispelling the after-burn of those desolate nights of the mind.

At first, and with one striking exception, the five misdirections seemed discouragingly like the points made by Advocate Cohen in attempting to persuade Judge Cloete to allow an appeal against sentence. Closer examination dispelled that thought. These misdirections were dressed in fine new livery, they sparkled with renewed vigour. The Emperor had regained the clothes that Judge Cloete had stripped away.

But it was the striking exception that was the real bombshell. The advocates proposed to tackle head-on the issue that had hovered in the background in the trial court. It was the issue of the pre-trial deal in which the State had agreed not to ask for a jail sentence.

The petition argued that the judge had been aware of the deal, had raised no objection and so was party to it. In effect, albeit in the politest of legal terms, Judge Cloete was being accused of reneging on an agreement he had implicitly approved. This raised for the first time the question of whether plea bargaining had a legitimate role in the South African legal system.

The petition began: 'To the Honourable the Chief Justice and the other Honourable Judges of the above Honourable Court the petition of your petitioner humbly sheweth…'

Such mock humility is what the opening ritual required. This was a battle to be fought mostly with lofty words committed to paper so there would be less of the cut and thrust of verbal duelling in the lower court. Disputatious voices would not dominate the halls of the Appellate Division of the Supreme Court of South Africa.

But the challenge in the petition could not be denied. Painstakingly, appellant Blank, assisted by his lawyers, outlined the circumstances. A series of meetings, beginning a month before the trial, had taken place between Blank's legal representatives and counsel for the State. A deal had been hammered out. The negotiations culminated in a meeting in the office of the attorney-general of the Witwatersrand, Klaus von Lieres und Wilkau, where agreement had been reached that Blank would plead guilty and the State would not seek a sentence involving any period of imprisonment. 'This term was considered by your petitioner to be fundamental since his standpoint was consistently that no arrangement with the State would be possible if it entailed a term of direct imprisonment.'

The other terms of the agreement were as they had emerged in the trial: Old Mutual would be repaid; Charge 49 would be dropped and Blank would pay a penalty to the Reserve Bank; the State would call for a substantial fine and correctional supervision; the defence would contend that correctional supervision was inappropriate. The fact of an agreement would be communicated to the presiding judge in chambers.

The full details of the agreement were provided to Judge Cloete two weeks before the trial, and he informed counsel that he would advise the judge-president that the trial would now be shorter than the anticipated duration of several months.

The petition continued:

> At no time prior to your petitioner's plea of guilty did the presiding judge indicate any disquiet or objection to the terms of the agreement aforesaid. The agreement reached with the attorney-general and the presiding judge's reaction thereto were decisive in your petitioner's plea of guilty. In the absence of an agreement, your petitioner would have conducted his defence differently and exercised his right to plead not guilty.
>
> While your petitioner is advised that South African law does not formally recognise the institution of 'plea bargaining', your petitioner is further advised that plea bargains do occur and that there is nothing improper in the State and defence entering into such agreements. The Court of Appeal has had to consider situations in which discussions akin to a plea bargain have taken place on several occasions.
>
> Your petitioner respectfully submits that the circumstances outlined above:
>
> 1. are of crucial concern to him personally;
> 2. are important in the administration of justice.

Predictably, the suggestion that the court was bound by the pre-trial deal angered two people in particular. One was Witwatersrand Attorney-General Klaus von Lieres und Wilkau. And the other was the trial judge, Tom Cloete. Both fired off missives to the Appeal Court setting out their positions.

Wrote the attorney-general:

> The terminology in the petition, more particularly the word agreement, may be misconstrued to mean that my decision not to request the court to impose a sentence of direct imprisonment was arrived at as a result of negotiations and/or plea bargaining. I explicitly informed the petitioner's representatives that I had no intention whatsoever of entering the plea bargaining arena. My view that a court was unlikely to impose a sentence of direct imprisonment in the

> light of all the relevant facts was conveyed to the representatives of the petitioner at the onset of the meeting. I had no intention whatsoever to interfere with the court's discretion.

Judge Cloete's response was equally emphatic. Talking of the meeting in chambers, he said:

> I at no stage inferred, nor was it either stated or suggested to me, that I was being asked to give an indication as to whether or not I would consider myself bound not to impose imprisonment. Had counsel requested any such indication, I would have terminated the meeting forthwith.
>
> I was careful not to say anything which could have led counsel for the State or the petitioner to form the impression that I had a view as to what I might regard as an appropriate or likely sentence.
>
> It was in no way indicated to me that the petitioner might decide to plead guilty depending on my attitude to a possible sentence of imprisonment. The contrary was the position. I was expressly informed at the beginning of the meeting that the petitioner had decided to plead guilty.
>
> I was not privy to any agreement which would in any way have fettered my discretion.

The appeal judge, E. M. Grosskopf, JA, had no difficulty in accepting the statements from the judge and the attorney-general. Sitting with him, fellow Judges of Appeal Kumleben and F. H. Grosskopf concurred. Appeal Judge Grosskopf's judgment said:

> The alleged irregularities relating to a plea bargain were not raised timeously in the proper form in the trial court, and moreover have no basis whatever. In the pre-trial discussions the prosecution intimated that it would ask for a particular form of punishment. If the appellant was induced by this intimation to plead guilty, he has no reason to complain. The prosecution did what it said it would. The trial judge was not bound by the attitude of the prosecutor.
>
> On the record of the present case, there is no indication that a plea bargaining took place. If the defence wanted to take the point that there was some irregularity or illegality in the proceedings in that a plea bargaining agreement had not been dealt with properly by the court or the prosecution, it should have done so by way of an application for a special entry on the record, supported by evidence.

> In these circumstances there clearly was no irregularity whatsoever and it is not necessary for me to consider what recognition should in general be accorded to plea bargaining agreements.

So the legitimacy of plea bargaining will have to be decided another day.

As for the other alleged misdirections by the trial judge, the arguments raised were similar to those raised in the trial court. They found as little favour. The Appeal Court ruled: 'The imposition of sentence is preeminently a matter falling within the discretion of the trial judge and a Court of Appeal can interfere only where such discretion was not properly exercised.'

Judge Cloete had exercised his discretion properly. And so that was that. Some non-legal questions remain unanswered. How did Greg Blank's original legal representatives come to believe so strongly that there was a deal to keep their client out of jail when the judge and the State insist there was no deal? Could this mistaken belief have influenced the handling of the entire defence case? Why was confidentiality on the pre-trial agreement observed in the trial, only to be broken in the appeal?

Might Blank have testified in his own defence if he had thought, even for a moment, that he was facing a long jail sentence? Might the argument for not sending him to jail have been delivered with more fire and fervour?

On Thursday, 15 September 1994 Greg Blank was on tenterhooks. This was the date on which the Appeal Court would announce its decision. His lawyers were so confident that they would win this time. It was also the most holy day of the Jewish calendar, Yom Kippur, and he had been accorded the honour of opening the ark at the Temple Shalom synagogue on Louis Botha Avenue. He fasted all day.

Finally he could bear the waiting no longer. He tried to call his lawyers but the phones just rang and rang. He had a small premonition of trouble. Finally, on his car phone, he got hold of Junior Counsel Gilbert Marcus, who had helped to prepare the appeal petition.

'Gilbert, it's Greg. How did it go?'

'No, no…it's been upheld.'

Upheld! The word meant everything to Blank. It was a word used frequently at racetracks. When an objection was upheld in horse-racing, it meant that the original result was overturned. The Appeal Court must have overturned Judge Cloete…

'Fantastic! So now I'm free.'

'No, Greg. The sentence has been upheld. You've got to go to jail.'

Blank felt the blow like a mulekick to the stomach. He went to his father's house because he didn't know what else to do. 'There were millions of people there and they were all saying how sorry they were. I just wanted to be alone. I went home to be by myself. I couldn't talk to anyone.'

That evening he went to see his new attorney, Stan Fanaroff, who introduced him to an aggressive young advocate called André Bezuidenhout. Bezuidenhout knew his way around the prison scene and said he would make arrangements for Blank to be admitted to Krugersdorp prison.

'Don't worry,' said Fanaroff, 'you've got seven days to hand yourself over. Get your affairs in order.' Blank went home. On Friday morning he rose early, put on his suit and prepared to leave for the office. Just then the bell at his Khyber Rock home rang. Two women reporters from the *Sunday Times* were waiting at the barred gate.

'Listen, I don't talk to the press.'

'No, we just wanted to come in and have a cup of coffee.'

Ever courteous, he agreed. 'They come in and all of a sudden they're taking pictures, and I said: "Listen, do me a favour, I'm very busy." So they left.'

Some time during that Friday Advocate Bezuidenhout contacted Blank.

'They're looking for you. The police are looking for you. I've just heard it on Radio 702. They say you've got to report to jail.'

'What the hell are they talking about? I've got seven days.'

'No you haven't. Don't even go home. I'll come and take you to the jail tomorrow.'

So Blank spent his last evening of freedom away from the comfort of his cluster home, darting from his partner's house to his brother's house. He thought: *Now I know what it feels like to be on the run. Even jail is preferable to this. The sooner I start my sentence, the sooner it will be over.*

PART THREE

15

And So to Jail

Two days after Yom Kippur, three days before his thirty-sixth birthday, Greg Blank reported for incarceration. He arrived at Krugersdorp prison at 6 a.m. on Saturday, 17 September 1994 in a cream Toyota driven by his legal representative, André Bezuidenhout. With him was his brother, Vaughan. It had been a jokey sort of early-morning journey, everyone trying to put a bold face on things, Blank superficially calm but inwardly stressed.

He had already decided that he would try to take jail as it came, flow with the tide. But it was more easily said than done. His original fears about prison were still there, buried in a compartment in his head. He had no idea what to expect, what he would have to do.

He knew only that he was going into a violent world with what he imagined to be the brutish rejects of society. From the moment he surrendered his personal freedom, his identity almost, he would be at the mercy of the State's warders. He wondered if they would be any less brutish than their charges. It was a frightening thought. All the stereotypes of prison life – from books, the movies, childhood imaginings – floated through his mind.

He saw some men in prison warder uniform marching on the square outside the buildings. They seemed cheerful enough. It reminded him of his days in army service. He tried to rationalise his fears. Could jail be much worse than the regimentation and restriction he had experienced as a serviceman in the South African Defence Force? Surely not. Well, he had survived that, he could survive this. It was just a matter of accepting reality, making the best of it.

He knew jail would not be for ever and that was a consolation. But something inside him kept saying: 'Eight years…eight years.' It seemed like a lifetime. The one thing he wouldn't do was count the hours or tick the days off on a calendar. That would drive him mad.

At first sight, the prison did not seem as bleak as he had feared. It stood on a large tract of ground just off a main east-west thoroughfare only a few kilometres from the centre of Krugersdorp. Of course, it was surrounded by high fences topped with barbed wire and there was a gatehouse on the west side which controlled entry and exit. It was never going to be mistaken for a pleasure resort. But the reddish face-brick was not so much brooding and ominous as cold and official-looking, more like a government school or building. There was even a hint of architectural grandeur about the structure that stood alone on the south side, enclosed by its own walls. This, he was to learn later, was a prisons museum as well as a training school for prison warders. It boasted an imposing entrance.

Across the large asphalt square stood the prison itself. From the southern perspective, it appeared to be a squat double-storey building, not so bulky as to seem forbidding. In the entrance foyer, a fountain played on the water of a free-form pond. Tubs of greenery muted the stark hallway. The decorative features looked slightly incongruous in so unwelcoming an environment. The floors were spotless.

To the left, a visitors' reception area, as bleak and unfriendly as a station waiting-room; to the right, a corridor, closed doors staring blindly out. Directly in front of him and three steps down, as he was escorted into his new home, was a metal door. Its featureless surface was relieved by only two things: a Judas spyhole situated at about eye-level for a very tall man and a knocker that jangled harshly – metal against metal – to summon the man behind the door.

Blank's escorts rattled the knocker. There was a sound of voices within, an eye appeared at the Judas spyhole and then there was another jangle of noise as a key was inserted into an interior keyhole and turned. He was surprised at how loud it sounded. The door swung open.

When it closed again, as it did almost immediately, there was something forlorn about the last booming clang. The way out was sealed. There was no going back, no final appeals, no hope of a last-minute reprieve. Four years, six months and ten days after his arrest, Greg Blank was finally in prison. He had not said goodbye to either his father or his mother. It was just too hard to do.

He was being locked up in what was one of the most violent prisons in the country with a sombre record of assaults and deaths in the cells. Society was about to exact its revenge on a wrongdoer. He was surprised to find that his welcome was mildly cordial. The major in charge came up to him and said: 'Good morning. How do you do, Prisoner Blank.'

Blank took stock of his surroundings. He found himself in a reception area about the size of a small domestic lounge. It had a table with bulky, dog-eared registers on it, two scuffed easy chairs and a notice board. Leading off it to the right was an office and reception desk. Authorised visitors checked in here, signed the register, waited for clearance. Natural light filtered in from tiny horizontal windows deep-set in concrete at ceiling level. The thought flashed through his mind that not even a baby could crawl through those windows. Behind him was the steel door through which he had entered. In front, about 12 paces away, was a wall of vertical steel rods about 10 centimetres apart with a barred gate inset. A warder with a large key hanging around his neck scuttled between the locked front door and the barred gate, responding to knocks and cries, unlocking and locking the one door before carrying out the same procedure on the other. Every now and then a prison staff member would emerge from the office in the ante-room and disappear down the long corridor.

Prisoners would appear at the barred gate, calling out: '*Hek asseblief. Dankie, bewaarder*' ('Gate please. Thank you, Warder'), as they sought admission to the reception area for some chore or other. A convict with makeshift floor-polishers attached to the soles of his shoes glided to and fro in this no man's land, polishing an already gleaming floor. It was about the only silent activity in the place.

All else was din. Vast corridors amplified and threw back the sound of voices, the squish of boots, metallic clangs, unidentifiable noises. Cacophony was to become a constant companion. In the months to come, the sounds would sometimes be reinforced by screams and groans from within the bowels of the prison.

Sounds become more indelible than sights in a prison because they speak of unmentionable happenings behind closed doors.

From where he stood in the ante-room he could see through the bars of the second barrier what looked like an interminable sloping corridor without windows. The corridor appeared to vanish into the earth. *Good God!* thought Blank. *Are they going to keep me underground?* The corridor was painted an unappealing ochre, pocked with angry black smudges where it had been scratched and scuffed. Graffiti ramblings, partly obliterated, defaced the walls.

The impression of a corridor into the earth was an illusion. It sloped because the ground sloped, enabling the double-storey building at the front to become four storeys at the back without affecting the skyline perspective.

Actually, Saturday was a good day to go to jail. Relatively speaking. Krugersdorp prison operated on a skeleton staff at weekends. The clerical staff who normally handled admissions were not on duty. Prisoners did not usually enter through the front door as Blank had done. They were sent to a reception area where they were processed as a group for the next 48 hours or so. By all accounts, it was not a pleasant experience.

Blank received rather more individual attention. He thought it was in part because Advocate Bezuidenhout put in a special word for him. Bezuidenhout evidently had contacts at the prison; they seemed to know him. For whatever reason, the admission process was quick and painless. He kept his civilian clothes because no standard-issue olive-green prison uniform was available. His tog bag was not searched.

Best of all, he was accommodated temporarily in the hospital wing, a small enclave only a few metres down the long corridor from the barred gate. It was an area of moderate comfort by prison standards; single cells for patients requiring isolation, hygienic kitchens, everything clean and neat. Well, not quite everything. The cell allocated to him was a fair size, but the mattress it contained was filthy. So were the makeshift sheets and blanket. He would have to do something about that. But at least there was the consolation of company in a common ward in those precious hours when the cells were unlocked.

He could catch a glimpse of trees and sky from the hospital windows. And he didn't have to descend that long corridor to the unknown depths of the prison proper.

He didn't realise it, but he had just learnt the First Rule of Prison Survival. You are at the mercy of the staff members. They can make your life a misery – or a lot more pleasant.

The new-boy prisoner found himself among young criminals, juveniles. Most seemed about 18 or 19. He rummaged in his tog bag and produced a couple of packs from the ten cigarette cartons he had stashed there. They broke the ice wonderfully. He introduced himself and learnt that his new and apparently amiable companions included someone convicted of rape and another convicted of attempted murder. They all wanted to chat to him.

At first he thought it was because he was such a pleasant guy. Then he realised it was the cigarettes. Within days he had mastered the Second Rule of Prison Survival. Convicts will do anything for you if you reward them. But don't make the mistake of thinking that they love you.

For the price of a few cigarettes, Blank found, his companions begged to be allowed to help him. In the weeks to come, they made his bed, did his washing, cleaned his cell. The only thing he had to be careful of was not to allow anyone to do a task already allocated to someone else. That would mean trouble.

Blank had had a slice of toast before setting off for Krugersdorp, and had been too tense to eat lunch. At three o'clock in the afternoon a warder came and locked them all into their cells. The sharp clunks sounded like death knells. Click – the barred gate. Click – the solid outer door with the small, gaping observation hole. Click – the end of the world. Blank felt desperate. He didn't know it then, but 16 hours of unpleasant solitude stretched ahead. He had no book to read, no radio to listen to. At home, solitude had meant a pleasant interlude with his own thoughts. In jail, it was a denial of his right to company. He missed the comfort of a telephone much more than he had expected. Telephones were the instruments through which he had earned his living. They were what his life was about.

He thought of the voices he would most like to hear in his present predicament and felt an acute twinge of deprivation. Without a phone at his elbow he was not a whole person. He thought back to his days as a national serviceman: *After a week, you were allowed the privilege of a phone call home, and you stood in a queue for three hours for your turn, and the joy when you heard a loved one's voice and it made you feel better just to tell someone how bad things were, how lonely you were.*

He thought of the other simple pleasures he had taken so much for granted. Lying back in bed and clicking on the TV. Getting up to make a cup of coffee or take a shower. Even turning a light on or off. In prison, the light switches are outside the door, out of reach of prisoners. By the end of his first week he had concluded, quite wrongly, that prison was a deprivation, not a torment.

He fell into a restless sleep, trying to block out the noise of prisoners shouting for warders, screaming at each other. At about 8 p.m. a warder came past. Blank felt a compelling need for conversation. They talked for about half an hour through the observation hole. He asked whether it was possible to obtain a newspaper and handed over R20 on the promise that the warder would deliver one daily. Somehow the night passed. On Sunday morning he woke up at about 6 a.m. and thought: *Where the hell am I?*

He got up, tidied his cell, began to do sit-up exercises on the floor. *I'm in jail*, he told himself, *I want them to see that I'm here, that I want to do the best I can.* The warders looked at him as if they thought he was touched in the head. He had no idea what was expected of him, what the jail routine was. Obviously the prison staff were not going to tell him.

At 7 a.m. a warder came and unlocked the cell doors. His new-found jail companions trooped off to the stark hospital eating room and he followed. It was breakfast time. The hospital inmates were queuing for food in their dressing gowns and grubby pyjamas. A kitchen hand ladled a gollop of a porridgy substance on to each plate. It was not the kind of porridge he was used to. No one seemed to notice or care that he was in track-suit trousers, not the olive-green regulation uniform for prisoners.

Blank was a mite uneasy. He had heard things about what happened in prison mess halls, seen the prison-life movies. He ate a couple of spoonfuls of the porridge-like concoction. At least it filled a gap.

The hospital contingent trooped back to the ward. The warder who had taken his R20 brought him the *Sunday Times*. It was the only newspaper that that warder ever brought him; in effect he'd paid R20 for a single copy of a single newspaper. Thus he learnt the Third Rule of Prison Survival. Never give money to anybody in jail unless you can be sure that you'll get your money's worth.

At noon, everyone went to lunch. Blank was given a steel plate and a spoon. He asked the kitchen hand what he was serving. 'Chicken curry,' came the response. Blank peered and saw a bone far too large for any chicken lurking in the murky brew on his plate. He decided he could live without prison lunches, and never touched another while he was there. He took a *kaalkop* instead. *Kaalkop* means 'bald head' and is what the prisoners call the food ration that consisted of a quarter-loaf of brown bread topped with what looked like some kind of white cottage cheese. It was, in fact, white margarine, and at first glance it did look something like a bald white pate atop a brown head. It tasted foul and greasy. He took the *kaalkop* back to his cell and ate the bread without its topping.

Eight years of this! he thought. *I'll never make it.*

Blank asked his new friends what time supper was. 'You've just had it,' said one. 'The bread is your supper. They give you two meals at once at lunch time.' So that was it, then. No more food until Monday morning. The cell doors clanged shut again at 3 p.m. Click, click went the locks. Blank stared at the walls. When next he woke he would have completed his first weekend in prison. It seemed a very long time indeed.

He was very conscious that he was still in the prison waiting-room, so to speak. The hospital section was insulated from the prison proper. Down that sloping corridor – that's where the real prison was. That was where the screams and the yells emanated from. Desperate men were down there.

Blank remembers: 'No one tells you what you can and can't do. Rather, prisoners tell you what they think you can and can't do. They're always telling you. But there are no rules saying you can't do this or that. You learn by trial and error.

'So now Monday comes and I want to show them what I can do. Greg Blank is not going to let prison get him down. I'm up at six and doing my exercises again. The warders still look at me as if I'm crazy. Actually, they're used to seeing crazies in the hospital section. When Weskoppies, the mental institution, is full, they sometimes send the overflow to Krugersdorp.

'Now you wait for the warders to open the cell. That's like the biggest thing of the day. Opening the cell! And going into the breakfast room. I know the routine now. I try to push out my chest. You have all these ideas about how you should behave in jail. Some guys are getting more sugar. Some guys are getting none. I get there and I get my porridge. No sugar or milk. So I say to the guy: "Where's mine?" He says: "What's in it for me?" So I give him R5 and – you can't believe it – sugar, milk, tea, second helpings, whatever I wanted.

'Finished my breakfast at 7.30, went back to my cell and…that was it! That was my day. I thought, here I am at 7.30 ready to do something. There must be duties to be done in jail, a gym to go to, workshops to work in. I say to the guy: "What do I do now?" He says: "Whatever you want – go to sleep, read a book." I spent the morning talking to the juveniles. At least it passed the time. By 11 o'clock I thought I would have a little sleep. You get tired from doing nothing.'

By the fifth day, Blank was fit to be tied. He returned to his cell after breakfast to find a big white man sprawling on his bed.

'Hey, what're you doing on my bed?' asked Blank.

'I heard you were in jail, and I want to put a proposition to you,' replied Felix Kramer, a stranger to him. That was when Blank learnt two things that were to change his life in prison.

The first thing he learnt from Kramer was something about the big rats that infested the prison. He had seen them, of course. Sometimes, in that first week when he became especially bored, he would take a little of his bread, crumble it, throw it to the rats that scurried across the roof below the hospital window, and watch them fight over the pickings. It passed the time.

Later he would develop it into a full-scale game he called hide-and-seek. That was his entertainment. Whenever the rats became aware of his presence, they would scurry to safety. So he would lurk out of sight behind the window until they had plucked up the courage to resume their activities. Then he would bob up and observe again, until they detected his presence once more. It made a great game. He thought of them as his little playmates.

But when Kramer told him he had seen the rats defecating on the raw porridge that was his staple meal, he resolved never to eat prison porridge again. That meant, after his decision to avoid prison lunches, going without breakfast as well.

For the next six weeks he lived on his quarter loaf of brown bread minus margarine and lost about 10 kilogrammes in weight. But he got to like brown bread – something he never ate at home – especially when it was enlivened by smuggled peanut butter or syrup. When he was lucky enough to gain access to these delicacies he would sit in his cell and dunk his bread until it was permeated with one or the other, or both, then gulp it down. It was bliss. He felt a kinship with the workers he had seen in his old life, sitting on pavements, eating hunks of bread.

The second thing he learnt from Kramer was more productive. Kramer, an inmate, was the chairman of the prison's recreation committee, a joint warder–prisoner operation designed to ease the burdens of prison life. He was serving a 13-year sentence and had boundless energy and was good with his hands, but lacked organisational skills. He had been trying for more than a year to get a recreation club off the ground. The efforts had been singularly ineffective for a number of reasons. Too little money, too little drive, too much inertia, too much resistance.

Kramer said he wanted Blank to join the recreation committee. 'Fine,' said Blank. 'What's your first priority?'

'We need television sets, something to keep the men occupied,' said Kramer. 'They've got nothing to do.'

'Okay, I'll get them for you,' offered Blank. But, at heart, he wasn't as certain as he sounded. The absence of specified rules made things difficult for the new-boy prisoner. Wanting desperately to ensure the shortest possible time in jail, he didn't want to put a foot wrong. But what was he allowed to do? He had already discovered one thing, and that was that the new title of the old prisons department was misleading. As his lawyers were later to report to the commissioner of the Department of Correctional Services: 'The term "Correctional Services", as it relates to him, was a misnomer – where was the correctional or rehabilitative element? All he witnessed was violence, aggression and unhappiness. He had never seen violence of this nature before – people beaten and stabbed almost every day right before his eyes.'

He arranged for a consultation with his legal team, Advocate André Bezuidenhout and Attorney Stan Fanaroff. Would it be taken amiss if he became actively involved in the social upliftment of his fellow inmates? he wanted to know.

By all means join the recreation committee, he was advised, but, to be on the safe side, keep the prison administration informed about what you are doing. Oh yes, and don't try to manipulate the system for your own exclusive benefit; that would be frowned on by the department.

Relieved, he called an old friend, a top Johannesburg businessman, and asked for help. The friend responded instantly. No one realised it at the time, but it was the beginning of a process that was to turn Krugersdorp into a showpiece prison. For Blank, it was also memorable for another reason. He had been able to use a telephone! As a member of the recreation committee with access to top potential sponsors, it made sense to everyone that he should be able to make phone calls.

He was back in touch with the outside world. It was a watershed moment. He sat down and wrote to his mother, his first letter from prison.

> Dear Ma,
>
> I'm sorry that you did not come and see my new home, but I'm allowed three visits per month so I expect to see you. Thanks so much for the pictures, they brought tears to my eyes. You know that I do not cry easy. I really miss you and wish I could speak to you every day like I used to do. Just promise me you will be strong. I need you there for me when I come home.

They have made me treasurer of the recreation club, the most sought-after job in the prison. I'm going to use my time here beneficially. There are so many desperate people. Being here really makes one appreciate outside life. Nothing is taken for granted. You will not believe what people will do for one cigarette.

Anyway, I really miss you and hope to see you soon. Lots of love,

VIC (Very Important Criminal)

His mother folded the letter into her family diary. Tears in his eyes? That didn't sound like her son. It was a side of him she didn't know. She thought she would keep the letter to remind her of it. She was relieved by the little joke about the 'Very Important Criminal'. It told her Gregory was keeping his spirits up.

Time passed in the hospital ward, not entirely uneventfully. The occasional arrival of a disturbed mental patient ensured that. Once the man in the next cell from Blank began banging his head endlessly against wall and floor. It carried on all night, and Blank could not get to sleep. On another occasion, he recalls, 'there was this massive guy – he must have been about 6 feet 10 inches. He claimed to be an explosives expert. He tore the sink from the wall in his cell and forced his bed through the little window. No one could go near him. He used to sit in his cell totally naked with a little piece of string under his bum, and he said if anyone came in he would pull the string and everyone would explode. They took him away after a while.'

By now, in his new role with the recreation club – his title was changed from treasurer to the more appropriate 'in charge of special projects' – he was venturing ever deeper down the sloping corridor into the prison proper. The place where the real prisoners lived. One of these days, that would be his home too, down there, far from the barred gate and the hospital ward.

In the meantime, he was getting to know this nether region and its disturbing occupants. It was like getting a glimpse of hell.

16

Gateway to Hell

A week after he entered jail, the Department of Correctional Services found it necessary to issue a public statement saying that Blank would be treated the same as any other prisoner. 'All prisoners are treated exactly the same,' said official spokesman Brigadier Chris Olckers. 'But because of the publicity they have received in the media, some prisoners are obviously treated differently by prison officers. However, crime is crime regardless of whether it is white-collar or blue-collar.'

This profoundly enigmatic statement seemed to settle suspicions in some minds that Blank would receive favouritism. But, lest anyone should be left in doubt, a suggestion from Olckers that Blank could be transferred to Johannesburg in order to be closer to his family was never implemented. Being kept in Krugersdorp was not the kind of 'favouritism' anyone could misconstrue.

Krugersdorp prison was an ugly place to be. The International Committee of the Red Cross – which in those days inspected prisons nation-wide, primarily to try to assess how political detainees were treated – had rated it among the toughest prisons in the country. At one time there had been an average of two murders a month in the cells.

Beyond the barred gate, the bleak, sunless corridor with its sullied ochre walls and green-painted concrete floors led downwards, turning back on itself as if it was trying to burrow into the earth. Locked doors guarded the entrance to various sections, graded – like the prisoners – to reflect the status of the inmates.

Blank surveyed his new universe. He still lived in the relatively protected hospital ward, but, as a member of the recreation club committee, he was starting to venture deeper into what one writer has called 'the belly of the beast'. He could feel the tension between correctional services members and prisoners and between prisoners themselves. Racial tensions too. There was a sense of action without purpose. Warders moved with wary eyes through knots of convicts – they called them *bandiets* – standing sullen in corridors. There was, inevitably, some banter, even dark laughter, but it sounded false and ugly.

Despair welled up in him. He didn't belong in here. He remembered something the judge had said in his trial judgment about prison being harder on first-time, white-collar criminals – criminals plucked from warm homes in the comfort of suburbia. The judge didn't know the half of it.

It was the abruptness that jarred Blank. Suddenly, he was in an alien world. The faces around him seemed at first to have no distinguishing features, only the same dull eyes. He thought: *Among these people are murderers, rapists, thugs.* He had never, to his knowledge, been in the presence of a killer. Now he was destined to live among them. People he didn't know looked at him with the indifferent curiosity that passed for interest in a jail. A new face provided some kind of distraction, for a moment.

He wondered whether he should stare back or look away. What gave offence in jail? He had no idea.

He had read about the gangs – the Big Five, Air Force Three and Four, the 28s, the 26s and who knew what others – about how they were supposed to rule by fear. He knew about the ruthless punishments, the smothering to death in a blanket, the stomping to death in a crowded cell, the ritual punching of a man's belly filled with water. The gangs imposed rigid discipline, army-style. In some, it was an offence for a junior to talk unbidden to a senior officer. In others, a pointed finger could be interpreted as an insult, to be revenged. Young prisoners were taken as 'wives' by some of the gangs. Infidelity and other crimes were rewarded by gang-rape – brutal, repetitive, anal assault.

The ultimate offence was to snitch. It was called *piemping* and could lead to a death sentence from the prison's kangaroo courts. He was to remember that in days to come.

At first sight, to the young and nervous prisoner, gang law didn't seem possible in so controlled an environment. The prisoners looked so submissive, the warders so dominant. But that was superficial. Underneath – he could feel it – there was a crackling resentment, like a hidden ember waiting for a spark to ignite it. *That's scary*, he told himself. *I don't know what makes these people tick, any of them. Who should I be more afraid of, the warders or the inmates? Can I avoid giving unwitting offence to any of them? I don't belong here!*

At the end of his first week in Krugersdorp prison he saw his first murders. It happened with startling suddenness and the kind of ferocity he had never seen before.

It was lunch time, and there were about 600 prisoners and a handful of warders in the A-Section dining hall. There was nothing special about the clatter and clamour that accompanied the food. Prison was always like that, he had discovered.

Then, suddenly, one voice rose above the hubbub, one word was uttered. The word was 'Up!'

The members of the 28s gang rose as one, pulled out their home-made weapons and turned on two members of their bitter enemies, the 26s. It was a signal for a free-for-all. The hall erupted into a boiling cauldron of violence. Food and eating implements flew through the air as bodies seethed in furious conflict. Makeshift knives and daggers glinted. Some prisoners tried to flee and Blank ran with them. Others stayed to fight. Warders, heavily outnumbered, ran for reinforcements.

And then, as quickly as it started, the fury was spent, and it was over. Almost as if nothing had happened. Except that two strangely-still bodies lay amidst the debris on the floor.

The warders returned, heavily armed, and placed the bodies on blankets. In prison, the fastest way to move a casualty or a corpse is on a blanket, pulled across the highly-polished floors. The blanket-stretchers, like sleds on snow, vanished up the long corridor towards the hospital. But it was too late. The men were dead.

Blank found himself trembling. The sheer intensity, the unexpectedness, left him in shock. The calmness that had returned to the dining hall seemed eerie. He had been given a glimpse of hell and now it was gone, as if a gentle sea had simply closed over it. But hell was there all right. Just under the surface. He felt shattered. That was when he began to feel grateful for being double-locked into his cell at night. He recalls now: 'When I first went to Krugersdorp, the worst feeling was when they came and locked me in my cell. But, after a while, I began to look forward to being locked up. I could hear the awful noises everywhere, but in my little cell I felt secure. It was like being in a womb. No one could get at me.'

Sometimes, though, he worried what would happen if he fell ill, needed help. 'In theory, there's always a warder within calling distance. In practice, it's not like that,' he told me one day after several months in prison. 'When the guys need something they scream "*Dankie, bewaarder*" until someone comes. Sometimes it doesn't work. Then you hear them beating on their bars with any hard object they can find. It seems to echo right through the prison. It's a frightening sound.'

Much later, he became an A-category prisoner, his privileges were increased and he was moved to a section with only six single cells. Here, the cell doors were not locked at night and the inmates had the freedom of their own tiny enclave – cells, passageway, shower room, kitchen. The first few nights there, he couldn't sleep. The unlocked door presented a threat. 'I kept thinking people were going to walk into my room, and wondering what they were going to do to me.'

He looked forward to visiting times, and yet he didn't. It was so nice to see familiar faces, hear affectionate voices. But it was humiliating too. The visiting room was a barn with rows of uncomfortable stools, like bar-stools, facing each other across a counter-like structure, amid thick soundproof glass separating loved ones. Warders watched and listened balefully. There was never enough time, too much to say that could not be put into public words.

'The visits were what kept me going in the first few months,' he recalls. 'But it was so dehumanising. You're sitting behind the glass and there are about 50 people in the room with you and they are all yelling and shouting – you can't hear your visitors and you're trying to speak into the microphone, and your visitor tries to touch you, touches the glass. It's so sad.

'The visits go so quickly, just seeing the people keeps you going.'

The visitors don't know what it's like down the sloping corridor. Sometimes they get frightened by what they imagine it to be. Sometimes they ask questions. Blank wasn't always sure what to tell them.

Di Reynolds came to see him quite often. They had not dated for nearly two years, but there was a curious bond between them and he took comfort in her presence. They thought of each other as good friends. Sometimes Blank would think wistfully of what might have been between them, but he tried not to show it. One day, about three months after he entered jail, she told Blank: 'Gregory, you know that American I met? We're going to marry.'

And he replied with a wan little smile: 'I'm happy for you. I hope you'll be happy.' Two months later, Di Reynolds came to him in jail and said that the man she was going to marry was dead. He had been killed in an air crash. She was distraught. Blank thought: *She's been a comfort to me. Perhaps now I can be a comfort to her.*

Slowly, very slowly, they began to grow together again.

Alien sounds are always alarming. He heard the commotion down the corridor, men fighting, cries, groans, grunts. The angry noise seemed to come from everywhere and nowhere, enveloping him. In the claustrophobic atmosphere of the prison it seemed to him that the place was being torn apart, that he was being sucked into a vortex of ferocity. Which way to turn? He wanted to run, but curiosity got the better of him. He saw the brawlers – ugly, vicious, out of control.

Now, suddenly, the noise of thudding feet, fast and urgent. He knew what it was, he had heard about it. It was the prison's reaction unit, 30 strong men approaching at jogger's pace, batons upraised. In the lead, the kung fu and karate expert, Warrant Officer Karl Wagner, a figure to inspire terror. He was the prison's chief trouble-shooter. Sensitive about his baldness, he always wore a hat. When he was on a mission, with his hat pulled down to almost hide his eyes, he looked a fearsome sight.

The faces of the men with him in the unit were masks of purposeful anger. They went past him in a flash, approaching the disturbance, ready for action. The prison itself seemed to be still for a moment.

And then the plastic batons began to flail. Again and again, remorselessly. At first there was some resistance. The resistance was beaten down. The noise of the flogging – thud, thud, thud – overwhelmed all other noises, gradually subduing them. Blank watched, fascinated and repelled.

My God, he thought, *the warders are enjoying this! They actually like it.*

After a lifetime, it was over. Three black men lay slumped in a bloody heap on the floor of the prison. The men from the reaction unit stepped back a pace, eyes hard and cautious, looks darting here and there to see if the brawlers had hidden allies. No one spoke.

The beaten men were lifted to their feet. Dazed, they were forced to strip and were then half-carried, half-dragged to the showers. The cold-water jets were turned on. The reaction unit disbanded itself, its individual members returning to routine duty. Once again the inmates of Krugersdorp prison had been taught an object lesson. There would be no mercy for those who contravened the rules. Prison was much too dangerous a place to allow indiscipline.

The beaten men considered themselves fortunate. If their offence had been more serious, they might have earned a month in isolation, to sit and lie in a solitary cell, arms linked to legs by a long chain, permitted to exercise outside the cell – still chained – for only one hour in every 24.

Not that even that punishment would have broken these tough men. They understood what prison was about, asked no quarter, nor would give it if the roles were reversed. They were there because society was taking its revenge for their misdeeds.

They would suffer stoically because they expected nothing better. Prison was prison. It was not there for rehabilitation, as some officers tried to tell them sometimes. It was there for retribution. And retribution would always be fierce and fast.

Is that the way it has to be? thought Blank. *Is there nothing else but the inexorable law of the jungle? And if that is so, where does it leave me?*

Blank sensed something else. At least part of the brutality was born in boredom. Endless soul-killing days and nights. Krugersdorp was not designed for anything else. It was originally supposed to be a way-station; a place to keep awaiting-trial prisoners and convicts on their way to more permanent accommodation. It was not designed for long-termers. There were no workshops, no organised activities, nothing to do.

One day, soon after his descent into the nether jail, Blank discovered the communal cells. He thought: *Imagine if I had been put in one of those! Could I have survived it? Hope must surely die here.*

Hope was a scarce commodity in the over-filled communal cells. Men were meant to endure there, not to hope. There were criminals facing ten-year sentences, 15-year sentences, in these gloomy caverns. Each communal cell was about the size of a squash court and accommodated up to 39 inmates in narrow, three-tier bunks. Clothes hung from makeshift hooks on the walls or lay strewn in bundles on the floor. A narrow passageway along the foot of the bunks provided access to the beds, a recreation space. It was barely wide enough for two men to pace simultaneously.

The bunks were so close together that a prisoner could lean across and touch – or stab – his neighbour. Sex was a squalid fumbling in the dark, sometimes forced, sometimes not. Fights flared for little or no reason.

It was about noon one spring day in 1994 when Blank, going about his recreation club committee business, got his first glimpse of a communal cell. Peering through the opaque corridor window which was used by warders to keep watch over their charges, he could see that most of the inmates were lying listlessly on their beds. He felt the hopelessness contained in the cell.

From his vantage point, he could see at the far side of the cell another row of windows overlooking a bleak concrete quadrangle, enclosed by walls, empty and charmless. The communal cell was home for 20 hours out of every 24, the door kept firmly locked. There was nowhere to sit save the bunks, nothing to do but play cards, rape newcomers and smoke dagga.

Dagga! The air was heavy with the pungent odour of the weed, mingled with the scent of human sweat and smouldering anger. It seeped out into the corridors. No one seemed to notice or care. The authorities had long since given up trying to stop the smoking. Dagga peddling was a major activity in the prison. As fast as the stuff was taken out, it came in again. No matter, it kept the users stuporously inert most of the time.

Sometimes, in the brief hours allocated for exercise, the prisoners would play desultory football in the quadrangle, if they could locate a ball, if it wasn't punctured, if they could be bothered. But then it would be back to the 20 hours of unrelieved misery and boredom in a locked and squalid universe 20 paces long, seven paces wide.

Curiously enough, some of the inmates preferred the communal cells. At least there was company, a primitive sense of community. They had no higher expectations, so they had no disappointments. They were hardly human any more.

No wonder there are problems of discipline here, thought Blank. *How do you punish men who have so little to lose? And care so little? How do you rehabilitate them?*

The beginning of an idea began to germinate.

The eating hall at Krugersdorp prison was a dangerous place. That was where prisoners congregated and old frustrations gave way to rapid rages. A mug, a knife, a plate could make a formidable weapon. Even the steel tables, fiercely uprooted, would serve as battering rams when the mood was vicious. Sometimes the prisoners would come ready armed.

Until you've seen it, it's hard to imagine the damage that can be done with a metal padlock attached to a string or a sock. Faces explode. Blank saw it once. 'It happens so quickly that you don't even realise what's going on,' he says. 'They take this padlock and they swing it and – BOOM – it takes half your head off.'

He learnt to walk delicately round the pools of blood that were often to be found on the floor of the prison. He also learnt the wisdom of an old prison motto: 'Eat like a springbok drinking water.' It meant: look sideways, look behind you. Be ever alert. Especially at mealtimes.

It happened one morning about four months after his admission. It was just before breakfast and prisoners were standing in line in the corridor, waiting for the kitchen of the A-Section eating hall to open. Suddenly, too fast to see properly, three figures flashed past. Blank flinched, thinking they were coming for him. They began stabbing the man directly behind him in the queue. He knew the victim only as Kehla. Kehla was a bulky man, quiet spoken, a member of the Big Five gang, but not a leader. Somehow he always seemed to be in the centre of trouble when gang violence erupted. Someone had it in for him. He had the scars from earlier knife wounds to prove it.

Kehla screamed as the vicious little jabs penetrated his neck, his head, his stomach. Blood welled and spurted instantly, a fountain of bright red blood that rained down. It happened so quickly that Blank hardly saw the faces of the assailants before they fled. He would not recognise them if he came up against them in the days to come. It was a frightening feeling.

The nearest warder was still metres away when Kehla sank slowly to his knees, then toppled, still screaming. The blood pumped and pumped. Blank recalls: 'We shouted for some blankets and we dragged Kehla in the blanket-stretcher along the slippery floor to the hospital ward at the top of the corridor. By that time he was covered in blood. We thought he was dead. The medics did a wonderful job. They had their fingers in his neck, on his pulse, staunching the flow. They patched the stomach wounds and the head wounds as quickly as they could. We thought all the while: "My God, this man is going to die." But he didn't. The next day he was walking around with a big bandage on his head.'

Blank asked him if the wounds hurt. He said: 'Ja, it stings a bit.' Blank thought to himself: *Jesus, his blood went all over me. What if he has AIDS?*

Nobody else could, or would, identify the assailants either. But the warders staged an investigation and thought they knew who had done it. Final proof was unnecessary. They found the three prisoners they wanted and began to *bliksem* the three *bandiets*. The assault began with a sharp, urgent crack, the noise of an open hand smacking flat out against a skull. Repeated and repeated. 'When I first heard that sound,' Blank recalls, 'my blood ran cold.'

Then the batons began to thud. It was methodical and merciless. After they had finished, they told the victims: 'We are going to put you in solitary for a month. In chains.' The chains linked a prisoner's arms to his legs. They stayed on day and night, awake or asleep. The victims accepted their fate uncomplainingly. What else could they do?

Blank never got used to the sound of the beatings. Each time he heard it, it sent shivers down his spine. He determined that he would never do anything to earn such a beating for himself. And then he realised, suddenly, that there was no way he could guarantee that he would not be beaten. Retribution in jail was as capricious as it was swift. It could come from any source, warder or prisoner. It could be prompted by real or imagined suspicions and grievances. Merely keeping a low profile didn't guarantee immunity. He had never felt more vulnerable.

One day, when he had again witnessed the ritual of a cold shower forced on a victim after a beating, he stopped a warder.

'Why did you do that?' he asked.

'What?'

'The shower.'

'To make them clean,' the warder said.

'You mean, to wash the blood off?'

'No, man, to make them clean. They have had their punishment. Now they're clean again. They can start again.'

Blank came to understand that the warders were not all brutes. It was just that there seemed to be no other way to impose discipline. The prisoners were surly and intransigent. Some of them were hardened killers. Many thought of themselves as tough guys. It was a challenge of wills. The inmates expected nothing more. The warders responded in kind. It was the culture and the system. It was based on brutality because there was nothing to substitute for it.

The powers that be at correctional services headquarters might talk their fancy talk of rehabilitation and restoration. But what with? One social worker, one prison psychologist for every 2 000 prisoners?

Yes, it was true. On the ground, the law of the jungle prevailed. The fittest survived. 'Jail is about survival,' says Blank. 'You learn survival. How you survive is up to you. You can join a gang, or survive by smuggling, or isolate yourself. At the end of the day, only *you* can do it. No one's going to look after you. No one cares.'

Blank thought he could see a way to make the jungle less hostile. A way to survive – for himself, and for the other prison inmates too.

17

A Prisoner Comes Back

Krugersdorp prison is a scant 3 kilometres as the crow flies from Stephen Motingoa's office window. Were it not for the intervening buildings he would be able to see the charmless silhouette of the jail, squatting on the higher slopes of the terrain to the south of him. Motingoa will never forget that, in 1986, he was an unwilling occupant of a communal cell in Krugersdorp. The experience was short, just three months, but searing. It left him very angry.

Nine years later, in 1995, he returned to the jail as an honoured guest. His first instinct when he was invited was to say no. He had no wish to relive that dreadful experience. But he was persuaded that, occupying the position he did, it was fitting that he should go. After all, he was then mayor of Krugersdorp, representing all the people of Krugersdorp. The jail was in his domain. He had a civic duty to see for himself the changes that had taken place in the institution to which his city played host. So he went, reluctantly.

The reports were true. He had a basis for comparison because of his own experience, and he could see and feel that the transformation had indeed been remarkable. But he could not suppress a shiver as he crossed the threshold again. It brought the ugly old memories flooding back.

The memories came back again in November 1996 when I interviewed him in the mayoral office on the first floor in the north-west corner of Krugersdorp City Hall. There were no formalities as I entered the foyer. 'Just go up the blue-carpeted stairs, first door on your right,' said the security guard. Upstairs, the sign on the open door read 'Mayor's Secretary'. Inside, a stocky young black man was pacing about, saying something to the white secretary at her desk. He was dressed in blue-and-white sneakers, blue jeans and open-neck, grey-striped shirt.

'Mr Gibson,' said the secretary courteously, 'meet Mayor Motingoa.' The young man gave me a handshake and a disarming smile, promised to be only a moment and then vanished into his own office.

Motingoa was only 33 and just two days into his third term of office when I interviewed him. He was born on 26 May 1963 in Munsieville, a Krugersdorp township that was to become notorious for Third Force strikes against politically active residents. He left Khagiso Junior Secondary School after the death of his father. That was the end of his formal education. He became active in trade union affairs and this 'university' took him abroad for brief spells, fostering his political commitment, his management skills and his natural eloquence. He was placed in detention without trial under the state of emergency regulations on 12 June 1986, and was subsequently charged with subversion, sedition and assault. He was kept in prison cells for three years. After all that, the charges were dropped without explanation in 1990. He threw himself back into trade unionism and became branch chairman of the Transport and General Workers' Union. On 3 November 1994 he was first elected mayor of Krugersdorp.

Much as he hated the jail he once knew, he enjoyed the irony of his new position. Stephen Motingoa – symbolic landlord of Krugersdorp prison! 'I see you're wondering about this,' he said, waving a hand at his attire. 'I checked my diary this morning, and I've got no formal appointments. Not for a few hours anyway. I like to be comfortable when I work.' And what was he working at? Apart from being involved in the truckers' strike that was just beginning, his objective as mayor, he told me, was to broaden the culture of the institutions of Krugersdorp. He laughed cheerily at the suggestion that he might need more than three terms in office to change the culture of a city with conservative Afrikaner roots that run deep.

Then he said: 'You want me to talk about Krugersdorp prison?' and became sombre.

'Six days after the security police detained me,' said Stephen Motingoa, 'they took me and about 30 other detainees from the cells at Braamfontein police station to Krugersdorp prison. When we arrived, they handed us over to the warders who forced us all to undress, to be naked, in an open area. There was no reason for it. They seemed to want to humiliate us. It was very uncomfortable, especially for the elderly men among us.'

Krugersdorp prison, he discovered, was a haven for sadists. The 30 or so detainees picked up in the swoops that followed the 1986 declaration of a state of emergency were placed in one of the featureless communal cells deep in the heart of the prison. 'The one thing I liked, even then, was that the prison was clean.' What he didn't like was the consequences of even a speck of dirt. Their communal cell had to be kept spotless. The warders checked often and took malicious pleasure in enforcing rules of their own making. A fingertip rubbed along a window sill and coming up dusty would provide justification for denying food to all the detainees for the day. Protesting earned a beating.

At a time when the government was reassuring the world that detainees were being treated with kid-gloves, Krugersdorp warders were laying into their charges with boots, fists and flying batons. Some of the detainees were barely 16.

Motingoa was lucky. He knew when to stop being provocative. He endured only minor assaults and indignities, and the occasional short-term solitary confinement for offences like failing to make his bed. This punishment was meted out for trivial infringements, such as making a slight noise when the warders wanted their captives to make no noise at all. Offenders, usually after being beaten, were locked in a small, apparently windowless cell so dark that it was not possible to see the blanket on the bed, let alone the toilet a metre away. For the first 24 hours they received no food whatsoever – the warders also called the punishment 'three meals', meaning deprivation thereof – and after that, spare diet, silence and darkness for whatever confinement time the warders deemed appropriate.

Once Motingoa saw a detainee called from the communal cell and ordered to crouch in the corridor and keep silent. As the man crouched, a few loose coins fell from his trouser pocket and tinkled on the floor. The warders beat him until he fell, and then they trampled on him. 'When we asked why they assaulted the detainee, they told us to shut up. Each day we would say to one another: "Who's next?" If you dared to complain to a higher authority about an assault, the warders would come back the next day and beat someone up again. It was indiscriminate brutality. The warders were all white, and I don't think they liked political prisoners.'

One man, in particular, inspired fear. The inmates knew him only as Du Toit. It was his pleasure to beat people. He was not big, but mean-looking and well built, and he demanded – and received – submission because he was armed in the authority of a warder's uniform. Everyone knew that if they retaliated it would bring his fellow warders running, batons raised.

'It was vicious and needless,' said Motingoa. 'They seemed to assault the prisoners just for the hell of it. Sometimes they would invent reasons to give a beating. Speak English and you were in trouble. Talk at meal times and you were beaten – fists, batons, boots, everything. If you were hurt badly enough, they took you to the district surgeon, who didn't ask any questions. Some detainees took it so badly they wanted to kill themselves.

'Of course, we were a difficult lot, because we were detainees, and we demanded that we be treated as innocent men, not as convicted criminals. When they came to wake us up in the morning, we often demanded the right to sleep longer because we wanted to be treated differently. And, of course, the government claimed that detainees were treated differently, better. We read that in the newspapers we smuggled in. But we weren't being treated differently, not at Krugersdorp anyway.

'I must be honest. We were fighting back, but you can't fight back in a prison like that where you are absolutely helpless, and the warders will come and beat you like nobody's business.'

The detainees began to understand why, when the security police had interrogated them at the beginning, they would often say: 'You don't want to co-operate? Then we'll send you to Krugersdorp prison.' Krugersdorp prison was the ultimate threat. 'The warders had absolute power over us,' said Motingoa. 'We had the impression that there was a clear connection between the warders and the security police. The ordinary criminals in the jail used to say to us: "Yes, we're treated badly, but not as badly as you."'

When Motingoa was transferred to Diepkloof, the prison near Johannesburg known as Sun City, it was like going on holiday. To him, three years in a Sun City cell were infinitely preferable to his three months in Krugersdorp prison.

David H. was still young in calendar years, but his face had the look of a man who had known too many winters. He was not so much despairing as beyond caring. Life had taken his youth and squeezed the juices out of it.

He was back in jail for the third – or was it the fourth? – time. In a way, he was grateful for that. He didn't like it in here, but he didn't like it out there either. His family no longer came to see him, but he didn't mind that. They didn't have much in common; they had been apart too long.

He expected no visitors, asked no favours, sought no friends. When he thought about it, which was seldom, he didn't see himself so much a criminal as a victim. The warders knew him as a model prisoner. His fellow prisoners found him distant but not aloof. He did nothing to alienate or antagonise them. He did not require bullying nor make demands.

To some he seemed like a man who had come to terms with life. Actually, he had given up on it. It hadn't always been like that, however.

David H. had been what some would call a petty criminal. He was 15 when the Soweto uprising took place in 1976, and he joined in for fun. He came through unhurt. Afterwards he decided that he had had enough of school. Standard Five was surely education enough. His parents did nothing to dissuade him. They thought he was out of control. He spent his time on the streets of Soweto with other idle youngsters. Sometimes, for fun, they would steal little things: fruit from a barrow, chocolate from a spaza shop, clothes from a washing line. The boys didn't mind if anyone saw them stealing because...well, because it added to the fun and they knew the police would never come after them. The police had bigger things to do.

He found a girl and they made a baby and David H., a family man now, moved to Alexandra Township where a friend rented him a room. He decided to find some work, make some money. The factories and small industries in the neighbourhood could find plenty of applicants for their jobs and they turned down the young man with a Standard Five education. He became a caddie at Royal Johannesburg Golf Club. When he was lucky, he earned about R20 a round, but there were days when he earned nothing, and still had to pay R5 for the taxi fare to and from his home.

One day, when his baby was ill, he slipped into the changing rooms at the club and rifled some pockets. He got R37. It paid for the medicine.

He tried to find steadier work, but still nobody wanted a family man with only a Standard Five education. He sought a job as a gardener and got occasional piece work when unskilled labour was required. He stole money for food for his family from a casual employer, and got sent to jail for six months. He learnt no skills there, saw no social worker. When he came out his friends admired him for his rebelliousness – they thought he was defying apartheid – but his common-law wife berated him for being a poor provider. Nobody wanted to employ an ex-con with no references and a Standard Five education.

He stole a car and went to jail again. There he learnt some woodworking skills over two years. When he came out, nobody wanted to employ an ex-con with no references and a Standard Five education, even if he did have rudimentary woodworking skills.

He settled for crime and imprisonment as a way of life. At least it put a roof over his head and food in his belly. His common-law wife took his child and went away.

He touched rock-bottom in Krugersdorp prison. A psychologist saw him once, 18 months before, when he was admitted. His turn for counselling did not come round again. He built his closed world around a bunk in a communal cell and, because he was an old hand and still strong, his cell-mates learnt to respect his privacy and leave him alone.

There were no skills to be learnt in this jail, no hobbies to develop, no proper teaching to improve his Standard Five education. He cost the taxpayer R20 a day to keep and feed. He thought, in quiet desperation, that one of these days the jail authorities would kick him out again. It was not a pleasing prospect.

One day soon a man called Gregory Blank would help him to regain a little self-respect. Not enough, but something.

'See the guy by the door there?' Blank said suddenly one day as we talked in the visiting area. 'The one with the grey hair?' What looked like an old man had shuffled into the quadrangle in search of a patch of sun. 'He's blind. Almost blind. He can't see two inches in front of his face. He's an old guy, must be about 55.

'When he came here about six years ago they kicked his head so badly that he lost the sight in both eyes. They've been sending him away for eye operations – lens implants and so on – but the only way he recognises you is by your voice.'

'The world must be a frightening place,' I said, 'when you're in jail and feeling vulnerable, and you can't see.'

'In prison,' said Blank, 'there are some things it is better not to see.'

In truth, violence provided a break in the somnolent routine at Krugersdorp prison. If you were not involved, were at no risk, it offered sideshows for soul-killing days.

Many, perhaps most, prisoners were never beaten. Prison broke them in other ways. It taught them the virtue of being nonentities. To be a no one, attracting the attention of no one, was their highest goal. If they had chores, they did them quietly. They broke no rules. They made no fuss. They acquiesced in everything. The warders liked that, in an absent-minded kind of way. Placid prisoners made life easier. They could be safely ignored. They were mouths to feed and bodies to accommodate, and nothing more. They would rise through the ranks of privilege – earn their promotion from category to category, and ultimately their parole – by the simple means of effacing themselves.

Apart from the loss of freedom, the only real price prison exacted of them was that they should agree to destroy their own self-respect. It helps explain why so many released convicts return to crime. They have no higher expectations of themselves.

18

'The Miracle of Krugersdorp'

10 a.m., Monday, 5 February 1996. A visitors' day at Krugersdorp prison. It is more than 16 months since Greg Blank first set foot in this place with dread in his heart. From the outside, nothing much has changed. But inside? Ah, inside. This we shall have to see.

The sun beats down on the cars parked on the pavement outside the prison gates and on the hot tarmac parade ground that fronts the jail building. It's going to be a scorcher of a day. Some of the women visitors have taken pains to make themselves look fresh and attractive – colourful summer dresses, careful make-up, even a hat or two. Some have brought children, from babes in arms to teenagers.

They enter the jail building, walk past the free-form fishpond and the green potplants, turn right down the corridor with the eyeless doors. The green floors are, as ever, spotless and gleaming. At the end of the short corridor there is a door on their left. It is open. As the visitors walk toward it they hear a buzz of talk and the sound of soft music coming from within.

The open door gives access to a walled quadrangle a little smaller than a tennis court and open to the sky. Two warders sit at a table immediately inside the door. Each visitor must sign in. The reception is friendly and informal. For first-time visitors, the scene within the quadrangle is surprising, almost bizarre. It looks and sounds as if a garden party is taking place – a garden party in a jail.

A giant mural covers the entire eastern wall of this quadrangle. It depicts a seascape, waves breaking between two headlands, and the effect is almost three-dimensional. On the adjoining wall, another giant mural of mountains and streams. A psychedelic pattern decorates yet another section of once-ochre prison wall. A convict is painting the barred windows on the fourth side. He stops to ask Blank to admire his handiwork. Yes, the grim iron bars certainly look...well, not exactly welcoming, but certainly more attractive, less claustrophobic, after a coat of clean white paint.

White plastic garden tables and comfortable chairs dot the central green lawn and paved surrounds of the quadrangle. Above each table is a brightly coloured umbrella. The furniture and umbrellas have been donated by well-wishers. They give an almost festive air to the meeting place, make it possible

– almost – to forget that the walls of this quadrangle are topped by fierce-looking barbed wire.

Prisoners, black and white, talk animatedly to families and friends. They are dressed in the regulation olive-green trousers with a variety of sports shirts of their own choice: white, pink, red. Young children explore. There are one or two warders, but they are unobtrusive and unthreatening. There seems to be an unspoken rule that prisoners and their friends are accorded reasonable privacy where possible. The rudimentary prison shop – shelves, a counter, a fridge – in the south-west corner does a thriving business in cool drinks, chocolates, peanuts and pies. One wife has brought a home-cooked meal for her man, complete with crockery and cutlery. It looks like roast chicken and roast potatoes with gravy. She watches him proudly as he eats.

Sometimes, as couples meet and hold hands, there is a hint of tears, but mostly there is the cheerfulness of reunion.

In the north-west corner, the prison band has set up its instruments and is playing soft cocktail music. The leader of the group is a former Afrikaanse Weerstandsbeweging general, Allan van der Merwe, who tried to drive a truck into the World Trade Centre just before South Africa's first democratic general election. He is big and bearded and he plays guitar and sings a little like Kenny Rogers, so Kenny Rogers is what his band members call him.

Two members of his group are white, two black. They make sweet music together – so sweet that, for the first time ever, they were invited to play at the members' Christmas dance the previous December. That had never happened before: prisoners providing entertainment for the prison staff. It had been a great success. Soon the prison choir – 30 strong and growing – would be providing a different kind of musical pleasure for all.

It is said that the AWB general discovered in jail that blacks were people too, so he resigned from the AWB and now spends hours teaching and training would-be musicians, mostly black. The prison has a number of musical instruments donated by businessmen, and a steady procession of prisoners wanting to learn to play. Lessons are given by fellow convicts.

Not all prisoners are permitted to receive their guests in the garden-party quadrangle. This is reserved for only the most privileged group, those who have achieved A-category status. Less-privileged groups have to see their loved ones through the thick glass of the visitors' room at the other end of the prison, and hear them through the crackling two-way microphones. They cannot touch each other. Blank had received his first visitors in that room. It had left its mark on him. That's why one of his early objectives had been to try to make this 'so dehumanising' setting more cheerful, to brighten things with paint. Streaks of bright red, bright yellow – not much, but it helped a bit.

Those days have passed for him; he's A-category now, he's got privileges.

Greg Blank sits with Peter Reynolds and me at a table under an umbrella, and tells his story. His regulation trousers look neat, almost tailored. He is wearing a white short-sleeved sports shirt. His hair is shortish, from preference, not prison rules. He has just come from a session in the gym and looks the picture of health. He insists on buying cold drinks from the shop. 'Fanta or Coke? And what about a pie?'

He is joking about his last visit to the bank. Yes, they allowed him to visit his bank once to see to his affairs. With proper precautions, of course.

'I walked into the bank with my guard, in my prison chains. People hear these chains rattling but they just look the other way, you know. They're conditioned not to look because you must be a dangerous criminal. It's quite weird, actually.'

A warder approaches us as we speak in the quadrangle. 'Sorry to interrupt you, Greg, but could you just have a quick look at these?' He produces a schedule of some kind. Blank casts an eye over it.

'Very good, *Sersant*. You've done a good job.'

The warder smiles. 'Thanks, Greg.' And he turns to me: 'Sorry to interrupt you.' We get introduced and shake hands.

A little later a young prisoner – in jail for theft – brings Blank a sheet of paper on which he has laboriously written the names of 50-odd prisoners who have been selected for the prestige soccer squad. Some of the best of the players will be picked for the away games against other prisons and, if they're lucky, for the exhibition games against recognised NSL sides like Jomo Cosmos. Soccer is big in Krugersdorp prison. All in all, there are eight soccer clubs in the prison, each consisting of two teams. Competition is fierce.

'Right,' Blank tells the prisoner. 'Now go away and make a fixture list. You've got enough names for four teams of 13 each, including reserves. Work out when A will play B and C will play D and when we will have the finals and so on. Allow an hour for play each afternoon.'

The young man departs, glad to have a task to do.

Blank says he will try to organise a conducted tour of the prison for us. We are not allowed in without a member of correctional services as a guide. Blank approaches a warder on duty. 'Sergeant,' he says with careful courtesy. 'Do you think we could just show my friends the gym?'

The sergeant is unsure; he thinks that only the colonel can give permission, and the colonel is not here. Blank says: 'Okay, thanks,' and fishes a key from the key-ring he carries at his belt. He unlocks the door leading from the quadrangle into the prison proper and sets off in search of higher authority. Soon he returns with a lieutenant. After the barest hesitation, the lieutenant agrees to be our guide.

'*Dankie*, Lieutenant. I appreciate your giving us the time. This is my friend Peter Reynolds, and this is Rex Gibson. He's doing a book on me.' We shake hands. The four of us head off for the inner prison. The last thing we hear from the quadrangle is the prison quartet playing and singing 'Country road, take me home…'

The long corridor that leads into the belly of the jail, and which appeared to Blank when he first arrived to be descending into the very earth itself, has been transformed.

A prisoner is seated on a plastic chair just inside the barrier. He is putting the finishing touches to another mural, this time a Kruger Park scene. It is 20 metres long and 3 metres high. He is drawing and painting freehand, copying loosely from a magazine illustration on a stool next to him. The outline of a rhino in the bush gains substance as we watch. The prisoner-artist is introduced – he is a repeat offender serving a long term – and we shake hands. He is coyly proud of his work and seems almost to blush as we praise it.

Looking down the long corridor, the windowless walls look clean, bright and even cheerful. At the point where the corridor turns back on itself, there is a colourful mural depicting Table Mountain. It is as large as a cinema screen, and prisoners and staff believe it may be the biggest picture of Table Mountain ever painted.

It seems almost to beckon one to take that downhill walk. We go down the corridor, passing little knots of prisoners, an occasional warder. A ritual takes place. Blank and the lieutenant pause, Blank says: 'Hi Joe' or 'Hi George' and Joe or George says: 'Hi Greg, what's new?', Reynolds and I get introduced and shake hands and the lieutenant smiles. Blank enquires as to the progress of this project or that – new internal wiring, wall hooks for tools in the little workshop, painting of cell doors – and, after a few moments of chit-chat, we move on. He tells a technician-prisoner due for release three days hence: 'Make sure you've finished your work or we won't let you go.'

The technician is helping to rewire the prison's television network. The old wiring was simply laid across the roof, but the giant rats that infest the building quickly discovered it and gnawed it to shreds. The new wiring will be out of reach of the rats.

Television has transformed life for many in the jail. There are sets in every section, strategically placed in the corridors so that anyone who cares to can watch. Prisoners in single cells sometimes have their own sets, hired from the recreation club committee at R5 a night or R100 a month. We get no more than a perfunctory greeting from the corridor viewers. They are engrossed in the morning soapie. The prison subscribes to M-Net as well as the SABC, and shows one video movie a day.

A prisoner comes up to Blank in a state of agitation. 'What's happened to the gumboots?' he wants to know. The gumboot-dancing rehearsal is due to start soon. Blank had promised to organise gumboots and a place to rehearse. Why hadn't he done so? Blank sighs and says: 'All right. I'll see what I can do.'

We keep strolling. Every so often we come across a little bank of public telephones. There are always prisoners waiting to use them for they represent a lifeline to the world outside. Once the prison had only a few telephones for all its inmates; something like one phone to every hundred prisoners. Calls were forbidden unless a warder was present. Making a call involved a long, long wait. Now there are dozens of phones, strategically placed, and their use is unrestricted.

We pass the hairdressing salon. It's called 'Black Like Me', and the hairdressers were trained by staff members of the up-market chain after which this salon is named. Prisoners can have the latest in hair fashion if they are prepared to pay for it. Simple haircuts cost R5, while for up to R40 it is possible to have perms and even tints. The four chairs in the salon are all occupied.

Blank seems to know by name almost everyone we meet, and everyone seems to know him. With the prisoners, he is friendly and informal. With the warders he is friendly but scrupulously polite, almost deferential. There is a subtle and intriguing relationship here. It is clear that Blank, with his keen business brain and personal charm, is held in high regard by the prison officers, who defer to his judgment in some matters.

One of the arguments used in his trial against sending him to jail was that he would quickly establish an ascendancy over the average warder. Well, 'ascendancy' is perhaps too strong a word. He is careful not to overstep the boundaries. He takes no liberties. But, yes, there is something – an air of unconscious authority, perhaps – which seems to set him apart. He is very careful not to misuse it. Highly structured, authoritarian institutions do not take kindly to bumptious upstarts. Warders who have only their strutting authority to hide their vulnerability don't like the tables turned by their charges.

It is Blank's gift that he is able to walk this interpersonal tightrope successfully. For instance, the lieutenant is obviously in charge of our little party. He has the keys – and the status. But it is Blank who plots the course of our tour and gives the running commentary. 'What do you think, Lieutenant? Should we show them the communal cells?' 'What do you think, Lieutenant, should we go in here?'

Some sort of unspoken balance has been struck between the guard and the guarded. 'We're going to do this,' Blank says, spelling out details of another project on the drawing board. The 'we' embraces both prisoners and members; they are a team. It is evident that the lieutenant shares Blank's pride in what has been achieved. They exchange smiles as their two visitors marvel. The lieutenant says it's very important that prisoners are given back their dignity, their sense of self-worth.

A window overlooks the once-spartan courtyard with its single giant pole supporting a fierce light. Now there is a basketball court and a fully-equipped boxing ring. Baby Jake Matlala and Dingaan Thobela have visited for exhibition bouts, and boxing trainer Nick Durandt comes in twice a week to help with coaching. The prison championships are scheduled for the following month. There will be a big turnout of spectators.

Another prisoner, another problem. The boxing ring needs repair. It needs a new rubberised surface and something to glue the rubber to the base. 'We need a mine conveyer belt,' says Blank. 'Where am I supposed to get a fucking conveyer belt?' He rarely swears but sometimes the endless demands fray his nerves.

After a while, we come to the gymnasium, a sizeable room that was once a storeroom. A sign at the entrance proclaims 'Krugersdorp Health and Racquet Club'. State-of-the-art equipment nestles on richly coloured wall-to-wall carpeting. Full-size mirrors adorn the walls. A radio is playing, but its music is almost drowned by the straining and panting of the men pumping iron. They look in gleaming good health. They pause in their labours to say hullo to Blank and his visitors. On the wall is a roster setting out who may use the gym and when. The facility is much in demand. There are two other gyms, each equally equipped, in the prison.

We go to the room next door. It's about the same size as the gym, carpeted too. The sign says 'Krugersdorp Recreation Club'. The walls are splashed with cheerful cartoon-type drawings. Some inmates are playing pool at the quarter-sized table. There are a couple of card tables, some chairs, a few pinball machines, some magazines and games.

Not far away, the school is in session. Better-educated convicts are helping to improve the knowledge and the employment opportunities of about 300 fellow inmates who once rejected education, or perhaps were denied it. The voluntary students are concentrating too hard to notice our presence. The classes take place each weekday morning. Some of the pupils are discovering, for the first time in their lives, the joy of learning how to read and write.

For those higher up the learning ladder, there are ten education bursaries provided by the Midrand Campus.

Round the corner, two little 'factories' are bustling away. Men who had no appropriate skills only a few months ago are now making intricate lampshades and ornaments from carefully cut jigsaw segments of stained glass bound by lead. Their workmanship is painstaking, professional. Others are making belts, bags and assorted leather goods; and still others are making clothing at antiquated sewing machines. All seem touched by the interest of strangers. They display their goods with pride. Soon they will try to sell them to visitors in the garden-party quadrangle.

When they leave Krugersdorp they will take with them some skill that they did not have before; some slightly better chance of finding a job. It is not much, but it is a great deal better than nothing.

Down the next corridor, a prisoner is working at a personal computer. A warder and another prisoner are watching intently. The operator is clearly giving his two companions a computer lesson. 'All our recreation club records are computerised,' explains Blank. 'The money comes in, we know who's given it, where it's gone to. We run this prison like a business.'

Out in the fields adjoining the prison men are working on the hydroponic garden, which is the prison's latest project. It has been funded by the Liberty Life Foundation, with expertise provided by Dew Crisp Farms. One of these days, vegetables grown there will find their way to the prisoners' tables.

I get a sudden tingle as we make our way around Krugersdorp prison. There is something very odd about the atmosphere here, something is missing. It is hard to pinpoint. But then I identify it.

Where's the tension? The tension is missing! The four of us – Blank, the lieutenant, Reynolds and I – are alone in a building peopled by supposedly desperate men, and yet all our chance encounters are serene and good-natured. The lieutenant may be alert, but he is not jittery. He does not find it necessary to cast darting glances to rear and side. About 20 prisoners approach us determinedly; they have no warder, and they are talking loudly. They pass by without creating even a ripple of apprehension anywhere. The lieutenant looks on benignly as they go past. I am reminded, suddenly, of schooldays when one might encounter just such a group of amiable fellow pupils on their way from one classroom to another.

There is no tension! We do not feel threatened.

Can this really be the infamous Krugersdorp prison? And if so, what magical chemistry has transformed it? And could it really be like this all the time? Only the impossibly naïve or the hopelessly romantic could believe that all is sweetness and light in the prison. Jail is jail, after all. The environment is deliberately unnatural. When men are caged, frustrations inevitably build and flare. Not even choirboys could live together in the perfect harmony that we observed during this, our first few hours in the belly of the prison. And neither Blank nor the authorities would pretend otherwise. Violence still occurs.

And yet, and yet…there has been a sea-change at Krugersdorp prison. Something wonderful has happened.

Murders are a rarity now, gang violence unusual. 'The gang structures are still there,' Blank tells me. 'It's just that they are working with us to make this a better place. They are like armies; their discipline is superb. If they tell their members to stop fighting, they stop fighting. If you look at the various gangs, they really don't want confrontations. Now that there is something for the prisoners to do, there is no need for much of the violence.'

And then the clincher. 'What other prison has a gang general responsible for maintaining the peace? That's what General Ben does for us.'

Of course the tensions are still there. 'There's always a bit of hostility towards the Big Five, because they are pimps. Then there's hostility between the 28s and the Air Force, because the Air Force killed a 28 about three years ago in another jail and the custom demands that the vendetta go on and on. But we called in the heads of the 28s a little while ago and told them they were on notice: if anything happened they would be locked in chains in solitary. So we kind of pre-empted the situation.

'Air Force Three and Air Force Four are problems too. Their culture demands that members try to escape. When one gets away, it's another one's turn. It's very rigid. It makes life difficult. Besides, the black warders particularly are afraid of the gangs. Most of them live in the townships, and the gangs are just as strong outside prison as they are inside.'

Nevertheless, there is more peace. The notorious reaction unit is seldom if ever called out. Warders are able to walk alone in the very heart of the jail. The laughter in the corridors is no longer edged with menace and malice.

On 7 September 1995 Mr Justice E. L. Goldstein, a judge of the Supreme Court, visited the prison. He was so amazed at what he saw that the next day he wrote a letter to the head of prison, at that stage Major André Vosloo. This is what he said:

> As you know I visited your prison yesterday. I arrived in a dejected mood, weighed down too much, I am afraid, by a work load which I, at least, perceive to be too heavy. Here was an institution which, from visits to other prisons, I had come to contemplate with sadness and dread. But I left elated and exhilarated by what I saw.
>
> You, your staff and your prisoners (especially Greg Blank) have created through a variety of mechanisms which you know too well, an

> atmosphere of kindliness and caring which permeates your prison and which, I believe, holds the key to real and lasting rehabilitation of its inmates. In your prison I was privileged to witness one of the great victories of the human spirit, and privileged, too, to witness the essential goodness and gentleness of men who had lapsed severely but who, through your great and noble work now, probably for the first time in their lives, see light at the end of the tunnel.
>
> I have a dream for the prisons of South Africa: that one day we can replicate in them a thousand times over the miracle of Krugersdorp.

Judges are trained to be dispassionate observers, not given to flights of fancy. Yet here was a judge using the phrase 'the miracle of Krugersdorp'.

The senior medical officer of Her Majesty's Prison Service, England and Wales, came to see for himself and reported back.

> I have never been to a prison before where, surrounded by over 500 prisoners, I yet felt totally at ease. Not a single word of abuse, prisoners were busy doing their bit. There is an awful lot I have learnt from this prison... My own establishments can only do better with the ideologies and practices the commander and his staff maintain. This should be the benchmark of the South African prison system.

Something had indeed happened behind the brooding walls of an infamous institution. But what was it, and how did it happen, and what did a prisoner called Gregory Lex Blank have to do with it? That is what we must discover.

19

Where Dreams Die

Greg Blank did not set out to become a saint in jail. He set out to become a survivor. That meant he had to develop a philosophy for coping, and then a philosophy for achieving. Having a clear, logical mind helped him. All he had to do was marshal his thoughts, dissect his fears, come up with answers. Prison gave him the time for that. In any case, it wasn't as if he had to invent completely new ideas. The philosophic foundations were already there, built in the heady days of his stockbroking triumphs.

Don't anticipate problems, he reminded himself. *If you do you will never go forward in life. You'll become a recluse, go into a shell. That's why there are followers and there are leaders in the world. You've got the guys who take a chance. They're the guys who are going to do well.*

You get knocked down once, you get up. You get knocked down twice, you get up. You get knocked down for a third time and you start thinking: 'Well, what's it all about?' That's when you come to the crossroads. Either you disintegrate or you say: 'It's just another time, I'm going to keep on going forward.' I remember my favourite quote: 'What doesn't kill me makes me stronger.'

You have to understand: the more you've got to lose, the more you'll be knocked down and have to bounce back. If you've got nothing to lose, you get knocked down twice and you say to yourself: 'What the hell, I've got nothing. They treat me like nothing. I'll be nothing.' That's what makes hardened criminals.

Treat a man like a dog, he becomes a dog. The trick is not to become what they want you to become. You've got to keep your dignity and your pride. The thing that keeps a person like me going is knowing that I'm going to get out – one day. I've got a life waiting for me. Whatever they do to me, it's not going to destroy that spirit. Whatever happens, it's a step closer to getting out.

It's a day that's not going to come back. Life goes on, boy.

Nobody feels lonelier or more insignificant than a newcomer joining 2 500 criminal strangers for a prolonged time in a terrible place not of his own choosing. Once in, Blank's perspective was forced to change. He had to get his head together. The question was no longer: 'What am I doing here?' That was something to be filed away in a disused compartment of his mind. The only question was: 'How am I going to survive?'

He got some advice from an unexpected source. A prison officer, Lieutenant H. J. van Rooyen, decided to teach him some of the facts of prison life. One day soon after Blank entered jail, the lieutenant came to him and said: 'Hey, lend me R20.' Quick as a flash, Blank delved into his pocket and produced a note. The lieutenant declined to take it. For several days thereafter, the lieutenant asked for money and then refused to take it. Blank was puzzled, but then he twigged.

'He was trying to teach me a lesson,' Blank recalls. 'Every second person in jail comes up and says: "Hey, lend me R2" or something. The first month I was there, I gave something to everyone who asked. I had guys following me like I was the Pied Piper. I thought I was the most popular guy around. Lieutenant Van Rooyen was trying to show me that I couldn't buy my way through jail.'

The second lesson was by way of an early warning. Lieutenant Van Rooyen told him: 'Don't try and get privileges for yourself. You'll be a marked man. The other prisoners will get you.'

Blank took the warning seriously. By the time Felix Kramer, chairman of the recreation club committee, came to his cell at the end of his first week to seek his services, Blank had realised that if he wanted to help himself he had better make darned sure he was helping others too. There was a mixture of altruism and self-interest in the decision. Helping people would be good for him. But he had seen the rampant dejection in Krugersdorp prison, and he thought he knew what it stemmed from. And, yes, he would like to help his fellow inmates too. He felt sorry for them.

Fellow inmates? At first he gulped at the very thought. Fellow inmates, indeed. They were criminals. He was not; well, not really. He quickly recognised the danger in that line of thought. He was an offender against society, just like them. A judge had found him to be one. He'd better get used to it.

Later, the lieutenant taught him another object lesson. Blank was desperate to have access to a television set; he couldn't imagine life without one. 'I managed to wangle a set into my cell, I used to keep it under my bed. I had had the TV about three days when the lieutenant walked past one evening and saw the set through the peephole. He said: "What's this?" I said nervously: "It's a TV set." He said: "Listen, put it away. It's too soon. I'll tell you when you can have a TV set."

'So I put it away and went without TV for four months. It turned out to be for the best. People couldn't point fingers at me. If I had had something I shouldn't have had, everybody else would have wanted one too. It would have been chaotic, and I would have been in trouble. The lieutenant saved me from a lot of aggro.'

Piece by piece, Blank began to assemble his prison philosophy. First, he had to learn to slow down. 'There's one thing I had to accept, I had to slow myself down dramatically. I'm working at quarter pace here, and that's too fast. People wake up slowly, talk slowly, move so slowly. We don't do things today, we do them tomorrow, and if we don't do them tomorrow, we'll do them next week. It's a way of filling time. You spread out everything you've got to do.'

Next step: reconsider your values. 'You learn values so quickly here. I've come from a privileged background but you can't put on airs. I wake up in the morning and put on my prison-issue trousers and sports shirt, just like everyone else. I don't have to worry about what car I drive, where I'm going, who I'm talking to, who might see me. You're no big deal. You can stay in your bed and do nothing all day. You can scream and shout, and no one gives a damn. But it's better not to scream and shout because they'll lock you up in solitary and forget about you for a while.

'The trick here is survival. How you survive is up to you. Felix Kramer's visit in my first week showed me the way. I was going to survive by throwing myself into improving the prison. At the end of the day, you have to survive. No one's going to look after you. No one cares.

'You have to exist, and you have to learn to co-exist very quickly. Look at that AWB general who runs the band. He was extremely right wing. He thought all blacks were his enemy. But he had to come to terms with the fact that he is no better than a black prisoner in this place. Sure, some of the white warders might prefer him. But then he would still have to deal with black warders and black prisoners too. There's no escape from that.

'I've been lucky. Even in jail, I've been lucky. I'm able to help people and put something back into this place. I've always tried to help people if I can.'

There was another problem, the problem of longing – simple, old-fashioned longing. To be somewhere else, back in society. 'I want to get out of here, I don't want to spend an extra second I don't have to in this place,' Blank told me once. 'But time goes more quickly when I'm busy. I really enjoy helping to make this place better for all of us, but I don't have a hidden agenda and I'm not a hypocrite. I've told the people in charge I'm doing it because (a) it helps me, and (b) it helps everyone else.'

It wasn't always easy. There were many dark days when he thought he could take no more of prison life, its endless, futile routines, the stubbornness of bureaucracy, the ingratitude of prisoners who had forgotten how to be grateful, if they ever knew. There are very few Pollyannas in prison. He tried not to show his depression and, time and again, it lifted quite magically.

He discovered the Oliver Twists of jail, not innocent boys but cunning convicts. Old lags expect nothing, grasp everything. Never satisfied, they demand more and more. Either there is more, or there isn't. When there is more, they take it as a right. When there isn't, they accept the inevitable with morose bad grace.

Blank recalls a typical incident from his early days in prison. 'Gimme a cheque,' said a tattooed hulk who had shambled to his cell door while he was reading the newspaper. Blank didn't know the man, but he looked big and mean enough to command attention.

'A cheque?' asked Blank, thinking: *You don't need a cheque in jail.*

'Yes, a cheque.' The hulk pointed to the newspaper. 'That's a cheque.' So Blank gave him the paper.

'Gimme a tiger.'

'A tiger?'

'For a box.'

'A box?' asked Blank. 'I haven't got a box. I've just come here.'

'Naw, man. A tiger to buy a box of dagga. A tiger is ten rands.' The lag looked pityingly at Blank for his ignorance.

'No,' said Blank.

'Oh, all right,' said the tattooed hulk.

Blank discovered the ingratitude of those who had learnt to live with nothing. 'Expectation is a very dangerous thing to play with. When there was nothing, there was nothing to complain about. Nobody expected anything. Now, suddenly, you start adding to the quality of life and there are complaints every day. This TV doesn't work, that plug is broken, this is wrong, that is wrong, where's my soccer boots?'

He learnt to watch his words. 'If you say to a guy: "I think the soccer field will be ready on the 20th," and it's not ready, well, he goes mad. He says: "But you promised…" and I say: "I didn't promise, I said I think…" Last week I had a big argument about the grass on the soccer pitch. It wasn't growing fast enough. "What d'you expect me to do? Pray for rain?" I told them. If you say to a guy: "That's a nice shirt," then he thinks you want to take it from him. If you give him a can of deodorant, he says: "Why? Do I smell?"'

Sometimes he wanted to tell them all to go to hell, he'd had enough. But, mostly, he kept his tongue.

Blank found comfort in a remembered message from his rabbi, given to him two nights before his departure for jail. 'God never demands of you anything you can't handle.' He hoped that God had got a firm grip on how much Gregory Blank could handle. He remembered his reply to the rabbi at the time: 'Thank you very much, but do you think He could now pick on someone else?'

There were better moments. Not every prisoner was a malcontent. There were those who longed to be free and go straight, if only… If only they had a job, or a chance, or a skill, or a support system. They were mainly young, the first-termers. Life would knock the wishful thinking out of most of them before long. Blank sensed, however, that some of them retained an elusive quality, almost like a living thing, that gave them hope. Against all the odds, they had hung on to their self-respect, their dignity, in the cauldron of Krugersdorp.

He realised, quite suddenly, that he hadn't faced the full truth when he told the authorities that he wanted to help both himself and his fellow inmates. There was something deeper there. The full truth was that his own self-respect had taken a terrible beating. He could pretend all he liked, rationalise his crime, but the fact remained that he could not feel proud of himself for what he had done. He had sacrificed the regard of others, which was very important to him. But more than that, he had seen his own self-regard founder in the spotlight of notoriety, though he had resolved never to show it.

That's when he began to see the real power of self-respect. Making a contribution to the lives of his fellow prisoners could help to restore his own image of himself, allow him to stand proud again in his own eyes.

And if that was so, then surely it was so for everyone in the prison. Improving prison was not just about making prisoners more comfortable. It was about making them feel better about themselves. Self-respect, properly fostered, might work a little miracle. It could begin to erode the negativism that had grown with the neglect of human worth in this place where all dreams died in ashes. Blank thought it worth a try.

Idealism is fine, said a quiet voice. But is it practical? Eminently practical, considered Blank. The practical problem boiled down to one thing: boredom. Most of the prisoners had nothing to do, so the devil made mischief. But there was more to it than that.

They had nothing to lose either. If a man had no privileges to speak of and was locked in his cell for most of the day, how could you punish him for any misdemeanour? Lock him up for a few more hours a day? It meant nothing, a minor extension of a nothing existence. Take away his bed? He probably didn't have a bed at home anyway. Deny him food? It wasn't legal and, besides, there wasn't a lot of food at home. Beat him? Yes, but how often could you go on beating him?

On the other hand, prisoners with something to lose were much easier to discipline if the need arose. Imagine telling a prisoner that he could not watch the big game on Saturday. Or that he was barred from playing soccer. Or that he could not use the facilities of the gym, or the school, or the workshop. His life would shrink to nothing once again. He would not lightly take that risk.

Chances were that warders would find their lives became more pleasant. Brutality had merely bred more brutality. Now they would have a disciplinary weapon that was both fair and effective. It would surely mean that they could be more humane in their approach. Sadists might be disappointed, but Blank was pretty certain that the jail authorities would buy that idea. Why wouldn't they?

There was one problem he couldn't really deal with. It was out of his hands. He knew the cynics inside and outside jail would say: 'It's easy to be a prison reformer if you've got rich friends.' He would just have to live with that. But, from an outsider's perspective, it is possible to see that the criticism misses the whole point.

Certainly, he had rich friends. After initial reluctance – 'Why should we help the enemies of our own society?' – they did come up with donations in cash and kind. But they might as well have been throwing their donations into a cesspool for all the good it would have done if it were not for the X Factor – the will to change.

The problem with prison, you might say, is that it attracts the wrong types.

The convicts are criminals and some of them are brutes. Prison needs to be an ugly experience for them, that's its deterrent value. The prisons service – poorly paid, unglamorous – by and large attracts precisely the kind of person who approves of that concept. On top of that, no society anywhere in the world really wants to expend limited resources on making life better for its rogue elements. That's too much like pampering the predators who have preyed on it.

The result is a dreadful inertia. It is a rare individual, among inmates or administration, who actually contemplates reform and rehabilitation. And even for those that do, the budget constraints seem insurmountable. The entire prison structure is designed to reinforce the *status quo*. There is simply no money nor will to change. Without the resources of enough psychologists and social workers the process of redemption can barely begin. Without money, nothing much can be done to make a prison less bleak.

It is no accident that, until recently, conditions in South African prisons were kept secret – by law. The Prisons Act forbade newspapers to publish any unfavourable reports without taking 'reasonable steps' to establish their correctness. An obliging judge found, in the infamous Sixties trial of the *Rand Daily Mail* for revealing prison horrors, that a 'reasonable step' was to consult the prison authorities themselves. Result: for 30 years and more, virtually no reports of prison abuse were published because the authorities invariably denied the things they wished to conceal. Nobody believed that there was no abuse in prisons. Few cared much.

At the highest levels within the Department of Correctional Services are a few good men with a vision of prison as a place of rehabilitation. Down the line too, working in jails, there are officials with ideals. But simple discouragement, more often than not, casts its spell on them. It was Greg Blank's contribution that he found a way to tap the idealism – and the money. Without that, the little miracle at Krugersdorp prison could never have happened.

Even so, discouragement dogged his early efforts. Witness the case of the donated television sets.

Within a week of his being recruited to the recreation club committee, a bubbly Blank was able to report back that he had managed to wheedle seven television sets out of a former business contact and friend.

The club committee had been meeting, usually once a month, in the A-category visitors' courtyard. In the beginning it had consisted of a staff member, Blank's early mentor Lieutenant Van Rooyen, Felix Kramer, Blank and a third prisoner.

At Blank's instigation, the recreation club committee had been expanded. Representatives from each section, usually black and chosen democratically, were incorporated. Sometimes there were as many as 17 people at a meeting. They all brought complaints and problems from their different sections.

Blank insisted on a formal agenda and minutes, which were given to the commanding officer. The meetings were run by Kramer with business-like proficiency, thanks to Blank's prompting. Save for the clothing and setting, an observer might have been forgiven for thinking he was at a company board meeting.

There was an air of excitement when Blank reported that he had been able to achieve, in days, what the club committee had so far been unable to do. The sets would be delivered soon. It wasn't easy, he explained. The donors had taken some persuading. They didn't see why they should give presents to a bunch of jailbirds. Their initial attitude was simply: 'They committed a crime, let them pay for it.'

But Blank had lost none of his old eloquence. He had this dream that criminals could be rehabilitated, their lives made more bearable in the short term, more productive in the longer. It was the least society could do. Didn't people realise that most of the inmates had never had a fair chance of achieving economic independence in legitimate ways? That was surely a recipe for disaster.

In some instances in the early days, he could add a little bit of polite pressure. Didn't the donors remember their old mate Greg? Hadn't he done them many favours in the past? Wasn't it time now to reciprocate? His way with words on the telephone was, as ever, persuasive.

Within hours the grapevine carried the news about the donation of TV sets to the prisoners, distorting it along the way, of course. Expectations in the prison soared. Soon there would be more than the single set they had had to make do with, a battered old wreck of an instrument that was wheeled on a trolley from section to section and went on the blink more often than not.

The lucky ones among the 2 500 inmates – those who could jostle their way to a viewing spot at the right time on the right day – might get to watch a random television programme once every nine days or so.

Now there were going to be more sets, perhaps one for every section. It created almost feverish anticipation and inevitable exaggeration among the entertainment-starved wretches. Was it just seven sets? Perhaps they would get ten or a dozen. Maybe even 20. There was to be a network. A set in every cell. Entertainment. Sport. Movies. Something to see and do at last. But things don't work like that in prison.

The television sets were duly delivered to the prison office, where they were signed for and placed in temporary storage in the head of prison's office. Prisoners passing through saw them there, stacked behind the desk. In the prison, convicts were hard at work making the brackets to support the sets at strategic points in a corridor of each section. Others were drilling holes in the thick walls of the jail so that the necessary cabling could be installed. The activity, the prospect, made the inmates wild with anticipation.

How could they be expected to know there was a hiccup in the process?

One day Blank received an instruction to go to the major's office. An inspector from the Department of Correctional Services headquarters in Pretoria was there. The inspector had been asking questions of the major. Where was the paperwork to cover the sets? Who had ordered them? Who had paid for them? Where was the provision in the budget? Who had given permission? Had they followed regulations?

Now Major Attie Nortje, head of prison at the time, wanted to ask Blank the same questions.

'Bla-a-a-nk,' he said, drawing out the prisoner's name in his inimitable style, 'who gave you permission to bring these sets into the prison?'

'You did, Sir. Don't you remember?'

'No, I didn't.'

'But you must remember…'

'No, I don't.'

Suddenly Blank became aware that something had gone wrong. The major himself was under pressure from the headquarters inspector. There must have been some unwitting infringement of the due processes somewhere along the line. He knew that all donations over R1 000 had to be authorised by the provincial commissioner of correctional services; all donations above R5 000 by the national commissioner himself. Normally, big donations had to be addressed to the department, not individual prisons, and were parcelled out as headquarters saw fit. The way round that, they had discovered, was to make the donations to the recreation club committee and not the prison. Blank thought on his feet. He knew he had to get the major off the hook.

'I'm sorry, Major,' he said. 'It's my fault. I must have acted too quickly. It's my fault.'

The inspector seemed slightly mollified. He emphasised that proper procedure had to be followed. The major assured him it would be.

It took two and a half months to get permission to install the new TV sets in the jail. During that time, the men in the cells became frustrated and the rumours became fiercer. The prisoners had been misled. There were no extra television sets. The sets were defective. The head of the jail had banned them. The warders had stolen them. It was another raw deal for the damned. With hopes dashed, anger grew. It doesn't take a big straw to break a back in jail. The warders, sensing renewed hostility, grew more wary and angry too. Nobody seemed to realise the strain they endured when the mood among the convicts degenerated. Certainly, no one seemed to understand that tensions between staff and inmates fed on each other.

Then suddenly, one day the logjam broke. Permission came. By this time there were ten TV sets and cable and wiring valued altogether at R25 000. On top of that, there was an M-Net decoder and a year's contract. And a new video machine for the daily movie that was to be introduced.

There was a scramble to complete the wall brackets and lay the wiring. There was no money for outside technicians, and the warders, even if they had the skills, had no time to do the job. The prisoners would have to do it. This was an unexpected bonus for a handful of the inmates. They had something constructive to do at last. And they carried with them the fervent good wishes of the entire jail population.

Sturdy cables were led to carry power and pictures from a master set installed in Felix Kramer's cell. Carefully, the workers began to roll out the cable across the low roofs of the prison's satellite buildings. The big rats watched ravenously from their hiding places in the eaves as the prisoners laid out a feast of rubber and fabric for them. In time, it would lead to endless reception problems. But not for the moment.

Television had come to Krugersdorp prison in time for Christmas 1994, and it lightened the hearts of many who now had something to while away the long days. The mood in the jail relaxed perceptibly.

20

Christmas Behind Bars

December 1994 – Blank's first Christmas in jail. Warders were expecting the worst because the festive season in a prison is notoriously a time of seething misery and anger. Prisoners become more conscious of their plight, facing the pain of a family time spent alone and sometimes unremembered. It is the season for escapes. But this time, at Krugersdorp, things were destined to be different.

Looking back, Blank remembers the weeks leading up to Christmas as highly frustrating for the revitalised recreation club. He was new in the jail, and still impatient. 'It was like two steps forward and one step back,' he says. 'Except that sometimes it was the other way round: one step forward and two back.'

It was not that the old guard, under Prison Commander Brigadier C. P. le Roux and Head of Prison Major Attie Nortje, were opposed to reform in principle. They were not. Headquarters had urged them to do what they could to place an emphasis on rehabilitation and they were willing to try. Indeed, they encouraged the activities of the recreation club committee, fruitless as those activities mostly were before Blank came along. They tried to give what help they could, and they would leave their posts at this prison at the end of the year with a sense of progress.

But red tape and budgets had strangled their best efforts, as they had strangled prison reform throughout the country. Bureaucracy and budgets complicated everything, delayed change interminably. The truth was that the authorities were as much captives of the system as the prisoners. The inbuilt inertia had them in its grip. Everybody was discouraged before they even started.

Blank's memory fails him in one respect. The steps forward far outnumbered the steps back, even in those first few frustrating months. The club committee, in the month before Blank was co-opted, had managed to raise R100,83. Three months later it had raised a total of R250 000 in gifts and R38 000 in cash. The transformation of Krugersdorp prison had begun.

Old-time prisoners could hardly believe their eyes and ears. What on earth was happening? Apart from the television sets and a R3 000 sound system and speakers to boost the TV sound output, many other contributions flowed into the once-forbidding citadel before the festive season started.

They included eight full sets of soccer uniforms, valued at R11 200; 25 pairs of soccer boots; R30 000-worth of gym equipment; 54 rugby jerseys; 300 packs of playing cards and 250 draughts sets; ten garden tables and 60 chairs; a complete basketball set including poles and backboards; one complete boxing ring worth R30 000; 25 soccer balls and 25 basketballs; an R11 000 learning programme on M-Net; and a R15 000 computer with software and printer.

The computer was needed for the recreation club records. On it was composed the first issue of the club's activity report – a two-foolscap-page document that came out for the first time in December 1994. The document went to senior jail staff and the prisoner representatives. Oh yes, and a copy to the Department of Correctional Services headquarters. The powers that be needed to know what was happening.

Proudly, the first activity report spelt out what had been done:

> The Recreation Club under M. J. Kramer as Chairman, N. Shefer as Secretary and Treasurer, and G. L. Blank as Special Projects, has made gigantic inroads towards the general improvement and wellbeing of all the prisoners at Krugersdorp Correctional Institution. It must be stressed that the Recreation Club could not have even begun to function without the assistance of the members [of the Department of Correctional Services]. In this regard, credit is due to Lieutenant H. J. van Rooyen and A/O Brill.
>
> Since the positive inroads that have been made by the Recreation Club, the measures of violence recorded in the prison have abated drastically. The aim of all members of the Recreation Club committee being to ensure that the internal harmony of all prisoners is at an optimum level, therefore decreasing the need for violence, making it much easier for the members to discharge their duties.

There followed a full list of donations.

> All the procurements fall under the auspices of Special Projects, headed by G. L. Blank. Once again, it must be mentioned that none of this would have been possible if it were not for the guidance of the Chairman, M. J. Kramer, who has borne the brunt of most problems, and the co-operation of Lt. Van Rooyen, who recognised the need for a strong and successful Recreation Club.

Despite the arrival of television sets, tensions began to rise again in Krugersdorp jail as Christmas approached. The sound of carols made things worse, the merry jingles sounding almost like a taunt to the men behind bars. Other jails round the country were preparing for an increase in the level of agitation and violence. At Krugersdorp, the recreation club committee racked its brains to see what could be done to prevent this usual pattern, to make sure transformation didn't go into reverse. Then Greg Blank had an idea.

'Why don't we give the prisoners a special Christmas lunch?' he asked the members of the committee. 'We've got some money, I think I can get some food donated. Let's make it a special day. While we're about it, why not a New Year's Day lunch as well?' The idea found favour. The staff had tried in the past to do something special on Christmas Day, but never on the scale that Blank was contemplating. There had been no money for it, no drive to make it happen. But yes, Lieutenant Van Rooyen allowed, there was no reason why it shouldn't happen this year. And it just might improve the atmosphere in the prison at a difficult time. Blank got busy on the phone.

In the week before Christmas, trucks began to arrive with crates and packages: R10 000-worth of fruit and vegetables; R10 000-worth of canned fruit; 200 kilogrammes of rice, 100 kilogrammes of custard, 50 litres of cooking oil.

Carefully, the recreation club committee planned the menu. Christmas breakfast would feature unimaginable luxuries: white bread, white sugar, jam, fresh milk, fried eggs. All served on special plates and in special cups. And then there was Christmas lunch. That would be a feast. A roasted half-chicken for each prisoner, potato chips, rice, gravy, green salad. Followed by fresh fruit salad, hot custard, watermelon.

Spirits in the prison lifted on the day. If there was a hint of melancholy, that was understandable. Yet for those who had no choice but to make the best of things it was possible to forget their circumstances for a few hours. For the jailbirds, one thing really mattered: somebody had taken the trouble to remember them and try to make this day special. Somebody cared. It was more than most of them had learnt to expect, inside or outside of jail. There was good-natured banter and some laughter in the eating halls that day.

The second activity report from the committee was produced in the week between Christmas and New Year. It was able to claim: 'The feedback from all who received the meals was exceptionally positive and the Christmas period went off without incident, unlike the problems experienced in other prisons around the country. We are planning on producing a similar meal on New Year's Day.' By now the committee was beginning to enjoy the hospitality business. The newsletter added proudly: 'In early February 1995 the Recreation Club is planning to invite all their sponsors to visit the prison so that they can see exactly how the prison functions and where their donations have been utilised.'

Highlight of the New Year's Day lunch was a whole dressed ox, a donation worth R4 000. Blank and his committee colleagues stayed up all night in the kitchens, overseeing the cooking operation, ensuring that the cooks did not succumb to temptation themselves. Season of goodwill it might have been, but that didn't mean that someone might not be tempted to swipe a morsel or two of beef, or a slice of watermelon.

The new year of 1995 was born in a mood of buoyancy. It brought a changing of the guard: a new, more enlightened, commanding officer, Colonel Nico Lotter to replace Brigadier Le Roux, and a new head of prison, Lieutenant-Colonel C. J. 'Nollie' Nolte to replace Major Attie Nortje.

The newcomers were not only amenable to change, they were enthusiastic about it. They helped to make things happen. Working with Blank and the rest of the recreation club committee, they encouraged anything that might lift morale in the jail. It was clear to them that there was a double benefit: what helped the prisoners helped the warders too. The more contented the prison, the less strain there was for their own staff. Why, warders sometimes even smiled as they came into contact with their charges in the ordinary course of their duties. The improving goodwill gradually became infectious.

It was the beginning of an era of accelerated reform, with Lotter and Nolte authorising the charge and G. L. Blank of 'Special Projects' leading it.

One day in prison, Blank told me: 'Colonel Lotter is without doubt a man of compassion and understanding. He's the sort of man...well, the sort of man you don't expect to see in the prison service. He's got a degree, he and his wife are both in the service, he's pro-active and he keeps sticking his neck out to try and make conditions better. You know, he really is someone who cares. I sometimes wonder whether he would not have had a much higher rank if he'd been more like the others, not so radical. The old philosophy about prisoners was: "These guys deserve to be here, so why should we treat them with any kind of respect or dignity?"

'Anyway, he isn't like that. He's courteous with everyone, a little understated. Oh yes, he expects discipline, but to him it's a means to an end, not an end in itself. He would rather use intellectual persuasion to keep people in line. For him, the days of putting people under pressure and locking them up and beating them up are long gone.

'Now the head of prison, Lieutenant-Colonel Nolte, he's more of a disciplinarian. He'll discipline people to get them to co-operate. But at the end of the day, they both want the same thing. In some prisons, an inmate would never see the head of prison, let alone the commander, but both men have an open-door policy that means you can go and talk to them if you have a problem. And they both want to change things. I wonder whether they'll serve as an example for other prisons.'

For the inmates of Krugersdorp, the question was irrelevant. The big issue was that, in *their* prison, things were changing for the better.

Over the next 13 months or so, the recreation club committee raised about R600 000 in donations for prison improvements. Most of the donors were individuals, but companies contributed too. In just over a year, more than 200 contributions were received and more than 60 donors registered. Each contribution was meticulously recorded in the committee's records: date of receipt, type of donation, authorising officer. The biggest single cash donation was R10 000, the smallest R500. Most of the other contributions were in kind. Transformation now had its own momentum.

The third edition of the activity report came out in January/February 1995, about a month after the new regime had taken over. Once again it captured the spirit of revival within the prison.

> It has now been five months since the Recreation Club has been fully operational. Significant changes are to be noticed in the prison. Amongst those, we can highlight a reduction in the levels of violence, and a sense of co-operation between the prisoners and the staff. These two factors have enabled the prison to be run in an efficient manner and with less stress being levied upon the members.
>
> W/O Wagner has been appointed as the member responsible for the Recreation Club, and he reports directly to the Head of the Prison, Lt.-Col. Nolte. The latter, it should be pointed out, has taken a keen interest in promoting the activities of the Recreation Club.

The report went on to list developments: the gym had been completed and was open to all prisoners; staff members who wished to train after hours could do so for a monthly fee of R10; a fully integrated computer system was in operation and all records of the club were updated daily; two new table-tennis tables and some bats had been received, as well as equipment for basketball, running and other sports. No one actually made special mention of it, but the authorities had authorised the importation of a two-speed drill for use by the inmates. No need to hide hacksaw blades in cakes any more, joked some of the prisoners.

The future looked bright too. Four pinball machines were expected any day, and would augment the amenities of a proposed 'fun room' that was nearing completion. This room would offer a variety of indoor activities such as pool, table tennis, darts, board games and card games. Refuse bins were being placed throughout the prison to enhance cleanliness and order. The painting of murals 'creates an atmosphere conducive to the new-found spirit that is evident in the prison at present'.

The fourth report referred to the 'resounding success' of a champagne breakfast for sponsors and potential sponsors hosted by Colonel Lotter and Lieutenant-Colonel Nolte at the prison in March, and announced that total donations had reached R407 210. That was the last activity report to emerge from the prison. Distributing the document had had unexpected consequences. Each time it was received by headquarters in Pretoria, it created a flurry.

What on earth was going on at Krugersdorp? Had someone thrown away the rule book? An inspector armed with red tape was sent scurrying to this mysterious place where prisoners were supposed to be more cheerful and staff more amiable. At each visit, the inspector wanted an explanation for everything – and everything seemed inexplicable to him. The visits provided a regular reminder of the bad old days of bureaucratic obstructionism.

It seemed sensible not to encourage this kind of interest, so the activity report was quietly killed. Transformation went on.

The advent of the TV sets was a one-off affair, a symbolic event. Now there were more important things to do. Top of the priority list for the recreational club committee was to get a proper soccer league going. That would be close to the hearts of most of the inmates and would provide pleasure for players and spectators alike.

The old practice was to let inmates have an occasional game of soccer if they wanted. Often it was a pick-up game played in a stark, unequipped quadrangle with an old tennis ball and a few pieces of string to mark the goalposts. Because there was no organisation, no soccer boots, no special field, too few usable balls and too much energy required to put a formal game together, play was sporadic and chaotic. Most prisoners just couldn't be bothered.

'People think money can buy anything,' Blank mused one day. 'Perhaps it can. I've asked people outside to help and they have done so – because they want to, or because they think I can help them when I get out, or because they think I might open my mouth one day about their activities. It doesn't matter, the end result matters. Look at a soccer ball, it's nothing. But when the guys are playing with a battered, broken-down ball and they get a brand-new one, it's so important to them. They're so thankful.'

Getting footballs was one thing; creating a soccer league was a much bigger proposition. Proper organisation was vital. A special soccer committee was appointed and christened 'KIFA' – the Krugersdorp Inmates Football Association. It had autonomy in its own area, but reported to the recreation club committee, which tried to meet its needs. Quite quickly, KIFA created eight separate clubs with two teams apiece, and drew up a programme for a knock-out league. Then it struck a snag. It was all very well to have a fancy league, but where could they play? On an unequipped concrete yard with a giant lamppost in the middle? KIFA took its problem to the recreation committee, which was busy 'arranging for' – the euphemism for soliciting donations for – the equipment needed to get the league going. KIFA needed a proper football field. There was a suitable area outside the building but within the prison grounds which had been set aside for soccer, but there had been no money to develop it. The ground was rough and barren. It would need to be levelled and smoothed, and goalposts erected. Worse than that, it was unfenced. The prison authorities had no wish to provide the inmates with a golden opportunity to escape.

Felix Kramer offered to erect a fence and create a proper surface for the ground, if the committee were given the authority to acquire the materials needed. Agreed. And that's how it happened that Kramer and a few inmates voluntarily built a security fence for their own containment – surely a first in the annals of imprisonment.

The ground was levelled and top-dressed, and the Krugersdorp prison football league was ready to go. The difference in mood within the prison was striking. Suddenly there was a sense of sporting occasion, a spirit of competition. Vociferous supporters actually had a team they could cheer for. It encouraged involvement and healthy rivalry. On the day when the finals of the knockout tournament were played a large crowd gathered on the open ground around the football field. Only the fence that Kramer built was between them and freedom. It was sturdy but not impregnable. But no one tried to escape; no one dared.

'They knew,' said Blank, 'that the spectators and the players would have killed them for trying because an escape would have meant an end to the privilege of playing soccer in the open. Now that's what I call rehabilitation.'

Next on the list for development was basketball: five teams, regular matches arranged, equipment available. So said the laconic register kept by the recreation club committee. It disguised a renewed spirit of enthusiasm for activity, dispelling the apathy and lethargy that had been at the heart of much of the senseless violence that had once been endemic.

The opening of the first gym was an important occasion. The cells were alive with speculation about it. 'Did you know it's going to be carpeted, wall to wall?' 'There're going to be large mirrors on the wall.' 'The very latest in gym equipment.' It seemed almost too good to be true. Those who were in the section where the gym was located could watch the progress day by day. Those who were not were kept posted on the grapevine.

Soon opening day came and the rumours all proved true. The gym was indeed modern, smart and well appointed. It was the first of three to be established in the prison on the strength of public donations. For those into bodybuilding, and even for those who were just looking for a healthy body, it was a blessing. They could put their names down on a roster and, provided they hadn't infringed any prison regulations, their turn for exercise would come as surely as day followed night.

The number of infringements within the prison dropped. Gym and soccer and baseball, TV watching, learning crafts – these were privileges much to be desired; they gave meaning to life. Warders discovered to their amazement and delight that a threat to revoke privileges was far more effective than bludgeoning when it came to maintaining discipline. An astute observer might have noticed another thing about the prisoners in the gym or on the soccer field. It was not only their muscles that began to bulge. It was their own sense of self-worth.

The story of David H. – the recidivist who had never gone beyond Standard Five – began to haunt Greg Blank. There were so many like David H. in Krugersdorp prison. Unlike himself, they had never really had a chance. A few of them were totally illiterate and unskilled. Some could pick out a few words in a newspaper or book. Some would bring him their family letters and ask him to read them aloud.

In persuading donors to contribute, he had often pointed out that economic disadvantage was a potent factor in breeding criminals. Glib, fancy words, he acknowledged, trotted out to prick consciences. But did he really believe them? And if he did, could he do something about it? At first, it was difficult. Sporting activity had an instant appeal. It satisfied the animal in man. Improving one's knowledge, education and skill was not nearly so immediately alluring. The general feeling among the inmates was that learning was for the cowards who lacked the courage for crime.

And yet he sensed, beneath the bravado and resistance, a kind of yearning for improvement. It was seldom expressed, because many who had it did not have the words to articulate it. But it was there, all right. He found it in David H., who had not been able to find it in himself. He thought he identified it in others.

The stained glass workshop, the leather press operation and the sewing room were the outcome of his musings. So was the Black Like Me hairdressing salon. He would never have imagined that grown men, let alone hardened criminals, would happily seat themselves at sewing machines, making garments like so many women, or weave hair-raising spells on the heads of their fellows with scissors and comb. But his instinct was right.

Creativity was the lure, and the acquisition of skills that might, just might, be applied in life after jail. Visitors who were taken to the workshops during

1995 – that year of living splendidly at Krugersdorp – invariably noticed the air of purpose and pleasure they found there. Prisoners were working because they wanted to, not because they had been forced to. And, what's more, they glowed with pride when visitors admired their handiwork – an intricate leather belt; a casual bag of patchwork charm; a stained-glass lampshade of exquisite shades and tones. As the little mounds of handiwork goods grew, so did the pleasure – and the profit. There was a ready market for such goods, inside and outside the prison.

There was something very satisfying about that. It made the workers feel somehow better about themselves. Prouder.

Of all the projects introduced to Krugersdorp, the grandest by far was the hydroponic farming plant. It was the joint brainchild of Blank, the recreation club committee and the Liberty Life Foundation. The plant would cover 5 000 square metres in the prison grounds and would be administered by a specially created trust, the Prisoners' Education and Rehabilitation Trust. Here, in a single project, was an array of opportunities such as no Krugersdorp prisoner had ever experienced. This wasn't just a farm; it was a life experience. One day its produce would, perhaps, be available to supplement the diets of the prisoners. But long before then, the project would provide vocational training for the inmates; give them practical and theoretical training in business management; build self-esteem and a sense of accomplishment; provide extra income for some prisoners' dependants; and generate a cash pool from which released prisoners could borrow money to establish their own businesses in the world outside.

And yet the workshops and the salons and the gyms – and even the hydroponic farm – were not enough. There were still those like David H. who had a more immediate need. It was the need for basic education. Without education, there was nothing to keep them from crime in the future.

The Krugersdorp prison school was a puny thing, uncherished by staff or members, a token attempt by uninterested parties. Housed in disused rooms – perhaps once destined to be communal cells – in the heart of the jail, it lacked facilities, equipment, books and dedication. Its pupils were no less reluctant than its teachers. It had to be built into a sturdier creature because it offered a way of hope for many who had once sacrificed their own education – out of political zeal or plain ignorance, who knew? Today, thanks to the efforts of the recreation club committee, the warders and outside donors, it has been revitalised. Classes take place each weekday. The 300 pupils range from Standard Three upwards. All are there of their own choice. Teachers are drawn from the inmates themselves; they find satisfaction in helping others. The rudimentary equipment – and it is only rudimentary so far – has come from the Liberty Life Foundation and the limited funds of the committee.

The school has one particular course that is unique. Once a week, law students from the University of the Witwatersrand come to lecture the pupils on street law, a subject specifically created to help people whose only contact with the law has been unhappy and often painful. Street law is about teaching people their basic rights, the protection afforded by legislation, and how to use the law to help themselves.

David H. attends the Krugersdorp prison school, withdrawn as ever. He has a hope, which he hardly talks about, that it will help him to get a job the next time he is released. It is a very faint hope, but it is better than nothing. He thinks that Gregory Blank gave him that hope.

21

Gun Alert

It was during that heady time of early transformation, just before Christmas 1994. Blank had been in jail for only a few months when he saw the gun.

He had been sent to get some paint-brushes from a different part of the prison. He walked down a long corridor until he came to the door to E Section. As usual the door was locked. Prisoners were required to attract the attention of nearby warders if they wanted to enter or leave. There was no warder in sight. He lifted the cover of the peephole in the door and peered through to see if there was someone on the other side who would open up for him.

Then he froze. There was no warder but, framed in the peephole, he saw a cameo.

A prisoner was furtively handing what looked like a gun – Blank couldn't be absolutely certain – to another. It was wrapped in a semi-transparent packet. It was a glimpse, really, from a distance. He couldn't tell the make or calibre, but it might have been an automatic. He didn't see all that well without his glasses. The men were not in prison greens so he assumed they must be awaiting-trial prisoners. They didn't notice him.

The mere idea of a gun in the hands of a prisoner in a volatile environment sends shivers down the spine of old hands, staff and inmates alike. Guns are notoriously dangerous in prisons. Some old hands could remember the attempted breakout at Albany jail in East London the previous Christmas. Someone had had a gun in the awaiting-trial section. There had been a near-riot. Before the gun could be recovered, two warders were dead and about 20 people injured. A gun in jail spells unfamiliar danger, something out of the ordinary.

Whoever smuggled this gun in – if it is a gun – must have had a purpose, thought Blank. *Nobody keeps a gun in prison as a souvenir. Homemade knives and blackjacks – now those are commonplace. I've seen them myself. The users need proximity. But a gun can deal death from a distance, provoke riots. And the assailant might never be seen.*

Quickly, Blank considered his options. He could keep quiet, which would be sensible. Prisoners had their own way of dealing with snitches, and he had no wish to become a murder victim. Mind your own business – that was the survival law in this jungle. The gun was none of his business. Or was it? You could never guarantee a mood in prison. Although spirits had lifted with the arrival of the TV sets, the bad reaction to the delay in installing them provided a reminder of how febrile emotions could be. Besides, there were threats of strikes in the air, hints of gang quarrels about to break out. Rumours were circulating among inmates and staff that prisoners belonging to Apla, the military wing of the Pan-Africanist Congress party, were considering a mass breakout during the festive season. Apla had been a powerful if wayward force in the war against apartheid and its members were often mavericks, bent on wreaking their own kind of political vengeance on occasion. They were dangerous customers.

There could be pandemonium and disastrous consequences if shots were fired in such circumstances. It would be bad enough if prisoners were shot; imagine the reaction if a warder were killed. And the revelation of a firearm in the jail, however it was used, would undoubtedly usher in a new era of repressive control. The careful first steps towards reform would be halted. Things would go back to square one.

He really ought to tell someone, but he was fearful of the consequences. Had anyone observed him watching the little scene through the peephole? Did anyone know that he knew? He looked around cautiously. Everything looked normal enough, but then no one is ever completely alone in a prison.

He made up his mind quickly. Turning, he dashed back up the long sloping corridor to the front office. Major J. G. Visser was on duty.

'Major, Major, I think I've seen a gun.'

The major turned a cold eye on him. In prison, lots of people claim to see guns. They think it will earn them remission of sentence. The exchange turned into an interrogation.

'How did you see the gun?'

'Through a peephole in the door of Section E.'

'Are you sure you weren't inside?'

'No, no, I wasn't.'

'Didn't you give the gun to the prisoner?'

'How could I get a gun?'

'You prisoners can get anything. And you all lie.'

'I saw the gun. Through the peephole. At least, I think it was a gun.'

'You couldn't have seen it from that distance. You must have been there.'

'How could I have been there? I can't even get into that section! The door's locked.'

As time went by he discovered that prison officials disbelieve prisoners on principle. Major Visser explained it to him one day: 'I see prisoners every day and 99,9 per cent of them have hidden agendas and they all tell lies. If I had to believe everyone I spoke to I'd never get my job done. So what I do is I treat everyone the same. I don't believe them. I know that a small percentage are going to lose out, but that's the way it has to be.'

Eventually, grudgingly, Blank was half-believed about the gun. The reaction unit went into action. Thud, thud went the boots down the corridor. Cries of alarm. Shouts. Rough handling. Lounging prisoners bundled off their beds and into a huddle. It took about an hour and a half before the gun was located behind a cupboard in a basement. It turned out to be a Magnum 357. No one could figure out how it got in because all prisoners were searched before entry.

A few days later Blank was in the prison office on another errand. As usual, there were convicts around, doing chores.

'Hey, Blank,' said an officer, 'I believe you found a gun.'

His blood ran cold. 'I don't know what you're talking about.'

The officer's remark seemed to echo round the room like a loud cry. Who had heard? Some prisoner must have heard! For many nights after that he lay sleepless and anxious, wondering whether someone would be lurking in wait for him as he wandered the corridors of Krugersdorp jail. He kept glancing over his shoulder as he walked.

Later he was told that he might be in line for some remission of sentence for reporting the gun. By this time his fears about retribution had diminished and he was able to feel elation. 'At the time I reported the gun, I didn't even think of the remission,' he recalls. 'But when I heard that I might get it, I felt this...this joy...because then you've shown the guys your credentials, that you're willing to help. And maybe you'll get out of the place a little sooner.'

Four months later he was told that the regional commissioner of prisons had granted him a special remission of sentence of one year. The head of the prison had recommended two years. He had been awarded half of that. No matter, 12 months was 12 months, a whole year off his eight-year sentence. And that, with the six-month amnesty he and thousands of others had received in 1994, meant that the maximum he could be made to serve would be six and a half years. The six-month amnesty was credited to him in May 1994, long before he reported to Krugersdorp prison. As a sentenced offender awaiting the outcome of an appeal, he automatically qualified for it.

Curious, he thought. *They reduced my sentence even before I went to jail. And now, as if to make up for it, they've halved the remission recommended for me while I'm in jail. It really is a strange world, Master Jack.*

In prison, you don't try to make sense of things. You just live with them. He learnt one thing, at least, from the gun incident. The best thing to do about violence in prisons is to avert it. The committee enlisted the aid of General Ben, leader of the 26s gang. He was appointed mediator.

Blank told me one day: 'He goes around the prison looking for guys who might cause trouble. Only this morning, General Ben came to me and said the 28s gang was making weapons again. So we searched where he told us, and brought out two big knives.' This meant that that bit of potential violence had been snuffed out, but it didn't mean that there could be no more violence.

Days merged into one another. Blank tried to be patient – he knew he had to be patient – but the demands on his time and attention mounted rapidly. There were small highlights to break the sameness of the routine. In February 1995 – five months after entering prison – he was promoted to an A-category prisoner for his 'general conduct, contribution and commitment to the prison'. It gave him certain privileges, the best of them being contact visits in the courtyard with the tables and umbrellas. He no longer needed to talk to his family and Di Reynolds through thick glass.

In April of that year the government announced another general amnesty, which lopped a further six months off his sentence. With the previous amnesty and the special remission for finding the gun, this left only six years to go – on paper. But he knew that the correctional services practice was to release satisfactory prisoners after they had served a third of their time. Again and again he did the mental arithmetic. He had 72 months to go. One-third of his remaining sentence was 24 months. He had served seven months so he had 17 months to go. He could bear it.

In August he was made a monitor. He wore the special identity badge with his photograph. It entitled him, among other things, to leave the prison buildings and enter the prison grounds without escort. The recreation club committee had come up with the idea of a forger-proof badge after an inmate copied the previous, simple badge and walked out of jail one day. Now the committee had a laminating machine and a camera and made its own badges.

Once, wearing his monitor's badge, he was in the grounds listening to the prison choir – he loved to listen to the choir – when a pretty woman approached him and began to talk. Blank told her about the campaign to improve the prison conditions.

'What do you do here?' she asked, clearly taking him for a staff member.

'No, I'm a prisoner.'

'But you seem to be organising things.'

'No, really, I'm just a prisoner.'

Realisation dawned on the woman. 'You're not Greg Blank are you?'

'Well, yes, I am.'

'My boyfriend's here. He's in for armed robbery. He says you've done wonders for the prisoners. Things are so much better.'

'Oh, great,' said Greg Blank. He thought: *Things are better for me too.*

He had been in jail for only a short time but he had become the Mr Fixit of the prison, the miracle worker. He was on good terms with the prison officers. When he went to the prison commander's office, as he often did, he usually received a warm welcome. 'I walk in and the secretary is asking me to translate, and the typist is asking me to help, and another person is asking me to do something for him,' he recalls.

Prisoners sought his help for the strangest things. 'See that guy there, his name's Harry. He's here for housebreaking,' Blank said to me one day. 'He's an orphan who got adopted. He found out last month that he'd inherited R6,8 million, but to get his hands on the money he has to be married. Harry is not married and he's telling his sad story to everybody and – you see that other guy there? – he's a nice guy but a bad guy, and he organises for his girlfriend's sister to marry Harry in jail. But Harry's a simple kind of guy and he gets married in community of property. Now his new wife starts forging his signature on cheques and starts taking all the cash. He comes to me and says: "What can I do?" So I call my lawyer and ask him to help Harry. Get his marriage annulled or something; it's never been consummated.'

Blank's story ended abruptly. He didn't know the outcome. Harry came up for release quite soon afterwards, and disappeared. For all Blank knew, he had been able to save his inherited fortune. Or perhaps there never was a fortune anyway. Fantasy and fact form a potent mixture in prison. But there was no doubt in his mind that Harry believed himself rich – and ripped off.

Even outsiders sought the help of prisoner No. 94324143. One day he received a phone call from a man whom he 'didn't know from a bar of soap'. The man said to him: 'You're very elusive.' Blank thought that rich. Him elusive? In jail? 'I've tried five times to get hold of you,' said the man. 'I know who you are, I know your whole history. I've got two big schemes in the market and I want you to help me.'

Blank said: 'Do you know I'm in jail?'

The man said: 'Yes, I've got no problem with that.'

Blank thought it weird that someone should still be seeking his advice after all that had happened. He thought: *Here I am trying to act as normally as possible in an unimaginable situation. It's like I'm saying to myself, okay, you've only got one leg, it's a hindrance. But I'm still walking, trying to make the best of things. If you want to do something badly enough, you'll always find a way.*

Blank graduated to a single cell – most whites in the prison had cells to themselves – in a special section for A-category prisoners. He had achieved this privilege in six months instead of the usual year, but he was satisfied that he had had no special favours; he had earned it. Lieutenant Van Rooyen's early warning still stuck in his mind. He remained very conscious that he should not seek any extra privileges for himself.

The section had its own rough cold-water showers and a rude kind of kitchen. Although the interleading door was locked at night, as they were in all sections, the individual cell doors in his new section were not. The six occupants – three whites and three blacks – could wander round their little domain at will any time they wished. They pooled food and cooked dinner together in the kitchen. It made for a cosy atmosphere.

It's strange really how prison changes you and then changes you again, he thought. *In the beginning, I hated being locked up on my own at night. I felt trapped. And then, listening to the screams and the yells and the banging from dark places in the prison, I began to welcome lock-up. At least I felt safer. But now my cell door is left unlocked, and I love it. Not being locked in is very important to me now. I feel I am just that little bit more free, a little bit closer to normality. It's a step towards going home.*

Blank's cell, like the others, was tiny. Its small window overlooked the grim walls of another section. It measured 2,5 square metres, a step and a half from bed to wash-basin and seatless toilet bowl, three and a half steps from window to door. But he had tried to make it as homely as he could.

A small, cheap mirror hung on the wall. There were pale curtains edged with blue on the barred window, a blue duvet on the bed, a darker blue strip of carpet on the floor. The pale-lemon walls were splattered with colour photographs of sentimental value: family celebrations, racecourse triumphs, special occasions with friends. And Di Reynolds, of course. A special place, indeed places, for Di. He could see her face last thing at night. A single red rose was stuck to the wall alongside the curtain. It spoke of many things. His books stood on a plank attached to the wall that served as bookshelf and desk. His television set was on a wall bracket above the bed. A bedside table held tissues, a white, yellow and red coffee mug and a phial of what looked like vitamin pills.

'It's small, but it's become home to me,' Blank told me on our first voyage of exploration into the prison. 'One thing about jail, it makes you realise how unimportant some things are – big homes and the trappings of wealth. Look, a jail is not a holiday home. People don't come here to lounge on the beach. Losing your freedom to come and go is the worst punishment anyone can endure. But I don't sit and mope about being in jail. I just try to make the best of it.'

One day they came and took his tiny portion of semi-freedom away again. It nearly broke his heart.

It was eight months after he had been given the privilege of a single cell in this small, desirable section of Krugersdorp prison. A rare silence – or what passed for silence; the shouts and clangs were always there, sometimes more obtrusive, sometimes less – was suddenly disturbed by approaching footfalls. A posse of warders arrived. They had been told, said the leader, that someone was hiding liquor in the section. They would have to search. Of course, they found the liquor. Five of the inmates had a good idea who had hidden it there. It was the sixth man in their section, but no one said anything or betrayed anyone. This was not the sort of 'crime' that warranted disclosure to the authorities.

Retribution followed. 'We can't have anyone saying that Greg Blank and his friends are above the law,' said the major. 'You will be locked in your cells again at night.' The punishment was imposed on 19 November 1995. On that Sunday afternoon, and each afternoon thereafter, a warder came at four o'clock and locked each of the occupants into his solitary cell – first the barred gate, then the heavy steel door. It was as if a clock had been turned back, a prison sentence started again from scratch.

'When they locked me up on that first Sunday it was like my first night in jail. I couldn't go to gym or chat to my fellow prisoners in the section. I was left alone for 15 hours and more a day with my TV and my thoughts. I went back to doing push-ups and stomach exercises in the cell.'

But always there were the thoughts, the intrusive, morbid thoughts. He had forgotten how to deal with these solitary periods. Little niggling imaginings became mountains.

Why, he wondered, *is someone doing this to me? Is it a vendetta? Are they trying to get me?*

Unbidden, disturbing thoughts about his new, tentative relationship with Di popped into his mind. 'When I thought about Di, my thoughts became a nightmare. I was locked in prison, she was free. How long could I expect her to wait like that? What was she really doing with her endless free hours? Could I truly trust her? I hated the jealous feelings but I couldn't stop them.'

The punishment lasted only until 30 November, a scant 12 nights. It seemed like a lifetime. Then they left the cell doors open again at night and, for a while, that seemed almost as good as being released.

22

Grinding Them Down

You could see it happen. As the months went by, Greg Blank began to change in jail. Disillusion and cynicism began to do battle with what he felt was his real inner self – the perennial optimist, the kind and gentle guy, the Good Samaritan. It may have been his own impatient nature that began to change him. It may have been the seemingly endless and repetitive cycle of expectation and disappointment, dating from so long ago, from his arrest to his trial, to sentence and appeal and incarceration. It may have been the natural grinding process of imprisonment that wears away optimism as surely as it wears away hope. Or it may have had something to do with the meeting that took place between staff and inmate leaders in the A-category visitors' courtyard one day in October 1995. That certainly had a marked effect on him, as will become clear.

Whatever it was, something began to happen to Blank. He found it harder and harder to endure each day. It was not his style to complain, but he could feel the pressure building up inside himself. The fact that he needed to maintain a jaunty presence – the *bandiets* expected him to be jaunty – made it harder to cope with the pressure. Instead of the mild irritation that occasionally assailed him, he now found himself feeling, and suppressing, a kind of rage. Everyone expected so much of him, drained him of so much emotional energy.

But, being Blank, the work had to go on. He could not turn his back on the role he had created for himself. He felt trapped by his new persona – Greg Blank, the prisoner's friend. *From claustrophobia to schizophrenia,* he thought with wry humour. One day, talking to me in the warm visitors' courtyard, he said suddenly: 'I've become much harder than I used to be. That's not easy for me, because I'm a soft person. I like to help. But I'm sick of the same old stories: they need money because their brother hasn't got petrol money to visit them, or their brother has died for the third time, or their children need help again. They're psychopaths, they lie to your face, and when you go and ask them about it, they shrug their shoulders and walk away.'

But the next time I saw him he was talking enthusiastically about a project to paint doors inside the jail in bright and different colours. 'Coloured doors will help to cheer people up,' he explained.

He began to feel keenly the unreality of prison life. Everything seemed artificial about it – the new friends, the visits from old friends, the lifestyle, the happenings. 'You know,' he said one day about a year after he had entered jail, 'it gets quite heavy now when people come to see me. Not my family, but casual acquaintances. What can I talk to them about? I can't tell them what I did yesterday, or talk about the movie I went to last night. All you do is end up talking about the jail, and how you cut your soap up into little pieces to make it last longer, and how this guy is doing drugs and that one tried to kill himself. At first, it's interesting, exciting – a new way of life. But after a while it's just one's routine. That's all it is, nothing else. It's a world you can't expect people to understand.'

He earned two months' special remission for cutting down a man who had tried to hang himself in his cell. Blank had arrived just in time to save his life. Sometimes he wondered if he had done the man a favour.

'Each day I'm here seems longer, more drawn out. I'm tired of playing this game, of being someone that I'm not. You're always having to be subservient. The youngest warder here is a sergeant of about 20. I've got to treat him like a really important person. I'm so tired at the end of the day, you have no idea. From the moment I wake up in the morning the problems start. This guy says this is wrong, and that guy says that is broken...and they all expect me to do something about it. The more pressure you feel, the more the walls close in. Prisoners complain of the stress of being in jail. We try to defuse it, but the moment we stop doing things, no one will do it. The inertia comes back.'

Yes, but hadn't he built a lifestyle for himself in jail? Wasn't he finding satisfaction in helping his fellows? Hadn't he made new and unexpected friends? He pondered the questions. They seemed to depress him.

'Most friendships start from an early age, you know,' he said. 'The friends you make later in life are sort of mutually beneficial friends to a certain extent, and in jail the same applies. It's like the army. How many guys do you really see when you leave the army after your national service? Oh yes, you make all sorts of arrangements to meet, but you never do, because you're going back to your own infrastructure, your own friends. But you do make friends in jail, friendships born of necessity. It's one of the tools you use to get through. You have to try and find people you can rely on.

'Unfortunately, in jail, most of them have a hidden agenda. You know: "I'll do something for you, but then I might just call on you to do something for me." And then they'll come on Tuesday and say: "Remember what I did for you?" I've never been like that. I've always done something because I've wanted to do it. The scary part for me is that everyone says I'll come out of jail and I'll forget it. But I won't. It's like somebody's death. It's something I would like to forget but it's happened and I won't be able to pretend it hasn't. Some day I'll have to tell my children I was in jail.'

In his bleaker moments, the demands on Blank the miracle-worker seemed so excessive that he felt like King Canute, who had to prove to his followers that he wasn't all-powerful, that he couldn't turn back the tide. The system seemed so immutable. All Blank was doing was leaving footprints in the sand, to be washed away.

'There's no rehabilitation, no help, virtually no counselling. See that guy there? He's going home tomorrow. Except he hasn't got a home. He's 40, he's black and he's got nothing except the R150 I gave him. His mother and father live in Klerksdorp and they can't afford to keep him. He's been in for housebreaking. Second time. You can bet he's coming back. Now multiply him by thousands, tens of thousands. That's correctional services for you. It's nobody's fault. Just the system. But the department's title is a lie. In prison we all have to live this lie.'

In our many interviews, Blank had fixed ideas on what could be done, which was pretty much what he had been trying to do. He had codified it into a simple four-pronged plan. 'Step one: teach prisoners a trade. Step two: provide some level of practical education in jail. Step three: teach day-to-day living skills. Step four: find a man a job before you let him out.'

Of course, such a programme had to be incorporated into the system. It could not depend on the energy of a couple of transient prisoners. Nicro, the private organisation which concerns itself with the interests of former convicts and which had urged that Blank should not be jailed, was well meaning but underfunded, and seemed ineffectual. 'Perhaps, when it has completed its restructuring, things might improve,' Blank suggested, a wealth of weariness in his voice.

Sometimes he felt the tension between black and white prison staff, compounded by the political transformation of the country. 'The schism between them is incredible. You can understand it, of course. The blacks want recognition and elevation, and they want it now. The whites fear that their status, and even their jobs, are at risk. You'd be amazed at the level of stress among warders. They're always being put off by the doctors for stress-related illnesses. They need rehabilitation as much as any inmate.'

It was at about this time that Blank came to a conclusion that seemed to disturb him: a warder is every bit as much a prisoner as any inmate. When the gates close behind the prisoners, they close behind the members too. The system holds both parties captive.

'The warders are also locked in here,' he told me. 'They're locked in by pension funds and housing allowances and medical aid. They have no other job they can go to, no other training. Often, for the whites, it's a family thing.

Their parents and their parents' parents were in the prison service. And, of course, they're frightened of breaking out. Even if an opportunity occurs, they're scared to take the gap because most of them have families to support. They ask themselves: "What happens if I fail? I'll lose everything." But everything is nothing anyway, only they don't see it that way. They're scared of the prisoners, but some of them don't feel comfortable when they have to go outside the jail. The jail is their home. It's where the system saves them from feeling inadequate. The frightening thing is, they are different from the inmates in only one way. There's no parole and they don't have the option of escape.'

Blank was in the middle of a denunciation of warders' pay scales when a prison officer walked past and said: 'Hullo, Greg.'

Blank stopped him. 'Hullo, Lieutenant. Tell Rex what you earn.'

'I'm earning R2 700.'

'R2 700 – take-home pay,' echoed Blank, looking at me. 'He's a professional and he's got a degree and he's earning R2 700 a month. Some warders get R900 a month. Street cleaners get more than that!'

'It's my job,' said the officer. 'And, you know, we can take salary sacrifices for better pensions, and things like that.'

Blank addressed us both: 'These guys work! I mean they work seven days a week... Okay, every second weekend off. They work long hours. Their lives are in danger and their take-home pay's a disgrace. The lieutenant works 20 hours a day. Now you get another officer, he works half that much, he gets the same pay. There's no incentive. That's the sad part of it.'

The officer shuffled his feet, looking pleased and uncomfortable at the same time. 'You ask Greg, I could have got TV sets and cars and you-name-it from people who wanted to give it to me. Not paying me off, just to make it better for this prisoner or that prisoner. But I wouldn't take it. I try to help the prisoners as much as I can, but the problem is, people think you're on the take. It's the system.'

'Yes, it's the whole system,' said Blank. 'The system assumes the worst about everyone. Now, the lieutenant, he's a menacing-looking individual. He puts his hat right over his eyes, and he's big, and he comes across as very aggressive, but I keep telling him he's like a lamb. He doesn't like it but it's true, he helps a lot of people, he really goes out of his way to help.' The lieutenant decided it was time to go.

Blank, his faith in humankind restored, was reminded of another Krugersdorp success story. 'Remember I told you about the guy who led the reaction squad, Warrant Officer Wagner? The kung fu expert who used to enjoy beating up prisoners? He used to be one of the worst warders here in the Eighties. He used to beat up the detainees and even throw tear gas into the cells when there was trouble. Well, he's changed. He's a different man. He told me the other day: "I don't want trouble any more. I want to help these guys." He works with us now. He's a very nice guy.'

Racial conflict is not simply a warder problem. It seeps into the fabric of prison life. No longer are there white sections and black sections. Apartheid has gone, but tension remains. Silly quarrels blow up out of nowhere.

'There's this big fat Afrikaner, a real right-winger,' Blank recalls. 'I'd put him in charge of maintenance and given strict instructions that no one was allowed to tap into our TV cables anywhere in the prison because it destroyed our signal. Unbeknown to me, our recreation chairman had given permission to some black guys to tap the line. So Etienne – that's his name – goes to these black guys to stop them. Now the worst thing you can say to anyone in jail is "*jou ma se poes*" [politely translated: your mother's vagina]. It's the ultimate insult. So someone says "*jou ma se poes*" to Etienne, who's in there for rape, and he gets all over-sensitive and starts calling them *kaffirs* and they all start swearing at each other. And that's the sort of thing I have to defuse all the time.'

How did he do it? 'I like to get the guys together and I say to them: "Now listen, guys, what you're doing is absolutely bloody stupid. We've got to work together here, we're existing together. We're not the enemy here. They are – the members!" And so we defuse things before they ever come to the attention of the warders.

'Sometimes we can't avoid the authorities getting involved because someone is looking for trouble. If that happens, we just have the guy locked up straight away. Simple as that. We can't afford trouble. You can't stop 2 500 guys having an occasional altercation. But serious gang fights...we've got to stop them before they happen. We haven't had a serious gang fight here for more than a year.'

Blank often wondered how many contradictory emotions could be contained in one person. How could he go from elation to dejection so quickly? What did it mean when even praise began to pall?

The minister of correctional services, Sipo Mzimela, toured Krugersdorp prison one day, chatted to Blank and went away hugely impressed by what had been done. He told Blank he was determined that Krugersdorp should become a model for the country and even suggested that Blank might go from prison to prison to lead by example. *Thanks, but no thanks,* thought Blank. Heads of such prisons as Leeuwkop, Potchefstroom, Rustenberg, Klerksdorp, Westville and East London paid visits to discover how the miracle had been wrought. They all wanted reform, but when they were told that much depended on getting sponsors, they grew despairing. They weren't equipped to find sponsors. They had no rich contacts. The department was not going to be able to help. Prison reform seemed a hopeless dream.

Even if money could be found, there was another problem. Correctional services headquarters didn't like being shown up. Every time Krugersdorp was praised it was a mute indictment of other prisons under its control. If Krugersdorp could do it, why couldn't the others? It would have been severely embarrassing to have to say: 'Because there is only one Greg Blank.' The department didn't want to have to say that in public.

But the newspapers were saying it anyway. As early as March 1995 – only six months after his arrival in prison – the *Sunday Times* published a report under the headline 'Greg Blank: the former wonderboy who changed life on the inside'. It started: 'Things have been looking up at Krugersdorp prison since fraudster Greg Blank moved in.'

A few months later, on 6 August, under the headline 'The miracle of Krugersdorp prison', *The Sunday Independent* reported:

> A little over a year ago, Krugersdorp had the worst reputation for violence of any South African prison. Today it is a model of what a correctional institution can be. One startling phenomenon becomes immediately apparent: about 80 prisoners have been given a weekend off, and all of them returned on time. 'We have not had one prisoner absconding this year. We let them go home on a Friday and come back on Sunday at 3 p.m., and they have all returned,' said a prison officer.

The report gave fulsome praise to Blank, but drew a wider conclusion. 'Successful prison reform can take place without official budgetary increases but with close co-operation among warders, prisoners and the community outside. With modest additional funds and proper application, the prospects for meaningful rehabilitation of prisoners grows exponentially.'

If only it were that simple, thought Blank when he read the article. *But it isn't. The theory's fine, but in practice there are the constant obstacles of inertia and red tape and public uninterest. Many businesses don't really want to help. I've been fighting it for nearly a year now, and I'm tired. So tired.*

One day in October 1995 he saw a familiar face in the visitors' reception area, a face he could not place. The man was wearing a brigadier's uniform. He came up to Blank and said: 'Hullo, son. You don't remember me?' Blank racked his brains. Where had he seen him? The stock exchange? At some function or other?

'I'm Chris Olckers. I covered your trial when I was a reporter. Now I'm with the Department of Correctional Services.'

Blank thought: *From reporter to brigadier in one quick step. Now isn't that remarkable?*

Olckers, who handled press liaison for the department, told him that he knew the South African television channel NN-TV had been to the prison to film its advances the previous week. Now he had on his desk about 20 requests from media wanting to cover the Krugersdorp 'miracle', from newspapers, magazines, television stations, even *Time* magazine.

Blank had realised, months before, that constant exposure for himself would be counter-productive. That's why he had kept in the background when NN-TV came. He suspected that the authorities would resent him hogging too much limelight, as if he were taking all the credit. They didn't seem to realise how meticulous he had been in earlier interviews about stressing that reform could not have taken place without the full support and co-operation of the prison staff. Not for the first time – nor the last – he wondered what it was about himself that seemed to attract attention. Undue attention. He loved it, but he didn't go looking for it – it made life difficult for him. It never occurred to him that he had about him an aura that media people call 'newsworthiness'.

He made news because he was who he was; as simple as that. Visible, eloquent, a doer. Right now, however, he had a higher priority. He didn't want to do anything that might jeopardise an early release. He had to get out of this place!

Whatever the reason, Blank lost his cool the day Captain Van Rooyen – now promoted from lieutenant – called a meeting to lay down the law to gang leaders in the jail.

Trouble had been brewing for days. As so often, it had to do with sex. The centre of the dispute was a *vroutjie* (a male prisoner taken as a 'wife') whom one gang had commandeered. The other gang had different ideas and the upshot was a relatively minor clash in which two inmates received superficial stab wounds. But in prison you stamp hard on small incidents so they don't become big ones. Hence the meeting. On this day in October 1995, about 40 prisoners shuffled into the visitors' courtyard. They were apprehensive. It didn't help matters that they were lined up against the east wall, and the warders were lined up against the west. It made for a them-and-us confrontation. Captain Van Rooyen, a burly man, had drawn his cap down over his eyes. He looked particularly mean and threatening, though he was, in fact, a rather gentle man beneath the rough exterior. He was about to issue an ultimatum.

'Men,' he said, 'if you carry on behaving like this, there will be no privileges. Everything will be stopped. The TV, the football, the gym. Everything. Cell searches will be started. We'll make your lives a misery again.'

Among the prisoners was a weaselly man with a penchant for complaining. He had already written to an organisation called Sapohr (the South African Prisoners' Organisation for Human Rights) in which the dominant figure was an ex-prisoner called Golden Miles Bhudu. Its declared aim was to protect prisoners' rights. The burden of the complaint to Sapohr was that the recreation club committee hadn't been democratically elected, that its members received undue privileges, and that it was promoting apartheid and racism.

That complaint was to have echoes in the months to come. But right now the weasel was standing there, listening to the ultimatum, with almost a smirk on his face. And he was complaining again. Blank suddenly saw red.

None of these guys appreciate what we have done to improve their lives, he thought. *They have no gratitude. They take everything for granted. They don't care about the work we have put in. They are ready to put everything at risk for the sake of their own petty vendettas. We wired the whole of the A Section for radio and TV, and all the guys did was to pull the wires down and put in their own extensions and then come to us to complain that their reception was poor. We painted the doors of the prison to make the place look nicer, and they scratched all over them. Bugger them, then.*

He stood up angrily, aligning himself with Captain Van Rooyen and the other warders. He felt very emotional. 'Listen, guys. I'm very comfortable here. I don't need anything. I've made a life for myself. I've been doing what I have done for your sake, because I cared. But I don't need to do it any more.

'You see that guy there,' he said, pointing to the weasel. 'The money he's got in his pocket, I lent it to him. The shirt he's wearing, I gave it to him. The amplifier he asked for, I bought it for him. I even lent him my weights so that he could exercise in his cell because he didn't dare leave his section for fear of being stabbed. And here this man is turning against me. We do our utmost to help you and this is how you treat us.'

Blank sensed a shifting in the mood. The prisoners seemed to realise that he had been speaking from the heart, and that what he said was true. There was a muted murmur of anger from the assembled men. They began to turn towards the weasel, who was standing, uncomfortable now, in the middle of their ranks. The weasel felt the hostility. Silently, he slunk out of the courtyard, away from the wall of angry faces. He did not leave his cell for a long while. Peace returned to Krugersdorp prison.

On a certain day in that gloomy month of October, something happened to lift Greg Blank's spirits again. The depression went, his old energy returned. If no one noticed it, it was because Blank had made a lifelong habit of hiding his feelings. But inside himself, still carefully hidden, a buoyancy, an expectancy, began to grow.

His attorney, Stan Fanaroff, had come to him with a novel plan. Buried in the general directions of the Department of Correctional Services was provision for the commissioner to reward a prisoner for 'meritorious conduct'. This reward could be a remission of sentence amounting to somewhere between three months and two years. As far as Fanaroff knew, no one had ever used this provision to argue for an earlier release for an individual inmate. No one could dispute that Blank's conduct since his admission had been 'meritorious and exceptional in the extreme'.

Fanaroff said he would compile a document setting out why Blank deserved to be rewarded, and formally request the commissioner to exercise his authority in terms of the relevant provision. Blank had already had a six-month remission for meritorious conduct. Now Fanaroff would ask for a further two years and urge an immediate release on parole. It would be a first, and surely the commissioner would find it irresistible.

If it worked – no, when it worked – Blank would find himself back in his own bed within days.

Once again, he allowed his hopes to soar. He hadn't felt so optimistic since the days of the deal, since his watertight appeal against sentence, since… But he wouldn't allow himself to dwell on those high expectations and bitter letdowns. This time would be different. He was sure it would be different.

23

So Close to Liberty...

With great care, Stan Fanaroff set about compiling the document that would surely set his client free. By November 1995 it was ready to go to the commissioner of correctional services. All concerned agreed that it was a fine document, crisp and telling. The Correctional Services Act allowed for remissions of sentence for 'meritorious conduct'. If this particular provision had not been used quite like this before – to secure an immediate release for an individual – well, there had never been a prisoner quite like Gregory Lex Blank before. Nor a track record like his.

On 15 November, the commissioner received the petition – 33 foolscap pages and 12 appendixes, all designed to reinforce the message that Blank was deserving of exceptional consideration.

All the relevant details were there, the prisoner's background, his trial, his glittering career. Even some reference to the Old Mutual co-conspirators, some of whom had not only escaped the wrath of society but had gone on to greater things in the world of high finance and investment. But that was just scene-setting. The petition was really about Blank's extraordinary contribution to the reformation of Krugersdorp prison. There was a list of donors set up by Blank and their contributions; a catalogue of the recreational facilities introduced; copies of the short-lived activity reports detailing progress; enthusiastic newspaper cuttings; the letter from Justice Goldstein, who had written that memorable sentence: 'I have a dream for the prisons of South Africa: that one day we can replicate in them a thousand times over the miracle of Krugersdorp.'

Particularly gratifying was a letter from the International Committee of the Red Cross, whose prime function is to monitor the conditions under which people in detention without trial are held. The old South Africa had a dismal record on that front. And Krugersdorp prison was regarded by the Red Cross committee as among the worst offenders. The letter the committee's head of delegation sent to the prison authorities – including the commanding officer and the head of prison at Krugersdorp – on 18 May 1995 could not have been warmer.

> Compared to the last visit (24–27 May 1994), the delegates could observe an overall improvement in the conditions of detention, in particular:
>
> ▪ There was a radical change in atmosphere in the prison due to the recent arrival of a new Commanding Officer, Colonel N. Lotter, and a new Head of Prison, Lieutenant-Colonel C. J. Nolte. The latter spent several hours a day in the sections and was praised by both warders and prisoners. As a result, tensions between inmates and warders had decreased.
>
> ▪ Juveniles, who were visited last year by the delegates, admitted that their conditions had greatly improved.
>
> ▪ The access to medical care and the quality of medical care had also improved dramatically.
>
> ▪ The prison had opened up to the community and to outside organisations. With their support other initiatives to the benefit of prisoners could be implemented at almost no cost.
>
> All in all, the changes which occurred took the delegates by surprise. Krugersdorp has set an example for all prisons in South Africa plagued with humanitarian problems. It will therefore be remembered as a prison which has been able to change thanks to a totally new leadership and the remarkable initiatives taken by its new Head of Prison.

Not a word about the remarkable initiatives taken by its inmates and Gregory Blank, thought Blank. *But no matter. Senior prison officials know. The system is on my side this time. My captors actually want to see me go free. They think I deserve it. Just look at the letters they have written for my petition.*

In his cell, while awaiting the commissioner's response, Blank re-read these remarkable contributions. They reinforced his mounting optimism. A correctional services social worker, C. G. E. Krause, had written:

> This writer consulted investors who, without exception, confirmed that they regarded the prisoner as an exceptionally honourable man and that, notwithstanding the jail sentence he was serving, they still supported him...
>
> Prisoners who came into contact with him stopped their dagga smoking and became restored in self-esteem. Prisoner Blank had changed, once and for all, the prison community. He has been evaluated as a well-adjusted, balanced person. This writer is of the opinion that the prisoner is motivated by the ideal of goodwill to his neighbour. He is a humanitarian and although it was not necessary for him

> to do so much, still he went ahead in trying to spread his deeds to other jails.
>
> It is indeed the writer's professional opinion that the prisoner has achieved so much that his role has been played out. He is in truth not needed any more and other prisoners believe he is no longer important.
>
> A long-term continuation of prison punishment can lead to the deterioration of a prisoner's positive self-esteem. A prisoner must naturally not be rewarded with remission because he can establish negative circumstances, but it must be kept in mind that the purpose of punishment is not to destroy a person. The prisoner has suffered and lost a great deal in jail. He needs no further rehabilitation... It is true that the community expects that criminals should be punished, and that they should not be freed after a short time, but the community also takes into account that when a prisoner has used his sentence to better himself and others round him, then he becomes a suitable candidate for parole.

These sentiments were echoed in a letter by Lieutenant-Colonel C. J. 'Nollie' Nolte, the man who was part of the new-broom team that took over in January 1995 and quickly won the respect of the inmates. Now the compliment was being repaid. 'From my first meeting with Greg Blank, and during all our subsequent conversations, I was struck by his positive attitude and his acceptance of the punishment imposed on him.'

That the prison had been praised by international and national authorities, he continued, was 'to a great degree' thanks to the contribution by Blank. Despite his potential for great influence, Blank had kept a low profile. His manner with members and inmates was one of respect and courtesy. At no stage did he try to manipulate things to his own benefit. The result of this contribution was that gang violence had decreased markedly, assaults had been reduced by 70 per cent and prisoner complaints had declined. Co-operation between members and staff had markedly improved. 'Legions' of phone calls and letters from family and friends of prisoners had testified to the improved environment.

'During my time as head of prison,' he wrote, 'Greg Blank was a model prisoner who did everything in his power (and succeeded) to raise the living conditions of the prisoners and to restore their self-respect. I can recommend with full confidence that prisoner Blank receive the maximum reduction of sentence for his selfless contribution to making Krugersdorp the model prison of the RSA.'

If I don't qualify for parole, who does? thought Blank.

He re-read the next letter in the document. It was from Nolte's predecessor as head of prison, Major Attie Nortje. He reported that, soon after Blank's arrival, he had summoned a group of prisoners to his office to discuss prison conditions. Blank had remarked that there was very little for the prisoners to do to keep themselves constructively and creatively busy, and suggested that the recreation club committee be expanded. 'Blank got many donations and greatly changed the circumstances within the prison. The violence, which in a small way took place in the prison, was summarily reduced. The prisoners all respected Blank because of his unending efforts on their behalf. He meant a lot to them. The jail has become a more liveable institution.'

There was just one curious omission from the list of praise-singers; from the commander of Krugersdorp prison there was not a word. Nico Lotter – once Colonel, now plain Mr since the demilitarisation of the force – was the top man in the jail. An endorsement from him would carry immense weight. Everyone in the prison, Blank included, knew that Lotter had a high regard for the achievements his illustrious prisoner had made possible. Every time the commander made a tour of the cells he was confronted by some new evidence of progress. He knew that it could not have happened without Blank, just as Blank knew he could not have succeeded without the support of the commander. They were a team, Lotter and Blank, a damn good team. Yet when Stan Fanaroff had approached Lotter for a letter of support, the commander had said no.

Lotter had his reasons, ones that seemed good and simple to him. He tried to explain them to Fanaroff, who did not seem to understand. 'I told him: your petition is designed to persuade the prison authorities to release Blank before the proper time,' Lotter explained in his mild, friendly way. 'If I write a letter supporting that, I will be asking the department to break its own rules. That would not be helpful to Blank or me. People would ask questions. Why does Lotter want Blank released early? How did Blank persuade him? Is there some bribery somewhere? I told Fanaroff I would gladly recommend Greg's release when the proper moment came. But I would not do it before then.'

Lotter's caution proved prescient, but it did not do him any good. He was to be drawn into a bribery allegation in the months to come that would drag him into the mental wasteland of clinical depression.

In the meantime, Lotter notwithstanding, Fanaroff's document remained powerful. Seldom have custodians paid such tributes to a prisoner in their charge. It hardly seemed necessary for Fanaroff to say much more. But he did anyway, just in case the message had not been driven home that his client deserved an early release. 'Overwhelming evidence exists that the conduct of prisoner Blank since September 1994 has been meritorious and exceptional in the extreme,' he wrote to the commissioner. 'The general directions by the department provide for a reward for meritorious conduct generally for a period between three to 24 months. The head of the prison has already recognised the prisoner's conduct to an extent and granted him a six-month remission. It is respectfully submitted that in the circumstances outlined herein prisoner Blank should be suitably rewarded not only for his benefit but also as an incentive to other prisoners. Such action will give credence to the maxim that "justice must be seen to be done".'

Fortified by so eloquent a report and with his spirits uplifted, Blank threw himself back into his role of prisoner's friend. There were still many things to be done before he was let out. Let the work recommence. First, he worked on his mind. 'I used to say to myself: Gregory, instead of going out tonight, I'm going to stay in. It was a kind of mind game. It made me feel I had some day-to-day control over my destiny.' He received an unsolicited letter that enhanced his good humour. It said [I have suppressed the surnames]:

> Dear Greg,
>
> My name is Delene X, James Y's sister. I want to thank you for taking care of him in there and I also want to thank you for being kind and gentle to my parents. My own brothers do not give them love and affection like you do. You always hug my mother and have pleasant words to say to her when we come to visit James. It means a lot to them. I have a wish for you as a reward.
>
> I wish that you have six gifts in life, which are health, wealth, peace, wisdom, guidance and, last but not least, happiness. Once again thank you very much.

Then to more practical things. The 'chatterbox' project was looking good. Working with Telkom, the idea was to introduce even more payphones into the prison. The project would benefit prisoners and also help to boost the recreation club committee funds.

Christmas lunch 1995 was to be just as special as 1994: boerewors, viennas, rice, beans, peas, fresh tomatoes, custard, fruit. There was also going to be a Christmas stocking for everyone: a packet of biscuits, peanuts, toothpaste, toothbrush. 'When you think that only 300 or 400 of the 2 500 people in the prison usually get a festive-season visit, you realise how special it is for the others to have someone, anyone, remember them,' Blank explains.

The head of prison came up with a couple of 'treats' of his own. Some prisoners would be allowed home for a few days over the holiday period. (All returned.) Those who remained could have visitors every day for the four days over Christmas, and the visits would not be 'booked', meaning they would not be deducted from the total number of visits permitted.

A steady procession of dignitaries began to stream to the model prison of Krugersdorp. Cyril Ramaphosa, then chairman of the Constitutional Assembly and secretary-general of the African National Congress, reported: 'I've seen a few prisons but this is by far the best I have been to.' Spurred on by the reports he was getting, the national commissioner of correctional services, General H. J. Bruyn, visited Krugersdorp in January 1996 and wrote to the commander, Colonel Lotter, afterwards: 'I was impressed by what I saw. I would request you to convey my thanks to the recreation committee for their work, and also for the beautiful sketch that was given to me. In particular I would like my thanks conveyed to all the members at Krugersdorp for their good attitude and hard work. I am proud of you.'

Soon after that, Lieutenant-Colonel Nolte received an unexpected honour from the prisoners under his care when they heard that he was being transferred. Wanting to say thank you to him, members of the recreation club committee invited him and other officers to a braai. They gave him lamb on the spit. The party took place in the grounds of the training centre opposite the jail, but within the prison's perimeter fence. Before he departed, Nolte made a confession that was to imprint itself on Blank's memory. 'You know, Greg, I've been in the prison service for more than 30 years,' he said, 'and I never, ever thought I could sit down and have a braai with prisoners, and enjoy myself.'

The more Blank paged through the document setting out why he should get parole, the more convinced he became that the case it made was irresistible. He thought to himself: *This must surely do the trick.* He was wrong. The letter that came back from Commissioner Henk Bruyn in March 1996, four months after the application, was kind but firm:

> I have studied the documentation handed to me thoroughly. I have also taken cognisance of Mr Blank's meritorious conduct and the fact that special remission of sentence was awarded to him in this regard. As these decisions were already taken, it is not in my power to grant him additional special remission.
>
> According to the [Correctional Services] Act, Mr Blank is not eligible to be considered for parole before the end of June 1996. At that stage the Parole Board will consider his possible parole and they will make a recommendation to the Office of the Provincial Commis-

> sioner, Gauteng, where the final decision will be made. Mr Blank will be given ample opportunity to prepare his input to the Parole Board. You will appreciate that I cannot pre-empt a decision that cannot be legally taken now, nor can I interfere with the discretion of the Provincial Commissioner before he has had the opportunity to apply his mind.
>
> There is great appreciation for what has been done for recreation and to alleviate the living conditions at Krugersdorp Prison. I have understanding for the circumstances caused by Mr Blank's incarceration, but regret that I cannot be of more assistance at this stage. However, should the result of the June 1996 process not be acceptable, you are welcome to get in touch with me to discuss it.

That was it, then. The answer was no. After the anticipation, dejection. But at least the four months spent waiting for a reply meant four months less to wait for the end of June 1996 and the Parole Board hearing. Blank thought he could survive the remaining three months or so.

By chance, at about the same time he received a personal letter from Nico Lotter, whose title had been changed to commander, Krugersdorp area of command. It was not the kind of letter normally received by prisoners. It began: 'Dear Mr Blank' and went on to thank him for his efforts in obtaining bursaries for prisoners from Allenby In-Home Study. 'I want to take this opportunity to thank you for all your efforts to place Krugersdorp under the spotlight. This is just one of a thousand initiatives you have successfully pulled through.' The commander signed off: 'With kind regards.' The letter bucked Blank up a bit.

On 3 May 1996 Blank received acknowledgement for another 'first' he had initiated on behalf of the recreation club committee. The prisoners donated some of their hard-raised money to an outside charity called the National Council for Persons with Physical Disabilities in South Africa. Project leader Annelise Verster wrote to him:

> Dear Greg,
>
> What a wonderful surprise to receive R500 from insiders. Thank you for your donation and for thinking of other people being physically less fortunate than you and your mates. Disabled people might not be in jail, but their minds are entrapped in a body that has no bars. Your body might be behind bars, but your mind is a free spirit. Thank you for your generosity.

Cruel, vain hope was to flare for Greg Blank one more time. During May, his release papers were sent for formal approval to the provincial commissioner. Wanting to take no chances – the proposed release on parole of this rather unusual prisoner was, after all, a sensitive matter, requiring the utmost delicacy – the provincial commissioner sent them to the national commissioner, just so that he would be aware of what was happening. Finally, the release papers were returned to the Krugersdorp prison authorities, duly signed, in early June. The date of release was confirmed as 29 June 1996. A special note was attached to Blank's file. It said: 'Do not inform the prisoner [of his release date] until June 28.' The authorities didn't want to run the risk of the news leaking out too soon.

Or so they thought. They reckoned without the prison grapevine and the media interest. No sooner had the information been entered into the computer at Krugersdorp prison than several warders raced to tell Blank the news. The first one to get to him said: 'Hey, Greg, you're getting out on 29 June. Don't tell anyone I told you.' A short time later the Office of the Provincial Commissioner, Gauteng, informed Attorney Fanaroff that Prisoner 94324143's application for parole would be 'favourably considered'. Fanaroff told Blank, and warned him to keep it quiet.

Blank could hardly contain his excitement. He told no one – not even me during our penultimate interview in jail – about the pending release. He had this superstitious fear that if he broke confidence, something would prevent it happening. He wasn't going to take a gamble on that. But now at last, filled with suppressed excitement, giving no sign to anyone, he could allow himself to count the days to 29 June, even the hours.

What he was unable to count were the malignant fates that seemed to be ganging up on him again. Just when he thought that nothing else could go wrong, something did.

24

. . . Yet So Far

Secrets are made to be leaked. Just 22 days before Greg Blank's release on parole was to be formally confirmed, the confidentiality surrounding the move was broken by a daily newspaper. It was to fan a well-organised 'public outcry' and lead to the Department of Correctional Services revoking its own decision.

One morning early in June 1996 someone phoned Blank and said: 'Have you seen *Beeld* today?'

'No, why?'

'It's broken the news that you're to be released soon.'

'So? Big deal,' said Blank. 'It can't change things. Head office has assured me there'll be no problem. It's fine. Nothing can go wrong.'

Deep down, however, he was not so sure. Press publicity like that was the last thing he wanted. *Why me?* he thought. *Can't they leave me alone? I've paid Old Mutual back, I've paid the Reserve Bank, I've served my time. I'm getting released strictly in accordance with prison regulations. So why this fuss? I'm just another prisoner being released on parole. Why won't they forget me?*

He now knew the answer to his own questions, of course. The answer was simple. He made news. Everything he did seemed to make news. Isolated in jail, minding his own business, he still made headlines in all the newspapers. There was nothing he could do about it.

Perhaps nothing much would have come of the *Beeld* report if it were not for the subsequent intervention of his old adversary, Golden Miles Bhudu, the president of Sapohr. Bhudu was the man who had received the complaint about the 'undemocratic' recreation club committee – the complaint that had so angered Blank that he had turned on the weaselly complainant at that tense meeting in the visitors' courtyard the previous October.

On 7 June 1996, Bhudu issued a press statement denouncing the proposed move. It offered its own headline: 'Sapohr statement on the possible release of Greg Blank financial whiz kid.' It was a fiery piece of work, making up in emotion for what it lacked in grammar.

Blank and Bhudu had a history together that was to come out within days and would cast some light on Bhudu's possible motive. But when the press release was issued there was nothing to weigh against it. It stood on its own, its ringing tones making it quite clear that it was sounding the alarm ahead of a truly preposterous happening. Here, unaltered, are the opening paragraphs of the press release:

> The decision by the Department of Correctional Services (DCS) to release fraudster Greg Blank jailed for eight (8) years for fraud of R10 million is outrageous and totally unacceptable. This decision can only help fuel perceptions that the Criminal Justice and Correctional Services System views certain privileged and 'very rich' prisoners who through their fraudulent and criminal activities enrich themselves out of mere greed for money and wealth, better than those less privileged, who are in prison, because of crimes of poverty.
>
> Many inmates like i.e. Abdul Bhamjee and many, many others with less serious crimes are still detained for similar offences still languishing in jail without even a possible date of release. No wonder overcrowding has reached unacceptable propositions and inmates exposed to unconstitutional and inhuman living conditions.
>
> Sapohr don't believe that Blank's Parole conditions could be serve taken into cognisance over the fact even whilst in prison Blank continued operating a Multi-Million rands business, whilst most Black inmates are only allowed (12) telephone calls per annum for ten minutes each if they are lucky enough. The DCS must take full responsibility for the consequences of this release because prisoners and SAPOHR is not going to leave this one sleeping. We will use this opportunity to challenge the entire DCS release policy.

Bhudu demanded the intervention of the public protector to probe four things: the circumstances surrounding Blank's release; an allegation that he had made a R500 000 donation to prison officials; the special remission granted to him; and whether anyone had been charged after Blank had discovered the firearm in jail.

Here at last – or so thought some – was the authentic voice of the people, pulsing with indignation. 'Prisoners and SAPOHR is not going to leave this one sleeping.' Newspapers pounced on the suggestion that prisoners at Krugersdorp were ready to mutiny over the Blank affair.

The diehards who had bayed for Blank's blood at the trial now wanted to know why he was being released 'so early'. New voices joined the chorus. Since few had any working knowledge of the regulations governing parole, and all knew still less about the recreation club operation at Krugersdorp, their moral indignation far outweighed their store of information. It didn't serve to silence them.

Once again, Blank was woken up with disturbing news.

'Do you know what they're saying now?' said an early-bird warder.

'No, what?' said Blank sleepily.

'They're saying you bribed your way out of jail. They're saying you bought us a gym for R250 000, that you've bribed us with unlimited rugby tickets and given us gifts.'

'That's ludicrous,' said Blank. 'No one here, not even the commander, signed my release papers.'

'Ja, but the people outside don't know that.'

'What they don't know,' said Blank, 'is that you've got to qualify for parole. You've got to have a job and a fixed abode and good behaviour... I'm not worried. The commissioner has assured my lawyers that if there is no proof of these allegations, everything will go ahead as planned.'

From his office in Cape Town an African National Congress MP, Carl Niehaus, heard Bhudu's challenging cry, and a couple of whispers too. Since the voice of the people could not be ignored, he decided that Parliament was the place to put flesh on the vague allegations. Niehaus was chairman of the Parliamentary Portfolio Committee on Correctional Services and thought he had a duty to enter the fray. Allegations, he said, had been made that members of the Department of Correctional Services could have been unduly influenced by Blank. This could be because Blank had apparently secured free tickets to rugby matches at Ellis Park for senior prison staff, and arranged gym equipment worth about R250 000 for the staff recreation club. Prisoners had complained that Blank was allowed unlimited visits and free access to telephones, enabling him to run a business, buying and selling shares on a daily basis. Niehaus wanted to know why Blank was the only member of the recreation club committee granted special remission, and whether it was because of his role in raising R500 000 in donations to improve prison facilities.

It was clear that Niehaus thought Blank an unworthy beneficiary of prison benevolence: 'Time after time, the same question is asked: is this because this is a rich white man with money?' he told parliamentarians, adding: 'There must certainly be a snake in the grass if Advocate Jan Swanepoel, director of the Office for Serious Economic Offences, felt obliged to state that Blank's early release undermined the work of his already overworked office.' Niehaus demanded that the public protector, Selby Baqwa, and the correctional services minister, Sipo Mzimela, stage a full-scale investigation.

It was stirring stuff, made all the more stirring by the fact that Niehaus consulted no one but his own anonymous sources before speaking. Parliamentary privilege enabled him to air his suspicions without substantiating them. Blank couldn't believe what he was hearing. Was this the same

Niehaus who had visited the hydroponic farm at Krugersdorp prison not long before and apparently been so impressed? Inevitably, Niehaus's statements received prominent coverage in the press, as did those by Jan Swanepoel and others.

That's very odd, thought Blank. *Why is Swanepoel going on about my early release undermining his work? Doesn't he remember that the State didn't ask for a prison sentence for me? The State told the world that it didn't think jail was the right place for me. Now a State official is complaining that I should've spent more time in jail.*

Other papers weighed in with reports based on the Bhudu press statement and the Niehaus reaction. On 16 June, *The Star* recounted the claim that Blank had provided a R250 000 gymnasium to the Krugersdorp prison staff club – a clear implication that bribery might have been involved in the release decision. And the same day, *Business Day* quoted Niehaus as expressing concern at allegations that the prisoner had been running a stockbroking business from the prison. *The Citizen* featured prominently the call for a full-scale investigation by the public prosecutor.

In the midst of this turmoil, the Department of Correctional Services discovered that it had made a silly mistake, a technical error. Its decision to release Blank on parole at the end of June had not been taken strictly in accordance with the regulations.

On Tuesday, 18 June, Blank woke with an uneasy feeling. 'I wake up and I'm not feeling right,' he recalled later. 'I've just got a funny feeling in my stomach and I don't know what it is. I'm short with everyone, which is not like me, and I'm getting aggravated. Well, anyhow, I speak to the lawyers and they say: "Don't worry, things are going according to plan. You've got another eight, nine days to wait. Relax."

'Comes the afternoon and a woman lawyer says my advocate has been desperately trying to get hold of me, please will I phone him. I phone him and say: "André, how's it going?" and I can hear in his voice that there's something wrong. He goes all sombre, like someone's dying, and he says: "Your parole's been revoked." I promise you, it was like a knife going through my heart. Then I think he must be playing a joke and any minute now he'll say: "Ag, I'm only joking, it's all okay." But he didn't.'

On 19 June the department issued the following statement:

> The Commissioner of Correctional Services has declared Mr Blank's imminent release on parole null and void. Legal advice has pointed out that Mr Blank's case could technically only be considered as from and including 29 June and any decision taken before that date is thus administratively incorrect and in fact null and void.

> The Department wishes to emphasise that it will not and cannot impinge upon the rights of individuals as contained in the constitution and other legislation and therefore Mr Blank's case will be dealt with strictly according to law and the rules of natural justice which includes his right to privacy and a fair adjudication of his parole case.

The statement offered the reassurance that the 'serious allegations of criminal activities' made by Carl Niehaus in Parliament had already been referred to the police for investigation, and that the matter was also in the hands of the public protector. The department would co-operate fully with him.

The department's silly mistake amounted to this: in setting a date for the 'favourable consideration' of Blank's parole, the Gauteng provincial commissioner had fallen into precisely the trap that Commissioner Bruyn had warned against in March that year. He had jumped the gun on his own decision. Blank was not eligible even to be considered for parole before 29 June.

Johannesburg's main newspapers drew attention to the news with what Blank took to be almost gleeful posters on street corners. 'Blank Stays in Jail,' shouted the *Star* poster. 'Blank's Release Blocked,' said *Business Day*'s. 'Blank's Parole Null and Void,' declared *The Citizen*'s. The pro-prison brigade cheered.

In his cell, the man at the centre of all this publicity felt the bleakest of despair. The mask of good cheer that he wore perpetually was allowed to fall. It was his fourth desperate moment, and perhaps the hardest to bear. He had been so sure this time. He had even planned what he would do with his first day out: a nice breakfast with the family, a brisk sauna, a luxuriant bath. Everyone had assured him that nothing could go wrong. But now it had.

For 24 hours Blank was desolate. Twenty-four hours is a long time in prison. Twenty-one months is even longer. That was the amount of time he had already spent in jail. How much longer now? He stared empty-eyed at the walls around him and came as close as he had ever come to black depression. He found himself wondering whether his ill-wishers had indeed defeated him. After a long day and a longer night, he somehow shook off the mood and returned to philosophical acceptance. Whatever the length of his sentence, it could never be infinite. A day gone was a day closer to release. He could wait.

The mask was on again by the time the head of prison came to see him at six the next morning.

'Did you sleep okay?' he asked.

'I slept like a log,' said Blank.

'But are you feeling okay?'

'Sure,' said Blank. 'How do you want me to feel? I'm carrying on; I have to. I can't just sit down and have a nervous breakdown, you know. Sooner or later I'll be getting out of here.' But he couldn't shake off one thought that was going round and round in his head: *If the department can be forced to back down at this late stage, what other technicalities might crop up? Perhaps it will decide it's easier to keep me in jail than risk another outcry. I think I'm a scapegoat. They seem to think I'm a time-bomb waiting to blow up in their faces. Will this farce never end?*

I sat with Blank in the courtyard at Krugersdorp prison the day after the announcement retracting his release. He had regained his composure and, as we talked in the wintry sunshine, he tried to explain to me how he had felt the previous day.

'You've got to understand how the disappointments eat away at you. The first disappointment was before my trial, when they let Kenny Fouche and Stompie Coetzee off with admissions of guilt. I thought they'd have to do the same for me. They didn't.

'Then, before I went to court, I got told: "Don't worry, you can book for the health farm, we'll walk into court and we'll walk out of court. The deal's been done, you've paid the money back." And it was like this weight was lifted off my shoulders and I felt totally exhilarated because now, whatever they'd said about me, it was wiped out. Just when I was thinking how great that would be, the judge gave me eight years.' That was the second major jolt.

Then came the third false hope. 'When we got leave to appeal, my new advocates told me: "Don't worry, we've found the misdirections. The worst you could look at is corrective supervision." I told them quite defiantly: "I don't want corrective supervision, I want a fine, the same as everyone else." They came back from the Appeal Court and said things had gone fantastically. And then the Appeal Court turned down my petition. I felt shell-shocked.'

And then, when he felt least able to bear it, the fourth big shock had come: the cancellation of his parole. From where he sat, he couldn't know whether the Department of Correctional Services was being manipulated. He hoped it would stand firm on its commitment to deal with his case 'strictly according to law and the rules of natural justice', but he couldn't be sure. He couldn't be sure of anything. What did 'natural justice' mean exactly? He knew there were powerful lobbies that would resist his release.

'All of a sudden this weight comes back on your shoulders. It's like a woman who's been pregnant for nine months and she goes into labour and has the baby. And the baby is stillborn. It's something you can't explain...it's more than devastating.'

His brother, Vaughan, came with his family to see Blank on the Sunday after the big letdown. It was a surprise visit. He hadn't seen Vaughan and his family for six months because they had moved to Switzerland. They had expected him to be free, and the reunion to take place in the happier surrounds of the family home in Houghton. But all they got for their memory book was a meeting in the A-category courtyard of Krugersdorp prison. Blank felt desperately sorry for them. They had so wanted him to be out of jail.

Once again the thought came to him: his problem was that he was society's token villain, what newspapers had once called 'the fall guy'. He had to be punished, and punished again, because so many others had got away with things. All along, he had been made to pay the price not only for his own sins, but the sins of others too. The judge in his trial had said as much. If many others were as guilty as he, the judge had said, then all the more reason why Blank should get a harsh sentence so that others might be deterred.

'I'm a scapegoat,' he told me. 'If it had been anyone else, they would have been freed as planned. Nobody would have made a fuss if it was Joe Dhlamini getting out. But because it's me, everybody makes a fuss. For scapegoats, the established rules seem irrelevant.'

As our conversation in the prison yard continued, Blank reviewed his prospects. 'I'm told the commissioner's behind us. I think he feels for me. But what's he going to say?' He answered his own question. 'The only thing he can say is that he's having all the allegations against me investigated. What we've been trying to do is find out who the hell's investigating. We've phoned the police. No one knows. The police have phoned here. They want to know who's investigating. We'd welcome an investigation. We've got nothing to hide. We'd just say to them: "Here's our computer, here's our list of sponsors, check for yourselves." What scares me is, how can the press write these things without substantiation?'

A few days later, the prison commander, Nico Lotter, got a call from a policeman. He would like to start an investigation; when could he come? *What nonsense!* thought Blank. *Since when do policemen phone and ask for permission to investigate a crime? Are they taking this thing seriously or not?*

Somewhere, somehow, there was a hidden agenda, but he couldn't get a handle on it. At least he had one consolation. The media now knew the other side – his side. Almost in desperation, he and his lawyers had been driven to issue their own statement after the Bhudu press release and the subsequent allegations. Perhaps now he would get a fairer crack of the whip. They had followed up their media release with another document to the commissioner of correctional services.

The argument that Blank was being unduly favoured for release was easily dealt with in the statement issued by his attorneys. Blank's eight-year sentence had been reduced by 32 months through amnesties and special remissions. Finding the firearm had earned him 12 months; saving the life of a prisoner who attempted suicide, two months. That, said the statement, left a five and a half year sentence. [Actually, it didn't – it left five years and four months, but it didn't affect the argument.] Blank would have served 22 months by the end of June. That was one third of the outstanding sentence of 66 months. Prison regulations permitted parole after one-third of a sentence had been served. QED. Blank had got no special favours.

The fact that some people thought the regulations ridiculous was a different debate. Cape Attorney-General Frank Kahn thought them ridiculous. 'When a faceless bureaucrat slashes by half or even three-quarters a sentence handed down by a court, it makes a mockery of the judicial system,' he told the media.

Fair enough, thought Blank. *Attack the system then. But don't make out that I'm a special beneficiary of it.*

The innuendo that he had bought his way out of jail was more pernicious. The Blank press statement went to great lengths to point out that the inmate was an elected member of the recreation club committee and had not personally, directly or indirectly, donated anything to the Krugersdorp prison.

The presentation to the commissioner was more exhaustive, and was backed up by some documentary evidence. There was no dubious R500 000 donation to prison warders. Every donation made to Krugersdorp prison was approved in advance by a senior official and meticulously recorded in a sponsor register kept by the committee. Blank did not run a multi-million rand business from prison. An attached letter from stockbrokers Irish & Menell Rosenberg confirmed that his main accounts were wound down in September 1994 – the month he went to prison – and that the firm took over the management of the investments for the beneficiaries thereafter. (Blank told me later that the only 'business' he ran from Krugersdorp was to keep an eye on his own affairs. He kept in touch with the markets by reading the financial press.) Blank was not allowed free phone calls or exceptional telephone privileges. Thanks in part to his efforts, all prisoners had equal access to public phones in the jail. It was one of the things that had made prison life more bearable. Blank did not 'arrange for gymnasium equipment to be donated to the prison staff recreation club'. Records showed that the club bought its own equipment from a private individual.

The warders thought it all a huge joke. 'They'd come to me and say: "Where's my cheque? Where's my payoff?"' Blank recalled. 'Sometimes they'd say: "I read I got these rugby tickets. Where are they?" Head office has been here not once, not twice but ten times, checking up on us. Why must I stay in prison longer than I need to so they can do another investigation?

We're the only prison where the recreation club runs as a business. We've got records.'

If anyone had stopped to think about it, Blank told himself, *simple logic would have discounted bribery. I'd have got the Gump of the Year award if I'd tried to bribe the jailers at Krugersdorp when they're not the ones who take the decision. The province decides. And trying to bribe the Office of the Provincial Commissioner of Gauteng from a cell in Krugersdorp is not very practicable.*

As for special favours on remission, I'd have got the Gump Award plus Bar if I'd thought it a good investment to bribe people to give me 30 months less remission than the maximum permissible.

Still, he was puzzled by the way the media seemed to swallow the idea. They batted the idea of bribery around quite freely. It didn't seem to occur to them that bribery was a two-way crime: the recipient was as guilty as the bribe-giver. Accusing Blank of giving bribes was equivalent to accusing the entire Parole Board and the provincial commissioner of Gauteng of taking bribes.

Then there was the extraordinary suggestion that unrest had flared in the prison at the mere prospect of Blank being released. Who could have planted that one on Golden Miles Bhudu? An attached letter from the recreation club committee and dated 21 June gave the lie to it. It was individually signed by all but one of the 18 members of the committee, 11 of whom, including the chairman, were black. It read:

> This letter serves to confirm that the committee of the Golden Recreation Club [the new, fancier name for the old club] is fully in favour of the parole date given to Greg Blank and feels that he is fully deserving of the remissions granted him for the meritorious service he has given to Krugersdorp Prison which has improved the conditions for all the inmates.
>
> We are of the opinion that the allegations made against him are unfounded and that every effort should be made to ensure that his release is effected as per the commendations originally made. The fact that the parole system in prisons is not functioning efficiently should not cause him to carry the burden for other errors.
>
> The reported unrest in this prison is non-existent at this stage, and we do not anticipate that any action will be precipitated by his release on parole.

The truth was that someone seemed to be gunning for Greg Blank, and others thought it might be fun to climb on the bandwagon. It was time for

Blank's legal team to turn its attention to the author of the original allegations, Golden Miles Bhudu. What was he up to?

This is what they discovered. In September 1995 Bhudu, on behalf of his organisation, was invited to inspect the amenities at Krugersdorp prison. He was so impressed that he recorded his thoughts in the visitors' book: 'I would like to express my appreciation and compliments to the recreation committee for their efforts to improve the circumstances of prisoners and more particularly Sapohr members.' At some moment during that visit Bhudu pulled Blank aside. Two witnesses heard him ask Blank for R10 000 from the recreation club funds. He needed the money, he said, to avoid having the phones at his office cut off. Blank declined, saying the club's money belonged to the prisoners and had to be used to improve their lot.

'It is clear,' Blank's attorneys told the commissioner, 'that Mr Bhudu's allegations were untrue, unfounded, unreasonable, unfair and motivated by personal political gain and resentment against the refusal of Mr Blank to assist Mr Bhudu.'

So much for specific allegations. It was the smears and innuendos that really got to Blank and his legal team. It was time to deal with Mr Niehaus.

His comment that there must be 'a snake in the grass' if Advocate Jan Swanepoel felt compelled to say that the work of the Office for Serious Economic Offences was undermined by Blank's release sounded splendidly sinister. But what did it mean? What snake? What grass? On 12 June, Stan Fanaroff faxed a letter to Niehaus in the latter's capacity as chairperson of the Parliamentary Portfolio Committee on Correctional Services. It said, in part:

> It has come to our knowledge that your Portfolio Committee apparently intends to hear evidence regarding the particular circumstances relating to the granting of parole to our client. We are in possession of a body of evidence regarding each and every donation which has been made to the recreational committee of the Krugersdorp Prison; Mr Blank's meritorious conduct and the special remission of sentence which he has received.
>
> In the event that your committee intends to hear evidence, we have been instructed to record that we are authorised to represent Mr Blank at any such hearing, and to present evidence on his behalf. Please do not hesitate to direct any questions that you may have to us, and we trust that we will be of assistance in showing you total transparency and correct procedure. We would appreciate your earliest confirmation of the time and place at which the Portfolio Committee

> intends to consider the matter, so as to afford us sufficient time in which to prepare ourselves to attend such a hearing.

At the time of this book going to print, in March 1997, there had been no response to this letter.

On 1 July 1996, I had my last interview in jail with Greg Blank. We didn't know it, but he was 24 hours away from release. We talked of many things, such as the prison officers who had helped make reform possible. Apart from Nico Lotter and Nollie Nolte, there was André Vosloo, who had succeeded Nolte as head of prison. 'He saw what Nolte had done and he wanted to do even more. We couldn't keep up with him. He wanted more phones, extra visiting days, football games against other prisons. With him, everything's based on good behaviour. He's a very strict disciplinarian – if you behave, I'll look after you; if you don't, that's it! He's a big guy, very strong – they used to call him in if there was trouble in other prisons – but with a very kind heart.'

Then there was the assistant head of prison, Braam Wilken, 'a soft-spoken guy, easy to work with'. And Chris Jooste, 'a nice pro-active guy who wants things to happen'. And, of course, the black staff members like Dave Monge and Gabriel Lishu. 'The black warders saw what we were doing and they took an active part. They didn't see it as a threat to their jobs like a lot of the older whites; they saw it as something that made their jobs easier and better.

'You know,' mused Blank, 'you learn about the guys, their loves, their lives, and in a strange sort of way you become friends. It's almost like being a stockbroker – you become friendly with a person because you're doing deals for him, but do something wrong, and that's it. It's the same here. "You're my friend, I want to help you; do something wrong and then you know what happens." So you're always on your guard too.'

We talked of his fraying temper. 'In the last three weeks I could see my whole attitude changing. I decided I had better just remove myself, let other people take over, because I was starting to snap at people. I'm not like that.' We talked of little Sipho Ngwenya, who didn't know a thing about working out in a gym until Blank took him under his wing. Now they are training partners. And we talked about the interdependence that had grown up between members, inmates and sponsors. 'I couldn't have started what I was doing if the warders had not given me the latitude to do it. I couldn't get the latitude from the members without the sponsors and I wouldn't have got the good behaviour of the prisoners without the first two. So, you know, it's been a full-on team effort.'

We talked about the turning point in prison reform at Krugersdorp. Blank thought he could pinpoint the precise moment. It was when warders stopped saying: 'You're a prisoner. You can't tell me what to do,' and when they began to say: 'Wait a sec. Let me listen to you. Let's see if perhaps you can help.'

Blank told me he had stopped crossing days off on the calendar, something he had only started to do when he thought he knew his release date. 'It's like I've run a marathon and the tape is in sight and then someone tells me: "Sorry, Blank, the race is not 26 miles, it's 40 miles."'

25

When Despair Comes

Nobody said life was fair. By some quirk of fate, Greg Blank's chief captor – the enlightened commander of Krugersdorp prison – was destined to endure nearly as many tribulations and disappointments on the road to reform as his prisoner.

If the concept did not seem so ridiculous, one might almost say that Nico Lotter was born to the prison service. Or, at least, that some external power ensured that he stumbled into the job. He had just matriculated and had no idea of what he wanted to do when he found himself, on Christmas Eve in 1965, at a staff party on prison premises. Some time during the evening someone suggested that he become a warder and he said yes instantly. In more than three decades of service since then, he has never contemplated any other career and he has never lost his satisfaction in trying to help the wretches under his care. 'So many things happen in jail,' he says. 'It's a world of its own. Not one day is the same.'

In the beginning, and for much of his career, his concern for prisoners stamped him as a very odd fellow indeed. Being humane to prisoners was not part of the culture. Fellow warders who had been taught down the generations that prisons were jungles looked askance at this stocky man with the big hands and the soft heart who had an antipathy to the violence that was the norm. They would criticise him for his approach and he would say to them: 'I can't help it, it's my nature.' Not that Lotter was a softie; he could not have survived a day in the prison service if that were so. He was tough, morally, mentally and physically. He believed in firm discipline, but not aggression. He could not shake off the conviction that mutual violence was not the way to rehabilitate anyone. A deeply religious man, he hated needless cruelty and physical abuse. Salvation, he was sure, did not lie at the end of a boot or in the head of a baton. Prisoners were people too. He believed they would respond to a combination of firm rules and human warmth.

It was only when he took over as commander of Krugersdorp prison in January 1995 that he finally had an opportunity to test his beliefs fully. Krugersdorp, he knew, was a violent place. He discovered that the warders didn't actually want to change; they seemed to need the violence. Most of them had a simple philosophy that they enjoyed putting into practice: get the inmates before they get you, and don't be too fussy about the means. The prisoners reciprocated in kind. Gang wars were frequent, assaults commonplace, blood flowed freely on the spotless floors.

At first, most of the warders listened with surly incredulity as he tried to outline his new approach. 'Violence,' he told them, 'is not the way. You can be strict and still treat prisoners humanely.' The warders thought they knew better. Criminals were vicious. Warders had to be even more vicious, lest they lose a never-ending battle.

Lotter believes he can name the moment when warder attitudes began to change. It was in March 1995 – only three months after his arrival – when he decided that telephone calls made by prisoners would no longer be recorded in a book, as departmental rules required. 'It was silly,' Lotter recalls. 'We would have to allocate warders to monitoring duty whenever a prisoner made a phone call. The warders were white, and so most of them didn't even understand the language the black callers used.' He decided to 'take a chance' and ignore the regulations. Such a thing had never happened before. 'I think headquarters didn't intervene because the positive benefits of the change were quickly evident and they probably thought: "Ah well, let's treat it as an experiment, let's see how it goes."'

One 'positive benefit' was positively unexpected. As soon as the prisoners were free to make phone calls without surveillance, they took to reporting assaults by warders on inmates. They phoned their lawyers and their friends and the media. They even began to phone their own commander in his office high above their heads.

'You know, it's funny, but some people actually enjoy violence. They're not happy without it. After I stopped keeping records of phone calls, I had numerous calls from the cells complaining about assault,' says Lotter. 'On top of that, the media were getting reports and asking what the prison was going to do about it. The warders began to realise that they were no longer protected by the traditional secrecy of the prisons. If they beat up prisoners, the world was going to find out.'

As each new assault came to light, Lotter would summon the guilty warders to his office and dress them down personally in a firm but apparently mild way that was deceptive. No one was left in any doubt that he would stand no infringement of his new rules. Slowly the message was driven home: the commander was serious and the beating-up days were gone. Lotter had won his first victory.

Even then, he would not have been able to preside over true transformation if it were not for two things. The first was the political change in the country, which he believes created a climate conducive to other changes, such as in the age-old methods of treating convicted criminals. And the second was the support and assistance of 'a most extraordinary prisoner'.

'In all my years in the service,' he told me, 'I have only come across two inmates of such quality and strength. Two prisoners who actually wanted to change things and set about doing it themselves. One of them was Hennie van der Walt [the former deputy cabinet minister who was sent to jail for fraud in the Eighties] and the other was Greg Blank. Of the two, Blank was the more outstanding.

'People say that it was just because Greg had money and rich friends that he was able to help in the transformation of Krugersdorp, but that's not true. He had much more than that. He had organising ability and lots of drive and a personality that won over everyone he came across. He knew how to get things done. Most of all, he had a vision. He didn't do things just for himself. When I first arrived at Krugersdorp, he came to me and said: "The prisoners have nothing to do. That's why there's so much violence." I agreed with him and told him to go ahead and do something, but always to get my permission first. He suggested that we have a champagne breakfast at the prison and invite potential sponsors so they could see what we were trying to do. The media got involved, and they began to comment on the positive things that were happening at Krugersdorp. After that, you could see the prison change for the better almost every day.

'What I specially liked about Greg was that he didn't argue or take offence. If I said no to a proposal, then no it was. But he didn't give up. He'd come back with a slightly different proposal and say: "Well, if I can't do that, can I do this?" And I would have to consider it all over again.'

For the commander, the progress was the good news. The bad news, he says, was that some of the old guard at headquarters seemed to resent what was happening. Lotter felt himself being regularly harassed by inspectors looking avidly for fault. Because the inspectors refused to believe that a prison could voluntarily transform itself, they searched for hidden agendas and underhand malpractices. Lotter made no secret of the fact that he didn't mind circumventing red tape or ignoring certain regulations, if he thought he could improve conditions in his jail. He didn't mind being considered 'a bit of a rebel' because, he thought, the cause of a better prison was more important. But sometimes he wondered about his principled stubbornness – it brought him so many hassles with his own bosses. In his bleaker moments he asked himself: 'Is it worth it?'

More and more, he asked that question as his tormentors began to read deeper, more sinister, messages into his actions. What funny business was going on between captors and captives? What rule book could they throw at this upstart commander with his fancy new ideas? Why was he trying to show up his colleagues at other prisons? Worst of all, was Blank manipulating him, trying, perhaps, to bribe his way to a more comfortable life in jail?

'Greg was very supportive,' says Lotter. 'He saw how I was being harassed and he used to come to me and say: "Don't worry, we've got nothing to hide. They'll soon see that everything's above board."'

But some could not, or would not, see. Lotter found himself under suspicion when the bribery allegations against Blank were given a semblance of credence by people like Golden Miles Bhudu and Carl Niehaus. If Blank was giving benefits, who was getting them? Inspectors came to Lotter's office to inspect a souvenir on his wall. Within a plain frame, roughly 40 by 30 centimetres, stood a memento of the South African rugby triumph in the World Cup – small fabric badges of competing countries so arranged that the Springbok badge stood at the pinnacle of a pyramid under a headline that proclaimed: 'The road to the final'. It was the sort of souvenir that might be found in any rugby pub, valuable only for the sentiment it embodied.

Blank had somehow acquired it and, on behalf of the recreation club committee, had offered it to Lotter to brighten his surrounds. Lotter had protested: 'But you know, Greg, I'm not allowed to accept any gift from the prisoners. Thank you, but I can't take it.'

'It's not for you, Colonel,' Blank had said. 'It's for the commander's office. To be left there when a new commander comes. It's for the prison itself.'

Lotter looked at the landscape painting on the east wall of his office. It too had been a gift – offered by a grateful artist who had sold pictures to warders. The previous commander had left it there when he departed. That commander had also known that he could not accept a gift in his personal capacity, nor take it away with him when he went. If such a distinction was acceptable then, it was surely acceptable now. So he found space for the memento alongside the framed certificates, commendations and prison memorabilia that adorned his western wall.

Then the cold-eyed police came in August 1996 and told Lotter they were investigating a charge of bribery against him arising from the gift. Lotter was devastated. Thirty-one years of honourable service, a transformed prison, and now this! 'What was I being bribed to do?' he asked himself in anguish. 'I wouldn't even write a letter to support Blank's petition for early release because I thought it would be improper to do so. I had nothing to do with releasing him. That was the general's decision. If I felt I had anything to hide, I could have taken the souvenir to my home and no one would ever have known.'

For the first time in his life, he fell into deep despair. He read up the symptoms of clinical depression and discovered that he had all of them. He didn't go to a doctor or psychiatrist, but turned to his faith. One day, he recounts, he had a conversation with God. He can recall the words precisely.

God said: 'Are you guilty?'

Lotter replied: 'No.'

And God said: 'So why worry?'

Almost instantly, the depression lifted. Lotter was able, once again, to continue enthusiastically with his transformation programme. With Blank long gone, the programme has not faltered. Inmates and members are committed to it. One day soon, Lotter expects to hear from the attorney-general whether he is to be prosecuted and for what. He faces the prospect philosophically. What will be, will be. He is saddened but not embittered. He knows he will always have Krugersdorp prison as his living memorial. If there is a prosecution, or if affirmative action costs him his job, no one can take that achievement away from him. He is content with that.

PART FOUR

26

A Kind of Freedom

On Tuesday, 2 July 1996, Greg Blank was woken unexpectedly by André Vosloo and Braam Wilken, his deputy, shortly before four o'clock in the morning. It was pitch dark and freezing outside. He had no idea why his sleep was being interrupted. He wondered whether it was another cell search.

Vosloo told him to prepare himself for release. 'When?' said Blank. 'Now,' was the reply. Blank wanted desperately to believe it, but was fearful of yet another disappointment, so he resorted to bravado. 'It's too early for jokes. Wake me up at seven-thirty please,' he said. He got up and paced his cell, still unbelieving, telling himself that if this was some cruel joke, the only difference from his normal day would be that he had risen earlier than usual. So what? Big deal. Vosloo returned 20 minutes later and said: 'I'm serious. Pack your things.'

Blank washed, shaved and brushed his teeth at the cold-water basin in his cell for the last time. He dressed in the same clothes he had worn when he entered prison – track-suit trousers and a top – discarding at last the olive-green, prison-issue trousers that had been his normal wear for nearly two years. He wrote a note and left it on his bed. It was what he calls 'a kind of will'. In it, he bequeathed almost all his prison possessions to fellow inmates; his radio to this prisoner, his dressing gown to another, his duvet to a third. When he had done that, there wasn't much left to pack – a few books, toiletries, the sentimental photographs that adorned the wall. The picture of Di. The single rose taped to the plaster. When he had finished he cast an eye round the small, bare cell and wondered how he had ever come to think of it as home.

At about 4.30 a.m. Vosloo came back to escort him out. 'Ssssh!' he said, and Blank pantomimed a finger to his lips. Suitcase in one hand, his portable TV set in the other, he was led for the last time through the series of locked doors, along the long corridors to the formal prisoner reception area on the west side of the building. The prison was sleeping, as near to silent as it ever got. It was too early to say goodbye to anyone. *They'll understand,* he thought. The familiar noise of doors clanging shut and locks clicking behind him seemed like a farewell dirge. 'Jail is really all about doors,' remembers

Blank. 'Every 50 metres there's a door, and another door, and another. When eventually the doors run out, that's when you're free.'

It took nearly two hours to process his release papers. He sat in the reception area, oblivious to the winter chill, his mind numb. Now that the big moment had come, his emotions surprised him. There was none of the elation he had expected to feel. No bands played in his head. It was all too ordinary. Warders on duty said a friendly goodbye, but their minds were on other things. This was an all-too-familiar ritual to them. The whole event seemed almost anti-climactic.

He thought perhaps it was because he wasn't really going free, not like other people out there. He was being released on parole. That meant house arrest and surveillance. He could go to work, but he had to be in by 6 p.m. on weekdays, 2 p.m. on Sundays. His movements would be monitored. Inspectors would call day and night to see that he was observing to the letter the conditions of his parole. He would still have to report in from time to time.

He knew how it would have to be. After all the controversy, the Department of Correctional Services would be super-zealous. It wouldn't dare open itself to the charge that parole conditions were just a charade, that being on parole meant Blank was free again.

His advocate, André Bezuidenhout, arrived at about 6.40 a.m. Bezuidenhout had been told in advance that his client was to be released that day, but had decided not to tell Blank for fear that 'garrulous Greg' would talk about it to someone, and another row would blow up. Now, when release was only one door away, Blank said: 'I'd better let my father know I'm coming home.' Bezuidenhout replied: 'He knows already, I've told him. He's waiting for you.' Together they carried the suitcase and the portable television set to the white BMW parked in the prison grounds. As the car moved slowly out of the gates of Krugersdorp prison Blank felt at last the surge of joy he had expected to feel from the beginning. He was driving away, and when he came back, as he determined he would, it would not be as a prisoner. He discovered a sure-fire way of telling that he was out of jail – his nose cleared. 'For the last 22 months my nose had been blocked, almost as if I was cutting out the smells of the jail. People used to say to me: "Jees, what a terrible smell!" and I would say: "What are you talking about?"'

On his way to the much-loved Houghton home to see his family – father, mother, sisters – he heard Radio 702's seven o'clock news on the car radio. The main item was about his own release. *How on earth did they know?* he asked himself. *No one was supposed to know. So much for all that secrecy. So much for Bezuidenhout not telling even me.* He phoned Di from the car and she said she would join him at the Blank home.

There was no special breakfast. The release had been too unexpected for that. There was just hot tea and the warmth of togetherness. At 10 a.m. the reunion was interrupted by a phone call from the Department of Correctional Services. Someone had overlooked a parole formality; would he please return to Krugersdorp forthwith? Di drove him back. He signed a paper and listened to a debate on whether he should have to report to the department in Randburg or Krugersdorp. *Let it be Krugersdorp,* thought Blank. *I know the people there.* But Randburg it was, because – after someone had been sent to follow him home to measure the distance – the Randburg office was closer to his house. The episode was a sobering reminder that he was not, indeed, his own man. It cast a little shadow.

Later that day, when he returned to his own home in Khyber Rock with Di, he didn't feel like celebrating. For him, it was enough that he could reacquaint himself with the comfort of his own home, his own bathroom, his own bed.

Whatever the burdens of parole, he thought, *this has to be a thousand times better than jail. I can begin my life again.*

When Blank left jail, controversy travelled with him, yapping at his heels. He saw the headline in the copy of *The Star* that was delivered to his home on the afternoon of his first day of 'freedom'. He had made the front-page lead story. The headline said: 'Blank is free – and union calls a strike'. It was his old friend Golden Miles Bhudu at work again. The tone of the report was breathless with portent.

> Fraudster Greg Blank was released from the Krugersdorp Prison at 7 a.m. this morning after serving 21 months of his eight-year sentence, and the South African Prisoners' Organisation for Human Rights (Sapohr) have called a national protest strike of their members (currently in prison) for tomorrow.
>
> This follows the furore caused by Blank's initial parole which was granted three weeks ago and then turned down by Correctional Services Commissioner Henk Bruyn after he was asked by the ANC's Carl Niehaus to explain why the early release was granted.
>
> Sapohr spokesman Golden Miles Bhudu warned Correctional Services that 'they had gone too far this time'.
>
> Said Bhudu: 'If Blank can be released after only 21 months, then thousands of prisoners should be eligible at the same time. Blank's case highlights the gross imbalances and inequality in the release policy. We are made to hear that he has been released without any

> scrutiny and without any investigations into the allegations against him.'
>
> Correctional Services spokesman Barry Eckstein said that Sapohr's calls for a national strike were 'totally irresponsible'. He added that the investigation was being conducted by the police and that Blank could be put back in prison if any substantial wrongdoing came to light.

Blank's father, Robby, was quoted as saying: 'I am so pleased that the commissioner kept to his word that Greg's case would be reconsidered at the correct time. He is entitled to this.' His son, he said, was not willing to speak to the media until he had 'relaxed and got a little genuine sunshine'.

Blank thought to himself: *Here we go again. They're talking about early release, as if I haven't been released strictly in accordance with prison regulations. They're talking about an investigation into serious allegations against me. They're talking about me going back to jail. Where's the investigation? Why hasn't anyone been to question me? My lawyers have been trying to find out who's doing the investigating but the police don't seem to know. Nobody seems to know. And what's Carl Niehaus got to do with it all? Has he been asked to provide his evidence for saying what he said?*

No strike by Sapohr's convict members took place that Wednesday, nor any other day. Prison authorities reported no untoward incidents at all. However, the *Star* report confirmed at least one thing that many were beginning to notice. It came in Bhudu's own words: 'Blank's case highlights the gross imbalances and inequality in the release policy.'

Other publications picked up the theme. In the second week of his freedom, Blank found himself confronting his own caricature on the cover of the *Financial Mail* of 12 July. There he was, captured by a cartoonist's pen with someone else nearly as notorious: Abdul Bhamjee, the National Soccer League official who got a 14-year sentence for stealing R7,4 million in soccer sponsorships and TV rights. Bhamjee was released on the same day as Blank after serving less than a third of his sentence.

Now the two of them – dressed in a cartoonist's idea of prison garb, arm-in-arm, smiling wickedly – were gracing the cover of an eminent financial magazine. Below the drawing was a headline which said: 'How to get 75% off your prison sentence'.

News magazines love to 'personalise' the issues they deal with. The accompanying article argued cogently the widely-held view that the prison system was in disarray, that too many hardened and vicious prisoners were being released simply because jails were too crowded to contain them, and that the commissioner had capricious powers to undermine justice by reducing sentences enormously. It also said that prisoners who were white and rich tended to be more visible when it came to parole time. It quoted Blank's old adversary, Frank Kahn, as saying: 'The prison authorities play with semantics. They say they are converting the form of punishment when they put someone on parole. But, in effect, they are freeing them because they don't have the staff to police them.' Kahn, said the *Financial Mail*, got 'choleric' on the issue of blanket remissions of which there had been at least six since 1990 – 'when then President F. W. de Klerk and later President Mandela's Government of National Unity started releasing convicts to celebrate democracy'.

Said Kahn: 'We spend millions of rands and years of effort to get a criminal in jail, and then Nelson turns 77 or something and the crook is out before you know it.'

He too seemed to have forgotten that he had been part of the team which specifically recommended at the trial that Blank should not be sent to jail. Ah well, there is merit in the argument offered by the *Financial Mail* and Kahn. No doubt Mr Justice Cloete, the judge in Blank's case, concurred. The release policy is whimsical. But it is equally true that the presentation in the *Financial Mail* promoted the impression that Blank and Bhamjee were uniquely privileged by an iniquitous system. Bhamjee can argue his own case. Blank simply sighed resignedly and made the obvious point to anyone who would listen. He didn't make the rules. He was released strictly in accordance with them. What was he supposed to do? Demand to be put back behind bars?

At the heart of the debate over the release of Greg Blank are simple questions which cannot have simple answers. How much time in prison does it take for a wrongdoer to repent? Which are more likely to punish and rehabilitate a criminal – his first days in jail, or his last?

Merely to pose the questions is to show the folly of a regimented system that allows no room for individual assessment and judgment. For the hardened offender, there is no stigma in going to jail, no special hardship in staying there, very little likelihood of rehabilitation. The interests of society might therefore be said to be paramount. The habitual criminal must stay inside until he is cured or defeated. But for a first-timer from the 'respectable' world, the mere fact of going to jail is usually the ultimate punishment. A first-timer will remember for ever his first day in jail.

In such cases, society's justifiable demands for vengeance and protection will eventually come into conflict with another important principle. The purpose of prison is not to destroy but to rehabilitate. At some point, someone has to reconcile the conflicting principles, but it will always be a subjective decision. Judges can't take it, because they have no way of keeping track of individuals they have sentenced. Prison authorities alone should not have the decision, because of the danger of bias and prejudice. Social workers are probably too soft and prison warders too tough. Parole committees are unwieldy and mere regulations tend to be inflexible. That doesn't alter the fact that someone must decide when and where parole is appropriate lest the prison system itself descend into barbarity.

David Gleason mused on these matters in a column in the *Financial Mail* written in October 1995, nine months before the release. He had small personal acquaintance with Blank, no axe to grind. 'Should the country's most famous white-collar criminal be allowed to leave prison early?' he wondered. His first reaction was no, certainly not. Then he had second thoughts.

> We now live in a country in which individual rights are paramount. And I have to presume the constitution does indeed reflect society's moral and social values. On this basis, a number of arguments come to mind. First on my list when judging Blank is whether a moral balance existed in his prosecution and subsequent sentencing. As we all know, Blank was a member (true, an important member) of a large gang of men intent on squeezing benefit from commercial fraud. But is it really right, or in the interests of society, that the prosecution bags one member of the gang while allowing the others either to escape or negotiate immunity?
>
> Does this mean society is happy that Blank should go to jail while many others involved in the same crimes now hold well-paid and comparatively high-profile positions? They were never prosecuted and never called on to pay a debt to society. Blank was punished. I have no argument with this. Too many white-collar criminals walk the streets of our cities with impunity. They know they are safe from prosecution because the vast number of crimes and their complexity has overwhelmed our ability to bring them to justice. So, yes, I think it right Blank was sent to jail. But the dilemma is that he carried the burden alone.
>
> The law says each man is separately responsible for his actions. But I have difficulty in accepting that one man is behind bars and the many others involved stroll on the Hermanus beach.
>
> Blank has been in jail a year, a year in which I (and you) have paid for his board and lodging. But I don't want to go on paying for Blank. I cannot believe that he is a violent threat to society: it is said that he has rehabilitated well and that he is demonstrably capable of making his own way acceptably in the world. My instinctive reaction was that

Blank should serve out his sentence. My more measured response is that he should be set free to pay taxes again, like the rest of us.

With her feet curled under her, Di Reynolds sat on the giant double bed in Blank's master bedroom in his Khyber Rock cluster home. A few metres away, Blank sat sprawled on an occasional chair, his bare feet on a stool, his manicurist at work on his nails. Blank had been out only two weeks, and he was still indulging himself, luxuriating in the comfort of his own house. Every now and then, the cell phone or one of the two fixed phones would ring and he would become engrossed in business conversation. Business was brisk and Greg Blank was very busy. He was doing the work he loved: giving financial and investment advice, setting up deals, making things happen.

He was still feeling his way as far as reaction to his imprisonment went. His own attitude – 'I've paid my debt to society, life goes on, you can choose whether to associate with me or not' – seemed to smooth the way. So far, he had picked up no negative vibes. The people he chose to deal and work with seemed glad to see him again, as if he had been on a long trip and was now returned. His horse-racing associates had welcomed him back and he was to be seen again at race meetings. Soon, as a racehorse owner, he would be given back his racing colours. Some people he met amused him. They would say: 'When you were away, Greg…' or 'While you were on holiday…' and Blank would stop them. 'I wasn't away,' he'd say, 'I was in jail.' And the acquaintances would laugh sheepishly.

On the face of it, he had slotted back into his old lifestyle. But faces can be deceptive. Di could sense the tension, the unrelenting strain of behaving 'normally' again.

'I think he's found coming out of jail a lot harder than he thought it would be. The whole adjustment thing is a lot more difficult. When you're in jail, you fantasise about what it's going to be like when you come out, and when you come out…it's just very normal. I think it's quite hard for him. Even if he does go out now, to a business lunch or something, there are always people who whisper and say: "Look who's there" and "fraudster" and "jailbird". Because he's a proud sort of person, it must get to him. I think he's handling it the right way. He's got to confront that pain barrier. There's no question that he can hide away and pretend it never happened.'

Then there was the surveillance. 'They check on him, sometimes twice a night. They'll come and ring the bell in the early evening and then they'll come back at midnight or 1 a.m. Even if he's asleep, they'll just ring the bell. Then he has to go downstairs and say: 'Hullo' and sign the book. Sometimes he invites them to come in and have a drink.

'Weekends are worse. I mean, during the week he's allowed to go to work, but at weekends he's got to be at home. They've given him permission to go racing on Saturdays, because that's part of his business, but he must be home by 7 p.m. On Sundays he's got to be in by two o'clock. You think, when you come out of jail, you're going to be a free man. But you're not.' Blank asked his captors once why the late night/early morning visit was necessary. 'You can't believe,' was the reply, 'how many parolees go out after our first visit of the evening.'

Di thought she understood what was agitating Blank. 'He's obviously worried about the investigation. Not that they'll find anything, I know he's not guilty. It's just a worry that they could somehow find a reason to send him back to jail. He couldn't take that. You know, I've had numerous battles with people who say Gregory's a crook. Even if he is, it doesn't change the way I feel about him or think about him. I respect him so much more now. I don't know why. Maybe because he faced up to what he did, and went to jail, and did what he had to do. I actually see him in a whole new light. It doesn't bother me at all that he's been in jail.'

And how were things between her and Blank? They had been honest with each other, she said. There was a kind of wariness between them. Blank was not by nature demonstrative; Di Reynolds needed to know where she stood. 'Right now I think I'm a bit insecure because I don't know what's going on. We're at a stage where we'll just wait and see what happens. Gregory's said to me that we shouldn't rely on the fact that we had a relationship before. Either it works now, or it doesn't. There must be no baggage from the past.'

She thought she was ready to make a commitment but Blank was still too raw, too bruised by his experiences. 'Maybe one day he'll find his feet and this investigation thing will be past, please God, and then...' She paused for a second. 'And then...well, I just live for the moment.'

She still puzzles about what drove Blank to commit the crime he did. 'He didn't need the money. I don't think it was a money thing. I think it was a power thing. Power was a kind of drug for him. It made him feel invincible.'

Invincible! A word from the past, Blank's own word. In his stockbroking days, he had loved the sense of power and invincibility. He could move markets and mountains. For a while, he had been a master of the financial universe. It had given him a sense of security. But power had proved to be a traitorous mistress, and had led him to jail. He had resolved that he would never fall prey to her again.

27
The Reckoning

Society has had enough. Those were the portentous words intoned by Judge Tom Cloete on that long-ago day in October 1992 when he sentenced Greg Blank to eight years in jail. Society is now entitled to a report-back. How stand the country and its white-collar criminals in February 1997? Has society been well-served by its watchdogs? Has it had its pound of flesh? Did it want it? It's hard to say, but let's take a look at the balance sheet.

On 2 September 1995, the *Government Gazette* recorded that Colin Harper, the former head trader at Old Mutual who had received indemnity, had forfeited R2,2 million; he was the last of the conspirators to reimburse the Reserve Bank for the fraud involving foreign currency.

Frank Kahn's investigation was able to determine the precise prejudice there had been to pension fund portfolios administered by Old Mutual, which refunded the full sums. Old Mutual in turn recovered almost all of this money from Blank, Celotti, Schapiro and others. Koos Stassen, Old Mutual's chief legal adviser, says: 'The chances of such frauds occurring again at Old Mutual are probably less than elsewhere. Management has come through the trauma with a deep-seated, common conviction that this should never be allowed to happen again.' The investigation had provided insights into tell-tale signs of collusive dealing, and had enabled objective control systems to be adjusted and updated. Other measures – including restructuring, peer review and regular inspections – had been introduced. 'The deterrent factor should not be forgotten,' says Stassen. 'It has been shown that collusive dealing between brokers and institutional dealers can be picked up and reconstructed in detail. It has also been shown that an institutional employer will risk the threats of negative publicity and scrutiny to bring fraudsters to book. The fact that people know that such frauds can be uncovered, and can lead to successful prosecution, is probably the best safeguard against a recurrence.'

The Johannesburg Stock Exchange also believes that a similar fraud would be much harder to accomplish today. There has been a general tightening up of controls and surveillance, while the advent of computer trading and the end of the 'open outcry' system have greatly reduced the opportunity for collusion. Where once brokers literally rubbed shoulders on the dealing floor, they now sit in solitary splendour staring at computer screens in their offices.

Bill Urmson, director of surveillance at the JSE, told me: 'What happened before was that you had a group of people who traded amongst each other on a daily basis, and they knew each other. They knew which brokers dealt for which clients and it was very difficult to hide the fact that you had quite a good order for an institution, whether it be a buy order or a sell order. Therefore there was the opportunity for other brokers to exploit the situation. It was a clubby environment, and although I'm sure a lot of the people were very ethical, practices probably grew which could facilitate individuals making profits to the detriment of their clients.

'Now it's a different picture. There's total transparency. If you want to sell, you've got to put your order in the book. The system keeps a record of when orders were placed. And there's something like 600 dealers who are able to look at the book at any time. As far as surveillance is concerned, we're into a different dimension. I think our system is one of the best in the world. All members have to keep their records on the JSE's central mainframe computer and the surveillance officers can access it at any time. If we pick up a pattern, we can go into an account instantly. We can look at every trade for the last year. We have better tools, so the opportunity to fiddle is reduced.

'What helps is that we have world-wide players in the game now and they bring a very structured management concept with them. For example, several firms are now subject to review by the internal audit departments of their international partners. And top world players don't want to see a headline in New York saying that a South African director is being investigated for malpractice. The whole culture has changed. Every firm has also got to have a compliance officer, whose job it is to ensure that the rules and practices of the JSE are followed. So everyone is now much more aware of the rules.'

Greg Blank agrees. 'Your biggest irregularities occurred on the floor. There was no way the authorities could police that because you had friends dealing with friends; friends selling shares to other friends and buying them back and splitting the profits at the end. They could never control it. Tuesdays were settlement days so you could have the same shares going round and round ten times and more between one settling day and the next, without any money passing hands. Only on settlement day would the eventual holder have to say: "Right, these are my shares, I'm going to pay for them."'

One new development has Blank smiling wryly. In the last quarter of 1995 – at the time of the stock exchange's 'big bang', when electronic trading was introduced and financial institutions were permitted to buy into stockbroking firms – the JSE was obliged to change its rules barring brokers from acting as principals as well as agents. Obviously, a financial institution that had bought control of a stockbroking firm could not be prevented from buying and selling shares for its own account.

The move is healthy, says Blank. It will eliminate undercover operations and bring a new fluidity to the market. But he cannot help remembering the trouble his advocate, Clive Cohen, went to at his trial to convey the precise nature of the crime. The dialogue still rings in Blank's ears:

COHEN:	And so, My Lord, in essence the accused is pleading guilty to having failed to disclose that he had a personal interest in the transactions which he was conducting on the stock exchange for the Old Mutual.
JUDGE:	Thank you, Mr Cohen. Mr Prosecutor?
MARAIS:	It is accepted as such by the State, My Lord.

So the 'essence' of Blank's offence was his failure to disclose that he was acting as both agent and principal. Yet, if today's regulations had applied then, the practice of stockbrokers selling their own shares would have been legitimate and widespread and Blank would have had a lesser need for a secret account. And that would have shifted prime blame to the co-conspirators at Old Mutual who cheated their own company while in a position of trust. Ah well, nobody ever said that life was fair.

Several ironies and oddities arose from the Blank trial. In his judgment, Judge Cloete dismissed Blank's claim that he had been blackmailed into joining the conspiracy as 'unjustified hyperbole', and made considerable play of evidence that one firm of stockbrokers, Martin & Company, had been subjected to similar pressure, but had resolved the problem by approaching Old Mutual. 'What should an honest person have done in the face of the threat from Schapiro?' he had asked rhetorically. 'Surely he should have reported this threat to his partners to enable them to send a delegation to the senior management of Old Mutual – the more so as, to the accused's knowledge, such a delegation had been sent previously and the threat had been averted.' In short, Blank had failed to act as honestly as Martin & Co.

It was a neat point, but one spoilt by statements published two days after Blank was sentenced. Martin & Co. denied that it had ever been put under any pressure by Old Mutual employees to act improperly; and Old Mutual denied it had ever received a delegation from Martin & Co. on such a matter. How, then, did the story come to figure in the statement of agreed facts presented to court? This minor mystery remains unsolved.

It was apparent that Judge Cloete gave Blank a severe sentence because he wanted to send a message that white-collar criminals would be treated with the utmost severity. Was the message received? There are, of course, no statistics to reveal who might otherwise have been tempted. White-collar crime has not noticeably abated, though there have been no high-profile trials in recent years. In any event, the message probably got lost in the furore over the foreshortened sentence. Criminals of all kinds may well have concluded that it didn't matter what length of sentence judges gave, as the government would provide amnesty and the Department of Correctional Services would provide parole. So much for deterrence.

However, another message went out in place of the judge's intended one. Thanks to Blank and his activities at Krugersdorp, society discovered that convicts are people too – and that it had turned a blind eye for too long to what its vengeance entailed. Not for at least 30 years has there been such a powerful spotlight on life behind bars. It has resulted in accelerated reform and intense public debate. The minister of correctional services, Sipo Mzimela, and his new commissioner, Khulekani Sitole, have promised major changes, and newspapers are probing again behind the high walls – something they were not able to do after the *Rand Daily Mail* was prosecuted for revealing prison abuses in the early Sixties and the legal shutters came down. Blank can claim some of the credit for today's tidal movement towards prison reform.

There was a second judicial message that got garbled. When the judge gave Blank an exemplary sentence, he intended to ensure that the young stockbroker with the soaring ambition and the hunger for power would not remain a hero of any kind. Yet the message that did go out was that wrongdoers can still become heroes if they're lucky enough, smart enough and compassionate enough to find opportunity in unpromising places. Such as prison.

Very likely, the judge will find satisfaction in Blank's redemption of himself. After all, it was sending him to jail that achieved it. The sentence was vindicated by the result. But it is also possible that the judge, like many others, will continue to wonder what might have happened to Blank had he not been able to turn an ugly and terrifying experience to advantage. If Blank had not created his own rehabilitation, would long years in a bleak and violent prison have done the job for him? It seems extremely unlikely. It is much more probable that prison would have broken him as it has broken so many others.

For Greg Blank, those issues are behind him. He has served his time and is building a new life. Business is going well, and – to his delight – many of his old clients are using him again. Nevertheless, the spectre of another prosecution still hovers. The allegation that he bribed his way out of prison has still not been cleared up, half a year after his release. Blank has not been interrogated by any policeman and no questions have been asked of him or his lawyers by anyone. As far as is known, the Parliamentary Portfolio Committee on Correctional Services staged no investigation of its own into the Niehaus and Bhudu claims. The 'body of evidence' offered by Blank's attorney, Stan Fanaroff, remains unexplored by the committee. Niehaus departed to take up an ambassadorial post abroad without referring to the matter again – either to confirm or to retract the allegations he relayed to Parliament. For a short time at Krugersdorp prison, a policeman poked around in a desultory way to see if he could find some incriminating evidence. A police docket is supposed to be with the attorney-general, awaiting his decision on whether or not to prosecute. Bribery being a two-way offence, the State could hardly prosecute Blank without prosecuting the prison official, or officials, who allegedly took a bribe.

Blank is unconcerned. He knows there was no bribe. 'I've always been optimistic. I was optimistic when I got arrested, I was optimistic in jail, I'm optimistic about the country now. Life is for living. It's not a rehearsal. The rabbi said to me that so many people are practising their lives, and when they die they have forgotten to live them. I'm not going to forget to live mine.' Blank has been back to Krugersdorp prison many times, to take donations, to say hullo, once to deliver a car that had been donated to the driving school that now operates in the jail. 'I want to try to help the guys. I sent them stuff for Christmas because I don't want to see what we built up destroyed. Besides, the beauty of going to visit guys in jail is that you can always leave.' The commander of the prison, Nico Lotter, says that the impetus for reform is still strong and Blank's release has not diminished it.

On his second day out of jail, Blank started working again, phoning his old clients, making appointments. Despite Prosecutor Petrus Marais's contention at the trial that Blank should not be allowed to resume life as a man of means, or even in a position of relative financial comfort, he flourishes. (It would hardly have been fair to prevent him flourishing after he had paid his debt to society.)

Intentionally or not, society has exacted a final price from Gregory Lex Blank. His long-time, on-off romance with Di Reynolds is over. She was the one who came to him in John Vorster Square police station on the morning of his arrest, and who gave him courage and comfort during the long, dark days in jail. 'She was fantastic,' recalls Blank. 'You couldn't have asked for someone with more loyalty.' But relationships can take just so much stress, so much pressure. In the tense days that followed his release, something, some ingredient, disappeared. The relationship 'just didn't work out'.

Blank will wonder for ever if things might have been different had he never been drawn into the Old Mutual conspiracy.

So much for the visible consequences of the Blank affair. There is a deeper issue. It seems Judge Cloete was mistaken when he said that society had 'had enough'. South African society has had nowhere near enough. It displays an astonishing tolerance for corruption that has its roots in the corrupt political system that prevailed for nearly 50 years, eating away at the very fibre of honesty and ethics in a once-upright country.

Bill Urmson of the JSE put his finger on an aspect of this legacy when he said of the business culture in Blank's heyday: 'If you look at the business community in Johannesburg, the whole sanctions era created a certain state of mind which argued that secrecy and deviousness were acceptable practices. People would say: "We've got to trade, and we may have to do it in a devious manner and it may not be 100 per cent – but who am I hurting?"'

Urmson doesn't cover the half of it. Every corrupt law corrupted those who acquiesced in it. The notion still prevails that the tax man and the exchange authorities and the sucker on the street are there to be cheated. The culture of connivance, crookery and the quick buck rules, not just in the JSE but everywhere. The old adage applies: get smart, don't get caught.

The truth is that the judge mistook a momentary kneejerk public reaction for a groundswell movement. The so-called 'outrage' at white-collar crime lasted for a brief while. Society didn't really want a moral crusade; it wanted a quick sacrificial lamb. If the lamb turned out to be a scapegoat, so be it. The reality was that society didn't want to be too bothered one way or another.

The further arrests and prosecutions predicted by Cape Attorney-General Frank Kahn in his contretemps with the *Financial Mail* way back in November 1992 came to nothing. Kahn said then: 'The due process of law which you bring into question can hardly be faulted when it leads to...an investigation which is so thorough that it has already led to three people pleading guilty, let alone the cases still to come.'

In fact, only one person pleaded guilty – Blank. Coetzee and Fouche signed admissions of guilt without undergoing a trial of any kind. As for the 'cases to come', there have been none.

That is not to say that everything came to a dead halt. On 4 December 1992, about three months after Blank was sentenced, the *Financial Mail* published an interview with Sidney Frankel in which it quoted him as saying: 'I'm satisfied that we acted within the rules at all times.'

Behind the scenes, however, wheels kept turning, and Frankel's 'satisfaction' turned out to be premature. On 17 October 1996, five years and seven months after the arrest of Blank and nearly four years after Sidney Frankel's pronouncement, the JSE and Frankel Pollak, as the firm was known by then, issued a joint press release.

Its opening paragraph said:

> Frankel Pollak (Pty.) Ltd. and three of its directors, Messrs Sidney Frankel, Geoff Rothschild and George Frantzeskou, have pleaded guilty to a number of contraventions of the usages and practices of the Johannesburg Stock Exchange and of its rules. These contraventions were identified by the JSE during the course of an extensive investigation into the affairs of the firm relating predominantly to the years 1989 to 1991. In this matter, the JSE took into account that Mr Sidney Frankel communicated to the JSE and others his suspicions regarding the activities of Mr G. L. Blank, a former director of the firm. Neither the charges nor the admissions related to complicity by any of the firm's directors in Blank's activities and the JSE is satisfied in this regard.

Having got the disclaimer out of the way, the press release went on to describe what the firm and its directors were guilty of. There were five admissions. Firstly, the firm had failed to establish reasonable controls to detect or ensure that transactions effected by a former director, F. J. T. Kruger, were not prejudicial to the interests of the firm's clients and the JSE. Secondly, the firm had failed to ensure that certain transactions effected between Kruger's accounts were adequately monitored. Thirdly, the firm had failed to detect the untoward operations of Capital Nominees, a sundry client account, by Blank in a manner prejudicial to clients. Fourthly, the firm had failed to comply with legal provisions, as a result of which certain transactions were not allocated from a suspense account in the time prescribed. Fifthly, the firm had contravened JSE rules by executing certain put-through transactions while knowing that staff or directors were party to them.

Frankel, in his personal capacity, admitted failing to institute sufficient controls to detect the Kruger transactions; to not sufficiently informing the JSE or the firm's own clients of his suspicions about Kruger's activities; and to failing to monitor adequately Kruger's activities. Rothschild admitted to the same faults, but added two more: failing to detect Blank's activities on the Capital Nominees account, and failing to prevent the put-through transactions involving staff and directors. Frantzeskou admitted failing to record in the prescribed way three transactions involving A. W. Bradshaw & Co. and a Frankel's client.

As to the consequences arising from this rather splendid list of failures, the joint press release was silent. Presumably, the clients whose interests were prejudiced have been placated or have gone elsewhere. No one seems particularly concerned.

Readers may note a superficial resemblance between the directors' admitted failures and some of Blank's lesser activities before his arrest, but clearly there can be no comparison. However, Blank's claim that some malpractices were prevalent on the JSE is given added weight by the admissions from his own firm. And the fact that it took five years to establish satisfactorily what had been going on indicates how hard it is to monitor or control stockbroking activities.

'As far as I'm concerned,' Frankel told the press afterwards, 'the chapter is closed.' Many on the stock exchange wondered out loud whether the game had been worth the candle. They drew the conclusion that the JSE authorities evidently regarded the offences as worthy of no more than a 'rap over the knuckles'. The firm of Frankel Pollak was fined R250 000, to go to the JSE's Guarantee Fund. Unless Frankel's has fallen on extraordinarily hard times since Blank's departure, this would represent only a minuscule portion of its annual turnover. Frankel and Rothschild were fined R40 000 each and Frantzeskou R10 000. It can be safely assumed that the guilty parties will not be unduly discommoded by their penalties. The JSE deserves credit for sticking so doggedly to its inquiry, but hardly anyone I spoke to believes that its findings will serve to deter future wrongdoers.

Such was the profound concern for routing out malpractice that the general sentiment on the JSE when the Frankel's affair was finally closed was: 'Ho hum.' On 20 October 1996, the *Sunday Times* quoted an unidentified stockbroker as saying: 'People couldn't give a damn. They are sick of the whole affair.' Frankel's went ahead to finalise a deal whereby France's second-largest banking group, Société Générale, took a 51 per cent stake in the firm. The banking group said the firm's infringements 'were not an issue in the deal'. So Société Générale, rather like society itself, was not too concerned about that episode either, it appears.

Blank still insists that it is the big institutions that lead the way when it comes to manipulating prices. 'They're interested in only one thing – performance – and they don't care how you get it. If they give you shares to sell, they want the highest price, and if they give you shares to buy, they want the lowest price.'

The ultimate in legal manipulation occurs in the practice known as 'window-dressing', which, simply put, means the artificial improvement of a unit-trust portfolio at quarter end to reassure unit holders that they have made a smart investment. Window-dressing is commonplace, though not all financial institutions engage in it. Old Mutual, for instance, says its core value of 'integrity in all dealings does not leave room for tolerance of deceptive inflation of share price, which is accordingly not allowed'. Nevertheless, some other institutions are not so scrupulous. The following typical market report, emanating from respected news agency Reuters, appeared in *The Star* soon after the close of the second quarter of 1996: 'Shares on the JSE ended broadly firmer on Friday as window-dressing at quarter ends of unit trusts provided a late fillip.' The headline said: 'Late snap to unit-trust quarterlies'. The activity attracts no particular attention, let alone censure. As far as the JSE authorities and the investors are concerned, window-dressing is okay. Father Christmas is allowed to visit four times a year at the Johannesburg Stock Exchange.

Only one question remains. It is not whether Greg Blank should have gone to jail. That is patently not in dispute. Wrongdoers deserve to be punished. What has to be established is whether, in the mild hysteria of the times, one man was singled out for severe punishment not so much because his crime demanded it as because some rumbling in society, peculiar to the times, had to be appeased. From the era of the Roman Colosseum, men were put to death or saved at the whim of public opinion. It was to avoid such situations that humankind codified its laws.

Was Blank a scapegoat, as he still believes – doomed to suffer alone so that the rest of society could, through him, achieve absolution? At the time of the trial, Judge Cloete made his views clear: the fact that others were also guilty, he said, was irrelevant. But was he right?

Whether Blank was a scapegoat can be tested against a simple moral rule. If justice does not pursue, with equal zeal, all those who offend against the values it defends, then justice is guilty of offering a mere sop to morality. By this test, Blank's view is vindicated. As the *Financial Mail* wrote after his trial: 'We have been treated to the sad spectacle of one man, alone, pleading guilty in the courts and receiving sentence for the crimes of a sizeable syndicate... There is a pronounced public perception that Blank is the fall guy for too many others.'

In the end, 14 people were identified as having been involved, to a greater or lesser degree, in the two scams for which two people paid admissions of guilt fines and one went to jail. Of the 14, eight were Old Mutual employees, one worked for himself and the remainder worked as stockbrokers or for one of the five other financial institutions affected. Most of their names appear at some point or other in this narrative. Some names do not because their role in the Blank proceedings – let alone their participation in criminal acts – was not deemed to be relevant. They got off scot-free. No one knows how many were engaged in similar malpractices and just quietly stopped when the bubble burst.

Conspirator A, identified as the brains behind the scam, was offered indemnity against prosecution for testifying against Blank. He lives an untroubled life at a Cape seaside resort.

Conspirator B was indemnified. His current whereabouts are unknown.

Conspirator C, an investment manager with Old Mutual, withdrew from the scam seven months before Blank was arrested. He is currently employed at a merchant bank in a similar capacity.

Conspirator D escaped prosecution and is now a portfolio manager for a large investment company. His CV, as published by his company, notes that he had been a portfolio manager for Old Mutual Investments until 1991. That was the year in which he joined his new employers and Blank got arrested.

Conspirator E is employed at the same company as Conspirator D.

Conspirator F is safely tucked away overseas, where he has considerable investments.

It is safe to assume that the background of the conspirators now in gainful employment is known to their employers, who seem comfortable in the knowledge. Some may argue that this is a tribute to these firms' forgiving natures. Others believe it is a commentary on their business ethics.

A single, cynical message emerges: if you're about to be nabbed, be the first to squeal to the authorities. Of the known Old Mutual conspirators, those who squealed first got indemnity. Their names have long since passed into history, buried with the State's official list of witnesses who might have been called if Blank had not made it unnecessary by pleading guilty.

Of the two who fled, one is dead by his own hand and the other is missing, believed to be in Italy. By the time those two decided they would like to squeal too, they had missed the boat. The State had its full complement of snitches.

I thought hard about whether the conspirators who have rebuilt their lives should be named again in this final chapter. Did they deserve that? On balance, I thought not. If the price they paid for their wrongdoing has been far lower than Blank's – well, that's hardly their fault. Society demanded no more of them. Now society has opened its arms again to them, which puts society itself on trial. Are we dealing here with forgiveness or expediency? Either way, the tolerance of corruption is enormous.

One person who believes that the villains of yesterday should be given a break is, ironically, Blank himself. One day soon after his release he said to me: 'People ask if I'm out for revenge, but there's no time for that. Those guys who want to pretend that it never happened, or pretend that they weren't involved, that's fine. I sleep well at night. I wonder if they do.'